ONLY IN

Duncan J. D. Smith

ONLY IN VIENNA

A Guide to Hidden Corners,
Little-Known Places and Unusual Objects

Photographs by
Duncan J. D. Smith

CHRISTIAN BRANDSTÄTTER VERLAG

I dedicate this book with love and thanks to Roswitha,
without whom the following pages could not have been written,
as well as to my loving parents Mary and Trevor,
brother Adrian and auntie Catherine;
also to my friend Cosmas Tembo and his family in Zambia –
and never forgetting Laurence who would have enjoyed
the bits about archaeology

Etched glass door at Berggasse 19, home of Sigmund Freud (see no. 84)

CONTENTS

Introduction

»Die Straßen Wiens sind mit Kultur gepflastert,
die Straßen anderer Städte mit Asphalt.«
(The streets of Vienna are paved with culture,
the streets of other cities with asphalt)
Karl Kraus (1874–1936)

Vienna is surely one of the grandest, and at the same time most compact, capital cities in Europe. It is also one of the most fascinating. The plethora of available tourist guidebooks offers the undemanding visitor a fabulous (and effortlessly accessible) array of museums, churches, palaces and eateries, reflecting the history of the city from Roman times, via the Habsburg Empire, up to the present day.

However, for those with a little more time on their hands, and for those who want to *discover* something of the place for themselves, this new guide has been expressly written. It only takes a few minutes of planning, and a glance at a decent street map*, to escape the crowds and the orchestrated tours and discover a different Vienna.

Based on personal experience, and footslogging all twenty-three of the city's districts (*Bezirke*), the author will point the explorer in a new and unusual direction. This is the Vienna of Roman ruins, medieval cellars and catacombs; tranquil courtyards and romantic fountains; unfrequented museums brimming with fascinating objects; secret gardens and astronomical observatories; Art Nouveau swimming baths and ornate public conveniences (!); film locations from James Bond and *The Third Man*; not to mention artist Gustav Klimt's recently discovered last studio.

It is also a city with a dark and sinister past, its forgotten Jewish cemeteries and Third Reich anti-aircraft towers still bearing grim witness to terrible times.

As would be expected, many of these curious locations, all of which are both visible and visitable, are to be found within the narrow streets of the ancient inner city (*Innere Stadt* or *Altstadt*), Vienna's 1st district, some of which still trace earlier medieval and Roman thoroughfares. However, an equal number lie outside the old city walls (today's *Ringstrasse* boulevard built by the Habsburgs), in both the inner suburbs (*Vorstädte*) of the 18th century (the 3rd–9th districts and the 2nd district of Leopoldstadt), and the outer suburbs (*Vororte*) laid out in the 20th century (the 10th–23rd districts). The latter lie beyond the old *Linienwall* ramparts (today's busy *Gürtel* ringroad) to the west, as well as the River Danube to the east. Using Vienna's exemplary transport network of trams (*Strassenbahn*), underground trains (*U-Bahn*), fast trains (*Schnellbahn*) and buses (*Autobus*), the explorer can quite quickly reach all the places described within the following pages – and that's without detracting whatsoever from the sense of personal discovery that each of these places has to offer. Indeed, directions have been kept to a minimum so as to leave the visitors free to find their own particular path. Whether walking on the slopes of the Vienna woods where Sigmund Freud pondered the meaning of dreams, relaxing in a tranquil Japanese garden in a quiet suburb, or gazing at what was once thought to be Montezuma's headdress in the very heart of the city, the visitor will hopefully experience a sense of having made the discovery for his or her self.

In embarking on these mini-odysseys in search of Vienna's tangible historical legacy the author would only ask that telephones be switched off in places of worship (which must not be visited during services), and due respect be shown in the quiet city courtyards that are home and workplace to many Viennese. Other than that, treat Vienna as a giant oyster containing many precious pearls – I just hope you enjoy finding them as much as I did.

Duncan J. D. Smith
Thassos, Greece and Vienna, Austria

* The ÖAMTC street map available from Freytag & Berndt, Kohlmarkt covers all 23 districts of Vienna and includes tram, bus and rail routes.

After each entry there is a selection of others within walking distance.

The dates given after the names of Austria's various monarchs are the actual years they reigned for, whereas those given after important non-royal personalities relate to their birth and death.

An alphabetical list of opening times of museums and other places of interest mentioned in the text can be found at the back of the book.

1 Harry Lime's Doorway

1st District (Innere Stadt), doorway at Schreyvogelgasse 8
on the Mölker Bastei

With the closing of the Second World War, Austria was for ten long years carved up into four zones by the occupying Allied powers (Great Britain, United States, France and USSR). Although the bombed-out capital found itself deep within the Russian zone to the east, it was decided to make the city into an international sector, patrolled by a representative from each of the four powers (the so-called »four men in a jeep« era).

It was against the resulting backdrop of black marketing, espionage and counter-espionage that Sir Carol Reed's classic 1949 film thriller *The Third Man* was set. Based on an idea by Graham Greene, and a resulting film script requested by Sir Alexander Korda, it concerns American writer Holly Martins (played by Joseph Cotten) who visits 1948 Vienna to look up his old friend Harry Lime (Orson Welles). On arrival, however, he witnesses Lime's funeral, having been apparently knocked down outside his apartment (in reality the Baroque Palais Pallavicini in Josefsplatz, well worth glancing at in the evening when its gilded ceilings and chandeliers can be seen from the street). Martins grows suspicious and discovers that Lime has been dealing in sub-standard penicillin resulting in several deaths, and that Lime's own demise was merely a stunt to avoid arrest. In the 57th minute of the film Harry famously re-appears, very much alive, in the doorway

(LEFT) The Riesenrad Ferris wheel in the Volksprater

(RIGHT) Harry Lime's doorway on Schreyvogelgasse

at Schreyvogelgasse 8 on the Mölker Bastei (see no. 24). After coming clean to Martins in his famous »cuckoo clock« speech below the Ferris wheel *(Riesenrad)* in the Volksprater (see no. 59), Lime is cornered by police in the city's labyrinthine sewer system and shot dead (the police enter via a steel hatch still visible in Friedrichstrasse on Karlsplatz; Reed's film crew actually used a metal cylinder-topped staircase on Lothringerstrasse). Filming took place in the covered section of the River Wien (20 metres wide and 8 metres high) that runs between the Naschmarkt and the Stadtpark, with a tense shootout at the subterranean weir below Friedrichstrasse into which the Ottakringerbach stream empties (see nos. 5 & 83).

Other notable scenes in the film include the Cafés Marc Aurel, now a stationery store on Hoher Markt, and Mozart, mocked-up on Neuer Markt, and the Casanova Revue Theater at Dorotheergasse 6–8, where Martins undertakes his late-night detective work. In addition to solid supporting roles from Trevor Howard and Alida Valli, and a memorable main theme played on the zither by *Heurige* musician Anton Karas, what makes *The Third Man* so special is author Greene's detailed depiction of post-war Vienna. He was briefed by his MI6 boss Kim Philby, stayed in the British-occupied Hotel Sacher and was shown around the city by Elizabeth Montagu, sister of England's Lord Montagu of Beaulieu (she also acted as the film's location advisor, English language coach to the Austrian actors and escort to Mr. Welles, who lodged at the Hotel Orient on Tiefer Graben). The only detail Greene didn't get right was actor Orson Welles's fear of sewer rats!

Note: see the original black and white film in the Burgkino at Opernring 19 tel. 01 587 84 06, where it has been showing since 1980, and experience the sewers first-hand as part of the guided walk *In the Footsteps of the Third Man,* tel. 01 774 89 01 or visit *www.viennawalks.com.* Fascinating too is the Third Man Private Collection museum of posters, books and music at Pressgasse 25 in the 4th district of Wieden; pride of place goes to the zither used by musician Anton Karas to record the film's theme tune (a second zither can be found in the Hofburg's Collection of Ancient Musical Instruments (Sammlung alter Musikinstrumente)). The last resting place of Karas can be found below a zither-shaped headstone in the cemetery at Sievering (*Friedhof Sievering*).

Other places of interest nearby: 2, 3, 4, 5

2 Turkish Delights

1st District (Innere Stadt), sculpture at the corner of Freyung and Strauchgasse

With the fall of Constantinople (modern Istanbul) in 1453 the Byzantine Empire had ended and within 40 years the burgeoning Ottoman Empire was expanding westwards towards the Danube. In 1526 Suleyman the Magnificent captured Pest in Hungary (now part of modern Budapest) and by autumn 1529 had advanced to the gates of Vienna with 300,000 men housed in 25,000 tents. Only the dogged resistance of the city garrison under Count Niklas of Salm (his Egyptian marble tomb is in the Votivkirche at Schottentor), the early onset of winter and re-supply problems forced Suleyman to retreat (see the wall plaque at the corner of Kärntnerstrasse and Walfischgasse marking the site of the old Kärntnertor gate where fierce fighting took place).

A Turkish horseman with scimitar on Strauchgasse

As a result, Ferdinand I (1521–64) erected new walls around the city (see no. 24) and moved the imperial court permanently to the Hofburg in 1533. It was at this time that the famous Swiss Gate *(Schweizertor)* was built.

Following the death of 50,000 inhabitants from bubonic plague in 1679, it was a weakened garrison of 10,000 that again faced Ottoman might during the second Turkish siege of 1683. This time Grand Vizier Kara Mustafa arrived with 200,000 men and laid siege to the city, against the wishes of his Sultan Mehmet IV who merely wanted the trade routes secured. In the meantime, a united Christian army under Duke Charles of Lorraine and King John III of Poland (Jan Sobieski) was formed and eventually routed the Turks at the Battle of Kahlenberg. For his disobedience Mustafa was strangled in Belgrade by the Sultan's emissary (using a cord of black silk), and Vienna was rebuilt in the triumphant style of the Baroque.

Dotted around the city are tangible reminders of these perilous times, such as the carved scimitar-wielding Turkish horseman on Strauchgasse, said to commemorate a baker who discovered Turkish tunnellers in a cellar here and alerted the Viennese guard thus saving the city. Although the story is unlikely there's no denying the stone Turkish cannonballs embedded in some of Vienna's old buildings (e.g. one at Sterngasse 3 shot from Leopoldstadt; three found during renovation work in 1963 in the medieval Griechenbeisel inn at Fleisch-markt 11/Griechengasse 9; one at Am Hof 11, subsequently gilded and displayed outside an inn; several embedded in the South Tower and walls of the Stephansdom – it was hit by more than a thousand! – one

A gilded Turkish cannonball on a wall in Am Hof

of which can be seen on the middle buttress of the nave wall with »1683« carved below; one at the corner of Linke Wienzeile and Morizgasse; and three outside a house on Sieveringer Strasse). Also from this period is the Stephans-dom's *Pummerin* bell (meaning Boomer!), the second largest free-swinging bell in Europe, cast originally in 1711 from 180 Turkish cannon captured in 1683 (of the type which probably reduced the spire of the Minoritenkirche to its present stumpy form during the first siege). Finally, there is the Upper Belvedere Palace with its skyline resembling Otto-man tents, designed by Lukas von Hilde-brandt for Prince Eugène of Savoy (1663–1736) who pushed the Turks back to Hungary; and that's not to mention the crescent-shaped croissants (*Kipferl*) so beloved of the Viennese (see no. 46), or the Turkish map of Vienna, drawn from memory, found in a Grand Vizier's secret archive in Belgrade in 1688, and now amongst other Turkish spoils in the Vienna Museum (*Wien Museum*) in Karlspatz. Vienna's Museum of Military History (*Heeresgeschichtliches Museum*) also holds a collection of Turkish trophies worth tracking down (see no. 40).

Formal reconciliation between Vienna and the Turkish communi-ty has been marked subsequently by an ornate, Koran-inscribed foun-tain at the top of Währing's Türkenschanzpark. The park's name, meaning »Turkish entrenchment«, marks the site of the Ottoman's final stand during the second siege.

Other places of interest nearby: 1, 3, 4, 5

3 A Most Grand Fire Station

1st District (Innere Stadt), the Central Fire Station and
Fire Brigade Museum (*Feuerwehrzentrale und
Feuerwehrmuseum*) at Am Hof 7/10

Whether it's a water tower (see no. 67), a swimming pool (see no. 65),
a gasometer (see no. 64) or even Friedensreich Hundertwasser's psyche-
delic Spittelau paper incineration plant (*Fern-
wärme Wien*), the utilitarian architecture of Vienna often takes on a grand appearance as befits a
capital city. Even the city's oldest preserved secular building, the little-known *Heumühle* watermill hidden in a courtyard at Heumühlgasse 9 in
the 4th District of Wieden, has delicate Gothic
windows incorporated into its battered old brick
walls.

The old watermill
in a courtyard
on Heumühlgasse

Vienna's fire station is no exception and can
be found in the largest enclosed square of the
Innere Stadt. The square's name of Am Hof
(meaning At the Court) reflects the fact that here
was the site of the original Babenberg palace of
Heinrich II Jasomirgott (1141–77) (see the wall
plaque at Am Hof 2). As first Duke of Austria he
built it when he chose Vienna as his ducal capi-
tal in 1156. Before that it was the site of the Roman garrison fort of
Vindobona (see no. 12) and later became the heart of the medieval
city. At number 13 is the Collalto Palace where the 6-year old Mozart
first showed his talents in 1762; number 12 is the lovely Urbanihaus
with its 1730s iron inn sign and the deepest cellars in Vienna; and it
was from the balcony of the Kirche am Hof that the end of the ailing
Holy Roman Empire was declared in 1806 (see no. 61).

Amidst all this history sits Vienna's fire station. The fire brigade
headquarters are at number 10 in the former 16th century Civilian
Arsenal (*Bürgerliches Zeughaus*). You can't miss the gable end with its
huge Habsburg double-eagle, sculpted suits of Roman armour and
carved weapons. It was the Baroque architect Johann Bernhard Fischer
von Erlach (1656–1723) (responsible for the Karlskirche, Hofburg
library (*Prunksaal*), Palais Trautson at Museumstrasse 7, Bohemian
Court Chancellery at Wipplingerstrasse 7 and Prince Eugène of Savoy's

Winter Palace at Himmelpfortgasse 3) who suggested building a city fire station to extinguish the numerous blazes that often threatened his work. However, it was not until the 1848 Revolution (see no. 14), when the mob stormed the Arsenal, that a fire department was opened here and the Arsenal itself moved to the outskirts of the city (see no. 40). At the time, fighting even broke out in the unlikely setting of the Stephansdom where a bullet hole can be seen near St. Leopold's Altar.

The fire station (left) and former Arsenal (right) in Am Hof

Next-door at Am Hof 7 is the palatial Märkleinisches Haus built to plans by the architect Lukas von Hildebrandt (1668–1745) (famous for Prince Eugène of Savoy's Upper Belvedere Palace, the Peterskirche and the Palais Daun-Kinsky at Freyung 4). It was into this Baroque building that the fire station proper was inserted in 1935, with its row of wooden double doors at ground level and a Fire Brigade Museum above.

Between 1534 and 1956 a telescope installed in the Stephansdom spire (*Alte Türmerstube*) was used for fire watching and a mock-up of this, together with fire vehicles and uniforms, can be found inside the museum. It certainly makes for an unusual sight to see Vienna's first steam-powered fire engine (*Dampf-Spritzenwagen*), dating back to the 18th century, displayed in a grand town house from the same period!

For those interested there is another grand, though purpose-built, fire station strategically located at Gumpendorfer Gürtel 2 from where the Mariahilf and surrounding districts are serviced.

Other places of interest nearby: 2, 4, 5, 7

4 The Lucky Chimney Sweep

1st District (Innere Stadt), effigy of a chimney sweep
at Wipplingerstrasse 21

On the corner of a building on Wipplingerstrasse, overlooking the exquisite Viennese Art Nouveau (*Jugendstil*) Hohe Brücke bridge (1903), is the enormous effigy of a white-capped chimney sweep with his ladders and coiled flue brush. The building he adorns however has nothing to do with his profession. It is in fact a lottery establishment – the chimney sweep being seen across Austria as a bringer of good luck.

Effigy of a chimney sweep on Wipplingerstrasse

From medieval times the open fireplace, and later the stove, was literally at the very heart of the home. The resulting soot-filled chimneys could ignite if not kept clean, posing a serious threat of fire in days when most houses were timber built. Owners deemed irresponsible in this respect could face the death penalty, and so it brought relief and a feeling of good fortune if a chimney sweep visited one's street. Although children often feared his blackened appearance it was believed he could avoid the attentions of the devil, thus bringing protection to households against danger and disease. The connection between chimney sweeps and good luck is celebrated every New Year's Eve (called *Silvester* in Austria, after Pope Silvester I who died in Rome on December 31st 335AD) when trinkets bearing his image (or hers – female sweeps are common today in this respected profession) are exchanged. Shiny chimney sweeps' buttons were once highly prized in this respect and the trinkets (*Glücksbringer*) may well be a development of this older custom. The link with New Year is because the sweeps would often render their annual account at this time, and with it a gratuity and New Year's wishes would be exchanged. Even now the Viennese believe that seeing a chimney sweep in the morning will bring the onlooker good fortune for the rest of the day.

Lucky pigs, again in the form of trinkets as well as in edible pink marzipan, are also exchanged at New Year, the pig being the holy animal of the old Germanic gods, as well as the sow being a symbol of prosperity and fertility in many European cultures. In olden times when meat was scarce, the man who owned a pig was lucky indeed! Another unusual New Year custom, observed on January 6th (*Heilige Drei Könige*), is the chalking-up of the initials of the three kings – Caspar, Melchior and Balthazar ($C + M + B$) – on house doors, together with the year, to bring protection and prosperity to Christian households in the coming year. It is often forgotten that the three initials stood originally for *Christus Mansionem Benedicat* (Christ shall bless this house).

Other places of interest nearby: 3, 7, 8, 9

(ABOVE) The Three Kings' initials on a city doorway

(BELOW) The White Chimney Sweep Restaurant on Weihburggasse

Note: for those wishing to delve deeper into the world of the chimney sweep there is a dedicated museum (*Rauchfangkehrer Museum*) at Klagbaumgasse 4, where it forms part of Wieden's District Museum. There is even a plush restaurant in the *Innere Stadt* called *Zum Weissen Rauchfangkehrer*, or The White Chimney Sweep at Weihburggasse 4.

5 Underground Vienna

1st District (Innere Stadt), the Esterházykeller at Haarhof 1,
off Naglergasse

In Middle Eastern archaeology many ancient cities are termed »tell«
sites, that is to say they are built up over time, layer after layer, on
exactly the same spot. To some extent the same can be said of Vienna's *Innere Stadt* that today sits on top of a 9 metre-thick layer of cultural debris, including ancient Roman (see no. 12) and Jewish (see
no. 8) layers with those of the medieval and later periods above them.
Periodically these layers are brought to light, as during the construction of the U-Bahn, when a medieval chapel was found in Stephansplatz (see no. 21) and the old crypt of the Minoritenkirche, off Land-
hausgasse, was revealed and preserved for posterity. Similarly, during
the excavation of the Freyung car park, a 12th century cobbled pavement was found and re-laid at present ground level for visitors to
examine.

Excavations in 1992 in the Michaelerplatz *(Archäologisches Gra-
bungsfeld Michaelerplatz)*, still visible today, revealed Roman buildings with frescoes and under floor heating (1st–5th centuries AD),
medieval houses and a deep well (13th century), walls of the former
Imperial pleasure gardens (16th–18th centuries), vaulted cellars (18th–
19th centuries) and part of the Old Burgtheater, demolished in 1888 to
make way for the Michaelertrakt (or wing) of the Hofburg (an old
doorway from the theatre, where Mozart's *Le Nozze di Figaro* (1786)
and *Così fan Tutte* (1790) were premiered, can be seen inside the
Michaelertor on the left-hand side). Also revealed was a finely-construct-
ed drain made of bricks stamped with the Habsburg double-eagle
motif, making up a tiny part of Vienna's labyrinthine sewer system
that was made famous by the film *The Third Man* (see no. 1).

The city's drainage statistics are incredible – 1,826 kilometres of
channels provide a storm sewer system, with house sewers adding an
extra 5,063 kilometres of which 182 kilometres are man-sized. Other
curious aspects of this subterranean world are the crypts (see no. 30)
and cellars punched deep into the Viennese clay to gain valuable extra
space in the increasingly cramped city. The peculiarity here, of course,
is that in those cellars running to several levels (up to five is known),
the deepest are the most recent! Tostmann's traditional Austrian outfitters *(Trachten)* at the bottom of the Mölkersteig near Schottentor

Medieval cellars on display in Michaelerplatz

has a staircase leading down to an amazingly extensive cellar system that can be visited on request. It may be legend that a woman locked in here in 1940 emerged the next day at the Stephansdom many streets away, but it does demonstrate how the construction of cellars was both uncontrolled as well as uncharted. Below Demel's famous cake shop (*Konditorei*) and café on Kohlmarkt, a cellar was found to be connected to the Hofburg by an ancient tunnel used subsequently by thieves to break into a bank vault half way along – it has now been sealed!

Many of Austria's Baroque monasteries possessed labyrinthine, multi-levelled cellars in Vienna, where they stored wine produced from their own vineyards (e.g. the Zwölfapostelkeller at Sonnenfelsgasse 3, the Augustinerkeller at Augustinerstrasse 1 and the Melker Stiftskeller at Schottengasse 3). These old and intricately brick-vaulted wine cellars have now become uniquely Viennese taverns that are truly one of Vienna's most unexpected discoveries. A wonderfully atmospheric example well worth visiting is the Piaristenkeller at Piaristengasse 45 in the 8th district of Josefstadt, its 300 year-old cellars housing an opulent restaurant as well as the Emperor Franz Josef Hat Museum (*Kaiser-Franz-Josef Hutmuseum*). By appointment the candlelit monastic cellars that housed the Imperial wine collection (*k.u.k. Weinschatzkammer*) may also be seen. Another extensive cellar is that belonging to the Heiligenkreuzerhof Monastery at Schönlaterngasse 5.

The deepest wine cellars in Vienna are below the Urbanihaus in Am Hof (see no. 3) whilst just nearby is the celebrated *Brezlg'wölb* (Pretzel Cellar) at Ledererhof 9. The oldest cellar is the Esterházy-keller in the bowels of the Esterházy Palais at Haarhof 1, where since 1683 Hungarian wine has been sold from the princely estate of that name. There are many other cellars nearby filling what was once a deep ditch (now called Graben) that ran around the Roman fort (see no. 12).

Not surprisingly, cellars also made ideal air raid shelters in the Second World War, identified by the letters *LSK* (*Luftschutzkeller*) painted on the wall outside (e.g. Spittelberg Gasse 26). Tragically, a direct hit on the Philipphof in Albertinaplatz, home to the exclusive Jockey Club, killed hundreds when the cellars there gave way – the victims were never recovered and the site is today marked by the Monument against War and Fascism (*Mahnmal gegen Krieg und Faschismus*) erected by Austrian sculptor Alfred Hrdlicka in 1988.

Other places of interest nearby: 2, 3, 6, 7

6 At the Sign of the Black Camel

1st District (Innere Stadt), Zum Schwarzen Kameel at Bognergasse 5

Until the reign of ›Empress‹ Maria Theresa (1740–1780), the names of the streets and squares of Vienna were not officially recorded, but rather recognised only by oral tradition. There were also no official house numbers, instead domestic dwellings were given either the name of their owners, or were identified by figurative signs. As many inhabitants could not read or write, shops were identified by striking and unambiguous symbols. The Vienna Museum (*Wien Museum*) in Karlsplatz contains some fine examples of this early street art, both from shops (e.g. an eagle carrying an ornate key from a locksmith's workshop) as well as houses, such as a red hedgehog (*Zum roten Igel*), the eye of God (*Zum Auge Gottes*), and a beautiful 18th century wrought-iron lantern (*Zur schönen Laterne*), that once hung at Schönlaterngasse 6 (a 1971 replica now hangs here to remind visitors how the street acquired its name; both were made in the former Old Smithy – *Alte Schmiede* – at number 9).

In 1771 a continuous numbering system (*Conscriptionsnummern*) was established in the *Innere Stadt* (running to well over 1000 and used originally to aid recruitment) and not until 1862 were individual streets finally numbered, as part of a system still in use today. Occasionally an 18th century building can still be spotted bearing its old continuous house number, carved or painted onto its lintel, often side-by-side with the more modern street number embossed on a metal plate (e.g. Kleeblattgasse 5, Köllnerhofgasse 3, Fleischmarkt 16, Ballgasse 8 and Kohlmarkt 11, all in the *Innere Stadt*; and Rechte Wienzeile 15 alongside the Naschmarkt).

Despite these improvements, and the fact that the populace is now highly literate, Vienna has hung on to many of its colourful house names. These include golden lions at Wiedner Hauptstrasse 36 (*Zu den zwei goldenen Löwen*), black ravens at Rotenturmstrasse 21 (*Zu den drei Raben*), a club-wielding caveman at Währinger Strasse 85 (*Zum wilden Mann*), a playful seal at Währinger Strasse 6–8 (*Zur Robbe*), white horses at Josefstädter Strasse 85 (*Sechsschimmelhof*) a spouting whale at both Lerchenfelder Strasse 29 and Piaristengasse 58 (*Zum Walfisch*), the biblical »Flight from Egypt« (»*Zur Flucht nach Ägypten*«) at Piaristengasse 56–58, and the mythical basilisk whose lair was below Schönlaterngasse 7 (*Zum Basilisken*). Similarly, some commercial establishments retain their symbols, for example a red hand above the old glove-makers (1854) on Schottengasse, a pipe-smoking Turk over the door of tobacco importer Adolf Lichtblau at Hermanngasse 17, innumerable hanging keys denoting locksmiths around the city and even a pair of wooden Lederhosen outside Grün-angergasse 12! A few also retain their old names, such as the Black Camel (*Zum schwarzen Kameel*), founded in 1618 as a spice store at Bognergasse 5 by Johann Baptist Cameel (a relative named the Camelia flower!), where both Beethoven and Lord Nelson shopped, and the Blue Carp (*Zum blauen Karpfen*), a former Baroque inn at Annagasse 14 founded c.1700 by Georg Kärpf.

The sign of the Black Camel on Bognergasse

In the late-19th century numerous shops revelled in their exclusive appointments to supply the Austrian Imperial court, hence the *k.k.* (*kaiserlich-königlich*) (imperial-royal) designation still to be seen over the door of Lobmeyr's glassmakers at Kärntnerstrasse 26, Habig's former hat makers at Wiedner Hauptstrasse 15 and Ch. Demel's Söhne confectioners at Kohlmarkt 14, one-time supplier of decorations for the Imperial Christmas tree (their *Marzipanmuseum* is in the cellar here). Two final related curiosities are the distinctly non-Austrian crests above Knize's outfitters at Graben 13, harking back to when they supplied dress uniforms to the Turkish Sultan and the Shah of Persia (modern Iran).

Note: Following the so-called Compromise (Ausgleich) of 1867 the Dual Monarchy of Austria-Hungary was established, by which Hungary got its own parliament in Budapest and Emperor (Kaiser) Franz-Josef I of Austria was also crowned King (König) of Hungary. Consequently, everything Hungarian was prefaced k. (königlich) (royal), whereas in the rest of the empire the initials k.k. (kaiserlich-königlich) (imperial-royal) were used; meanwhile everything Austro-Hungarian was prefaced k.u.k. (kaiserlich-und-königlich) (imperial and royal).

Other places of interest nearby: 3, 5, 7, 8

7 The Clockmakers' Quarter

1st District (Innere Stadt), the Clock Museum
(*Uhrenmuseum der Stadt Wien*) at Schulhof 2

The huge church dominating Vienna's Am Hof courtyard (see no. 3) is like the Roman god Janus – it exhibits two very different faces. Known variously as Kirche am Hof, or the more colourful Church of the Nine Choirs of Angels (*Kirche zu den neun Chören der Engel*), its public face fronts the courtyard itself. Italian architect Carlo Carlone added this incredible Baroque façade in 1662, and it was from the balcony in 1782 that Pope Pius VI famously gave benediction. It was here too, on 6th August 1806, that a herald proclaimed the end of the Holy Roman Empire (see no. 61).

However, a short walk through an archway beside the church into Schulhof will reveal the other face of this intriguing building. Suddenly, the original and much older 14th century Gothic stonework appears, like a cake being stripped slowly of its white Baroque icing. Similarly, inside the church, the original Gothic Carmelite fittings have been masked by later Jesuit additions, such as attached pilasters and porticoes (this same effect is visible at St. Michael's Church when comparing its white-plastered Baroque front, facing the Hofburg, with its older unclad Gothic stonework to the rear, as viewed from the courtyard at Kohlmarkt 11).

It is typical of Vienna that in a few paces the informed visitor can escape a bustling courtyard and discover a peaceful back street. Schulhof behind the Kirche am Hof is no exception, and tucked in between the church's rugged Gothic buttresses are two tiny watchmaker's lockups reminiscent of medieval times, especially when a horse-drawn *Fiaker* clatters by on the cobbles (*Fiakers* were first licensed in 1693 and named after the *Auberge Saint-fiacre*, a Parisian inn outside which hire carriages have long drawn up). Even the buttresses themselves have been scooped out to allow carriages to pass more easily down this narrow thoroughfare. Opposite at Schulhof 2, in the 300-year old Baroque Obizzi Palace, is the Clock Museum of the City of Vienna, founded in 1921 and the oldest of its kind. Rudolf Kaftan, an early curator, together with the novelist Marie von Ebner-Eschenbach, accumulated the collection. Among the fascinating exhibits on its three floors are many curiosities, including the world's smallest pendulum clock that fits inside a thimble, as well as clocks that are concealed inside walking sticks and landscape oil paintings. There is also an incredibly complicated astronomical clock, one of whose hands is calculated to take 20,904 years to make one complete revolution! Such novelties make this museum of interest to everyone, and not just the specialist.

The Obizzi Palace itself, named the Harp House for its unusual shape, has an interesting history. It was once the property of Count Ernst Rüdiger von Starhemberg, defender of Vienna during the Turkish siege of 1683. During the fighting it is said that lead cannonballs were cast in the fireplace. The Baroque façade was added by Ferdinand Obizzi who commanded the city garrison in 1690.

Just around the corner at Kurrentgasse 2 is a window flanked with cherubs that illuminates a tiny, frescoed, late-Baroque chapel dedicated to Polish saint Stanislaus-Kostka, who once lived in a cell here. It is the smallest, and probably least well-known, place of worship in Vienna.

A Fiaker passing a watchmaker's shop in Schulhof

Note: Those wishing to investigate further the history of Vienna's Fiakers should visit the small Fiaker Museum on the second-floor at Veronikagasse 12 in the 17th district of Hernals.

Other places of interest nearby: 3, 4, 6, 8

8 »Out of the depths I cry to you«

1st District (Innere Stadt), the Judenplatz Museum
(*Museum Judenplatz*) at Judenplatz 8

Historical records from Upper Austria reveal a Jewish presence in that part of the country from as early as 903AD, and a Jewish community has existed in Vienna since the 12th century. In 1238 they were granted privileges by the last of the Babenberg dukes, Friedrich II (1230–46), as a result of which Vienna's medieval Jewish Quarter, focussed on the area now known as Judenplatz, began to flourish. It was home to the *Or-Sarua-Synagogue* that contained one of the most important *Talmud* schools in the German-speaking world. Its floor was set a little below ground level in accordance with a Bible verse from Psalms (»Out of the depths I cry to you«). The peaceful conditions offered to Jews in Vienna, whose services were highly valued, even provided a haven to those fleeing from intolerance elsewhere in Europe. However, in 1421 under the Catholic Habsburg Duke Albrecht V (later Emperor Albrecht II, 1438–39), Jewish property was appropriated to fill the Royal coffers in the face of poor harvests and threats from Moravian knights and the Protestant Hussites of Bohemia (now the Czech Republic). The result was an atrocious pogrom known as the first Viennese *Geserah*. Albrecht justified it by accusing the community of desecration of the Eucharistic Host, ritual murder and of being in league with the anti-Habsburg Protestants. The Synagogue was burned down, its stones re-used in the city's Old University (*Alte Universität*) and the Jewish community forcibly baptised. Those that refused were burned alive on the Erdberg, thrown into the Danube, jailed or expelled: many opted for mass suicide. The anti-Semitic feeling of the time is reflected in a notoriously offensive wall inscription at Judenplatz 2 (*Zum Grossen Jordan*) where the expulsion is gleefully recorded in Latin below a depiction of the baptism of Christ: »By baptism in the River Jordan bodies are cleansed from disease and evil, so all secret sinfulness takes flight. Thus the flame rising furiously through the whole city in 1421 purged the terrible crimes of the Hebrew dogs. As the world was once purged by the flood, so this time it was by fire.«

History relates how the Jews would eventually re-group in the Leopoldstadt ghetto of 1625 (see no. 58), the location also for their final ghetto under the Nazis (see nos. 13 & 52). It was whilst sculptress

Rachel Whiteread was planning her affecting Holocaust Memorial (*Holocaust Mahnmal*) in Judenplatz that the charred remains of the original medieval Synagogue were uncovered several metres below present ground level. The city council agreed that such deeply symbolic remains should be made accessible, which they now are via the Judenplatz Museum at number 8, occupying the ground floor of the Misrachi-Haus *Torah* school. This subterranean museum contains an excellent video reconstruction of the walled Jewish Quarter as it appeared in 1400, and of its Synagogue, whose hexagonal *bimah*, where the *Torah* lectern once stood, is marked out in Judenplatz directly above, next to Whiteread's memorial. To complete the sense of having come full circle, the statue of German playwright Gotthold Ephraim Lessing, a key figure in the 18th century German Enlightenment whose views on tolerance and humanism prompted the Nazis to pull it down, was re-cast by the original sculptor Siegfried Charoux in 1968 and now dominates Judenplatz once again.

Other places of interest nearby: 4, 6, 7, 9

The notorious anti-Semitic
inscription at Judenplatz 2

9 The Church of the Danube Boatmen

1st District (Innere Stadt), the Church of Maria am Gestade,
at Salvatorgasse 12

Of the many churches within the *Innere Stadt*, that of Maria am Gestade (translated variously as »St. Mary on the Riverbank« or »Virgin on the Shore«) is curious for a number of reasons. Together with the Stephansdom, it is one of the few Gothic churches not to have been altered in the subsequent Baroque period, retaining its delicate vaults, tracery and buttresses from the late-14th century. It can be

The filigree tower of Maria am Gestade Church from Salvatorgasse

identified from afar, especially when illuminated at night, by its unusual seven-sided filigree tower rising 56 metres into the air. Incredibly it escaped later demolition only because a contractor could not be found who would take away the rubble! Also unusual is the fact that the nave (the main seating area of a church at the west end) and the chancel (the area directly in front of the altar to the east) are of equal length (the former is usually longer), and that the nave is narrower and built slightly askew. This is due to the steep and restricted terrain here on the edge of a natural plateau, used as a natural defence by both the medieval town and the Roman fort, walls of which were found below the church (see no.12). Of great interest are the surviving fragments of medieval painted glass incorporated into the beautiful windows behind the High Altar. More would have survived had Napoleon's troops not used the church as an arsenal and stables during their occupation of Vienna in 1809 (see no. 61). In addition there is a side-chapel containing the mortal remains of Klemens Maria-Hofbauer (1751–1820), named the »Apostle of Vienna« by Pope Pius VII. A trained baker and a founder of the Austrian Congregation of the Most Holy Redeemer, Hofbauer also cared for the Czech community whose church this has been since 1912.

Outside the main west door, sometimes compared to the prow of a ship, is a flight of stairs that until the 16th century descended steeply to the Alsbach and Ottakringerbach streams which formed the town moat (now the street called Tiefer Graben, meaning deep ditch). This accounts for the popular name of Mariastiegenkirche (The Church of Our Lady of the Steps), as well as the building's age-old connection with the Danube raftsmen and bargees who once passed so close with their cargoes. Over the porch of a modern building in nearby Passauerplatz is a very effective sculpture of the boatmen themselves, who would have used the church.

The nearby Fischerstiege (Fishermen's Steps) also lead down to the riverside where there is a sculpture of fish traders reminding us that their docks and warehouses would once have been here (another sculpture can be found across

A sculpture on the Fischerstiege depicting Danube fishermen

the canal at Obere Donaustrasse 97). Similarly, on Vorlaufstrasse there is a sculpted salt merchant whose salt barge landing would also have occupied part of the riverbank. This accounts for the streets called Salzgries and Salztorgasse, the Salztorbrücke bridge and also for the presence of the nearby 12th century Romanesque church of St. Ruprecht (Vienna's oldest), Rupert being patron saint of salt miners and first Bishop of Salzburg from whence the valuable commodity came. His statue, hidden amongst trees behind the church, can be seen clutching a barrel of salt.

Other places of interest nearby: 4, 8, 10, 13

10   The Fountains of Vienna

1st District (Innere Stadt), the Andromeda Fountain
(*Andromedabrunnen*) in the courtyard of the
Old Town Hall (*Altes Rathaus*) at Wipplingerstrasse 8

Lovers of classical music will no doubt be aware of the colourful tone poem *The Fountains of Rome* by Italian composer Ottorino Respighi, brilliantly evoking the city where he settled in 1913. Like Rome, Vienna is embellished with a number of fountains (*Brunnen*), but they have yet to inspire such wonderful music – which is surprising since they make such an aesthetic and therapeutic contribution to the urban scene. By undertaking the following fountain-based odyssey, from the *Innere Stadt* down to Wiedner Hauptstrasse, the explorer will at the same time take in many of the city's major sights *en route*.

The Andromedabrunnen (1741) in the courtyard of the Old Town Hall at Wipplingerstrasse 8 was the last work of distinguished sculptor Georg Raphael Donner whose bronzework depicts the rescue of Andromeda by Perseus, son of Zeus, from a monster (Donner himself is the subject of a bronze on Schwarzenbergplatz); the Wedding Fountain (*Vermählungsbrunnen*) (1729) in Hoher Markt replaces a wooden monument erected by Emperor Leopold I on the safe return of his son from war, and depicts the marriage of Mary and Joseph; a small fountain at the top of Tuchlauben (1928) depicts a tailor cutting cloth (see no. 11); the Austria Fountain (1846) in the Freyung has allegorical figures representing the rivers of the former empire (Danube, Po, Elbe and Vistula) and is said to be stuffed with cigars smuggled in by the sculptor from Munich but never retrieved!; the Water Nymph Fountain (*Donaunixenbrunnen*) (1861) forms part of an M. C. Escher-like courtyard in the Freyung Passage.

The Volksgarten contains a contemplative memorial fountain (1907) to Elisabeth (*Sisi*), wife of Emperor Franz-Josef I; the Pallas Athene Brunnen (1902) outside the Parlament on Dr.-Karl-Renner-Ring has mermen figures representing the rivers Danube and Inn (front), and Elbe and Moldau (back); the *Augustinbrunnen* (1908) at Neustiftgasse 32 recalls the bagpiper of legend (see no. 16); Emperor Franz Josef I's former private garden, the Burggarten, contains a dramatic fountain depicting a man wrestling a lion; the Danube Fountain (*Danubiusbrunnen*) (1869) in Albertinaplatz has figures representing the rivers Danube and Wien.

Georg Raphael Donner's Andromedabrunnen in the courtyard of the Old Town Hall on Wipplingerstrasse

The Providentia Fountain (*Donnerbrunnen*) (1739) in Neuer Markt was Vienna's first non-religious public sculpture with figures representing the Danube tributaries Traun, Enn, Ybbs and March (its naked figures were originally removed by ›Empress‹ Maria Theresa's

Chastity Commission and may now be found in the Baroque Museum (*Barockmuseum*) in the Lower Belvedere).

The fountains in Michaelerplatz (1895–97) symbolise Habsburg might on land and at sea, whilst on the Graben are two fountains with lead figures by Johann Martin Fischer (1804), those on the Josefsbrunnen depicting *The Flight into Egypt* and the others, on the Leopoldsbrunnen, showing *The Discovery of St. Agnes's Veil*.

The Academy of Sciences in Dr-Ignaz-Seipel-Platz is adorned with two graceful wall fountains (1755) by sculptor Franz Josef Lenzbauer; in the quaint Franziskanerplatz, close to Vienna's smallest coffee house, is the *Mosesbrunnen* (1798) (although the original was melted down by the Nazis).

The Stadtpark on Parkring contains the Danube Sprite Fountain close to the famous golden statue of Johann Strauss, and nearby is the Venetian mosaic *Minervabrunnen* (1873) on Stubenring outside the MAK (*Österreichisches Museum für angewandte Kunst*) (it was exhibited originally at the World Exposition in the Prater); Josef Engelhart's *Borromäusbrunnen* (1909) is in Landstrasse (see no. 37).

The High Jet Fountain (*Hochstrahlbrunnen*) (1873) in Schwarzenberg Platz commemorates Vienna's first high-alpine spring water pipeline from the Rax and Schneeberg mountains 75 kilometres southwest of the city; a charming little fountain in Resselpark is adorned with water-spouting frogs.

And finally, off Wiedner Hauptstrasse, there is a dragon fountain (1846) on Rilkeplatz, the Viennese Art Nouveau (*Jugendstil*) Mozart Fountain on Mozartgasse, with its figures from *The Magic Flute* (*Die Zauberflöte*), and the *Engelbrunnen* (1860) in a charming square at Wiedner Hauptstrasse 56 – an ideal spot to finish the journey and enjoy a well-deserved drink under the trees!

Other places of interest nearby: 8, 9, 11, 12

11 Vienna's Oldest Frescoes

1st District (Innere Stadt), the Neidhart Frescoes
(Neidhart-Fresken) at Tuchlauben 19

On August 1st 1979, whilst renovating an apartment on the first floor of an innocuous-looking town house at Tuchlauben 19, traces of old wall paintings were discovered. The authorities were notified immediately that a sensational historic discovery had been made. Preliminary analysis revealed not only the early date of the frescoes (they are Vienna's oldest secular frescoes) but also the historical significance of what they depicted. Within a few months it was decided to conserve the paintings *in situ*, to convert the room into a museum (the Neidhart Frescoes) and, of course, to re-house the apartment's tenant!

In the land register of the *Innere Stadt* the house can be traced all the way back to 1370. In 1398 it was sold to a wealthy merchant called Michel Menschein who made his fortune in the textile business, indeed the name *Tuchlauben* refers to the street's former fabric arcades. This accounts for the small fountain at the top of the street that depicts a tailor cutting a piece of cloth. Despite the house being variously inherited and sold some thirty times subsequently, the style of the paintings points to the late-medieval period (1398) – and to Menschein as their instigator. Adorning the walls of what would have been his banquet hall, the frescoes take the form of a cycle depicting scenes from the life and work of the Babenberg courtly songwriter (*Minnesänger*) Neidhart von Reuental (c.1180-1240). His tomb, much damaged by Napoleon's soldiers, lies near the Singers' Portal outside the Stephansdom; its canopy includes a fox's head, an animal about which he once wrote a popular song.

A scene from the Neidhart Frescoes at Tuchlauben 19

The scenes in the house on Tuchlauben are surprisingly playful and direct and are set within a framework of the four seasons. Along the north wall is *Summer* (Peasant Brawl, Ballgame and Lovers, and Theft of the Mirror) and *Winter* (Snowball Fight and Sleigh Ride), whilst on the south wall is *Spring* (Violet Picking and Round Dance) and *Autumn* (Banquet and Landscape). Such a secular room decorated in this manner is unique in Vienna, although there are parallels to be found in France and Italy. The Vienna artist remains unknown, as could have the frescoes themselves considering the fact that in 1715 much of the building was demolished and rebuilt as a fashionable Baroque residence, concealing the paintings for more than 250 years.

Like many other great European cities, Vienna can boast a spectacular array of examples of the wall-painter's art at its best, especially on the ceilings of the city's incredible array of baroque churches (e.g. the Jesuitenkirche in the *Innere Stadt* and the Piaristenkirche in Josefstadt), palaces (e.g. the wonderfully exotic floral frescoes of the Berglzimmer in the Schloss Schönbrunn by the Bohemian painter Johann Wenzel Bergl) and other public buildings (see nos. 22, 27 & 71).

Two other curious examples of fresco work in Vienna are the *Biedermeier* period bespectacled cow playing backgammon with a

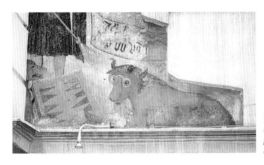

The Biedermeier fresco of a cow and wolf playing backgammon at Bäckerstrasse 12

wolf on a wall outside Bäckerstrasse 12 (thought to be a parody of Catholic-Protestant tensions) and the fragment of painted Roman wall plaster under glass in the permanent archaeological display in Michaelerplatz.

Other places of interest nearby: 8, 9, 10, 12

12 The Ruins of Vindobona

1st District (Innere Stadt), the Roman Museum
(*Römermuseum*) entered via shopping arcade
at Hoher Markt 3

Although the area around Vienna had been inhabited since prehistoric times, the history of Vienna proper begins in 15BC when the Romans under Emperor Augustus penetrated Celtic Noricum, thus incorporating the Vienna Basin into their province of Pannonia Superior. In the late-1st century AD they established a defensive line of military encampments along the Danube (known as the *Limes*) as a bulwark against marauding Germanic tribes to the north, as well as providing bases for their fleet along this important trading waterway. The provincial capital of Carnuntum, 40 kilometres to the east of modern Vienna, at the crossroads of the Danube with the amber trade route from the Baltic to the Mediterranean, received extra protection in the form of a garrison fort that the Romans called *Vindobona*.

They chose the so-called City Terrace on which to build the fort, a naturally elevated area that rises above the Danube's floodplain from Nussdorf in the north to Simmering in the south (see no. 83) – thus was Vienna founded. They built a classic square-planned Roman fort, whose walls and ditches have long since been replaced by the following modern roads: Rotenturmstrasse, Graben (meaning ditch, once the fort's southern moat) and Naglergasse (the curving street facades at either end still following the curved corners of the Roman fortress), Tiefer Graben (meaning deep ditch, along which the Alsbach and Ottakringerbach streams once flowed), and Salzgries-Seitenstettengasse (below which an arm of the Danube ran, now the Danube Canal). A walk along these streets permits an appreciation of the ancient topography, as well as the original extent of the fort.

Although nothing Roman remains above ground today, having been built over from medieval times onwards, a few tantalising windows have been opened on this ancient world (e.g. demolition of houses at Sterngasse 5 revealed a Roman bath house, a column of which has been re-erected next to the Theodor-Herzl-Stiege; below the fire station at Am Hof 7/10 is a section of terracotta drain (*Römische Baureste Am Hof*) that ran below the *Via Sagularis* and emptied into the Ottakringerbach, part of the fort's elaborate sewerage system; Roman walls were found below the church of Maria am Gestade (see no. 9); Roman paving slabs found during the construction of the Artis

Kino-Treff cinema at Schultergasse 5 are now displayed in the foyer; a shop window opposite Lichtensteg 5 contains excavated Roman stones; and a wall plaque at Naglergasse 2 mentions Roman walls uncovered during house-building in 1901).

There is also tangible evidence for a thriving civilian community that existed *outside* the walls of the Roman fort (e.g. during the excavation of an underground car park below the Freyung remains of buildings were found that once lined part of the main Roman road (*Limesstrasse*) east to Carnuntum (now Herrengasse), a map of which can be seen in the window of Herrengasse 16; in Michaelerplatz can be seen the walls of Roman houses that lay at an intersection of the main road with another leading down Kohlmarkt to the fort (see nos. 5 & 11); the 13th century Giant's Portal (*Riesentor*) of the Stephansdom has an inscribed Roman gravestone incorporated into its right-hand arch suggesting a deliberate attempt to Christianise a former pagan burial site; and on Rotgasse is a modern mosaic marking the site of the *Porta Principalis Dextra*, a gateway which opened out onto Wollzeile, that in turn led to a cavalry base east of the fort, fragments of which can be seen on both platforms of the U3 U-Bahn station at Rochusgasse).

However, the most impressive remains are those in the Roman Museum (Römermuseum) found below Hoher Markt, Vienna's oldest square and former fish market, where a pair of houses were found along one of the fort's two major streets, the *Via Principalis* (Hoher Markt–Wipplingerstrasse leading northwest to Comagena, Roman Tulln; the other main street ran along Marcus Aurelius Strasse – Tuchlauben southwards to Aquae, Roman Baden). They follow the usual Roman house plan of rooms set around a porticoed atrium and include under-floor (*hypocaust*) and through-wall heating. The houses date from a rebuilding of the fort in 180AD by the 10th Legion, the original having been built c. 100AD by the 13th/14th Legions but destroyed by Germanic tribes. Although driven back by Emperor Marcus Aurelius (who died either in Vindobona or Sirmium) thus

Under-floor heating in the Roman ruins below Hoher Markt

allowing the town to prosper and establish its first vineyards, the tribes later returned precipitating a full Roman withdrawal by c.400AD.

In 833AD *Wenia* is first mentioned, as part of the Holy Roman Empire founded by Charlemagne, and the old Roman walls and roads would in time provide a foundation for medieval Vienna (see no. 24).

Note: Most visitors go to Hoher Markt to see artist Franz Matsch's Viennese Art Nouveau (*Jugendstil*) clock known as the *Ankeruhr* (1911) with its midday procession of mechanical figures, one of whom is Roman Emperor Marcus Aurelius. Also worth visiting is the Vienna Museum (*Wien Museum*) in Karlsplatz for its fascinating collection of Roman statues, altars, lamps and frescoes.

The Jugendstil Ankeruhr clock in a corner of Hoher Markt

Other places of interest nearby: 10, 11, 13, 14

13 An Infamous Address

1st District (Innere Stadt), Morzinplatz

Following the first violent expulsion of Vienna's Jews in 1421 (see no. 8) and a second in 1670 (see no. 58), the Jewish community of the early-20th century had become a settled and vital part of Viennese life. A third expulsion seemed unimaginable and yet, between 1907 and 1913, the young Adolf Hitler (1889-1945) was in the city honing his own brand of fanatical anti-Semitism. Like Vienna's Christian Socialist mayor Karl Lueger, whom he greatly admired, he learned quickly that given a suitable scapegoat he could turn the envy and discontent of Vienna's *petit bourgeosie* to his own political advantage.

As a budding artist in 1907-08 Hitler lived in an apartment at Stumpergasse 29 in Mariahilf and then just around the corner at Felberstrasse 22. It was during this time, in between drinking coffee in the Café Sperl, that he was twice rejected as being »inadequate« by the Academy of Fine Arts (*Akademie der bildenden Künste*) on Schillerplatz. Increasingly disgruntled and without money he then occupied a flat on Sechshauser Strasse, a homeless shelter in Meidling and finally a men's hostel called the Männerheim at Meldemannstrasse 25-27 in Brigittenau. In May 1913 Hitler eventually abandoned Vienna for Munich and then Berlin, only to return to the Austrian capital 25 years later, in March 1938, as Führer of the German Third Reich. This time he spent the night in the luxurious Hotel Imperial on Kärntner Ring and proclaimed the annexation (*Anschluss*) of Austria from the balcony of the Neue Burg (see no. 56) before flying back to Germany. Within days the elegant Hotel Métropole in Morzinplatz was commandeered as the regional headquarters of the Nazi secret police (*Gestapoleitstelle Wien*) and Heinrich Himmler's henchmen began rounding up opponents of National Socialism. This included members of the preceding Austrofascist Party, Communists and Socialists. Men, women and children were taken to the hotel, via a back entrance at Salztorgasse 6, for interrogation, torture and dispatch to the concentration camps (see no. 76). Thereafter followed the first

wholesale rounding up of the Jewish population, culminating on 9th November with the notorious Night of Broken Glass (*Reichskristallnacht*), a ruthless pogrom during which more than forty synagogues, prayer houses, schools and cemeteries were desecrated. Of the 6,500 Jews arrested 3,700 were sent to the concentration camp at Dachau in Bavaria (see nos. 52 & 58).

Numerous plaques around the Jewish quarter in the 2nd district of Leopoldstadt record former synagogue and school sites, as at Leopoldgasse 13-15 and 29, and Große Schiffgasse 8 (see also Neudeggergasse 12 in Josefstadt). A plaque on the wall of Schiffamtsgasse 18-20 marks the home of one Dr. Arnold Deutsch, deemed undesirable by the SS (*Schutzstaffel*) and murdered; whilst another in a pretty schoolyard at Kleine Sperlgasse 2a marks the spot where 40,000 Jews were rounded up between October 1941 and March 1943. A total of 65,000 would eventually be murdered. Only the City Synagogue (*Stadttempel*) at Seitenstettengasse 2-4 in the *Innere Stadt* survived, due in part to its facade being concealed from the street (see no. 14).

Needless to say the world's first Jewish Museum (1895) was also destroyed, although today there is a new one (*Jüdisches Museum der Stadt Wien*) at Dorotheergasse 11 containing a poignant collection of charred ceremonial objects retrieved from the rubble of Vienna's synagogues.

Not far away, a plaque at Neutorgasse 8 commemorates Dr. Hans Zimmerl, a member of the Austrian Freedom Movement (see no. 18), beheaded in 1944 along with a thousand others, on a guillotine referred to chillingly as »Instrument F« in Vienna's oldest criminal court, the Landesgericht, at Landesgerichtsstrasse 11 in Josefstadt (not open to the public).

In the face of such horrors it came as some relief when the Hotel Metropole was razed to the ground by allied bombing in the last weeks of the war (a similar fate awaited Adolf Eichmann's Central Office for Jewish Emigration at Prinz-Eugen-Strasse 20–22, formerly the Palais Rothschild, from where the Nazis orchestrated their »final solution« for Vienna's Jews). The Métropole site is now occupied by the Leopold Figl Hof, named after Austria's post-war Chancellor (1945-53) who himself survived the Dachau concentration camp. The hotel's notorious former back entrance now leads to a memorial for members of the Austrian Resistance Movement (*Gedenkstätte für die Opfer des österreichischen Freiheitskampfes*), whilst in front of the building is a Monument to the Victims of Fascism. The latter is made of granite boulders from the quarry at Mauthausen concentration camp near Linz in Upper Austria, where prisoners hacked out stone for the cobbles of Vienna's streets. On it are carved the words »*Niemals vergessen!*« (»Never forget!«).

Monument to the victims of Fascism in Morzinplatz

A further poignant memorial to the victims of the camps are the three black paving slabs to be found on Lothringerstrasse, carved impeccably by Jewish prisoners and brought recently to Vienna from a former Nazi political building in Nuremberg.

Quite rightly there are no wall plaques recording the numerous

A wall plaque at Schönbrunner Schloss Strasse 30 marking where Stalin stayed in 1913

places Hitler stayed during his time in Vienna and they should not be treated in any way as tourist destinations: the history books serve well enough to remember his appalling »achievements« in the city. However, it is a little-known fact that just prior to Hitler's departure for Munich in 1913 his future adversary Josef Stalin arrived in Vienna. The young, up-and-coming Bolshevik stayed at Schönbrunner Schlossstrasse 30 where he wrote his paper *Marxism and the National Question*, before returning to St. Petersburg. A wall plaque of questionable taste still hangs there today, erected in 1949 when Vienna was in Russian hands and Stalin was still alive. Even more chilling is the fact that Hitler the artist is known to have visited the park at nearby Schloss Schönbrunn to paint. Is it just possible that two of the twentieth century's greatest monsters passed each other on the street without ever realising it?

Other places of interest nearby: 10, 12, 14, 15

14 The Architect who Feared his Wife

1st District (Innere Stadt), the Kornhäusel Tower
(*Kornhäuselturm*) at Judengasse 14 between
Friedmannplatz and the end of Fleischmarkt

Sandwiched between Vienna's magnificent Baroque/Rococo architecture of the 17th–18th centuries and the retrospective pomp of late-19th century Historicism (Ringstrasse Style), is the so-called *Biedermeier* period. The era it covers, between the Congress of Vienna in 1814–15 and the 1848 Revolution, saw Austrian Chancellor Prince Clemens von Metternich impose autocratic rule that effectively excluded the middle classes from political life. As a result they retreated into a cosy world of artistic and leisurely pursuits – Neo-classical architecture (see nos. 48 & 72), furniture (see nos. 17 & 44), decorated Christmas trees, Schubert and Waltzing. These privileged yet politically apathetic *bourgeosie* were satirised by a German author in the form of a fictional character called »Herr Biedermeier«, after whom the era and its decorative arts are named (*Bieder* = worthy/naïve; *Meier* = a common German surname).

The star architect of the period was undoubtedly Josef Georg Kornhäusel (1782–1860), remembered for his unobtrusively elegant neoclassical buildings. In 1826–32 he redesigned the Schottenkloster (Monastery of the Scots) at Freyung 6, notable for its stretched-out classical pediment. In 1822 Kornhäusel remodelled the Josefstadt Theatre

The Schottenkloster on the Freyung re-designed by Josef Kornhäusel

(*Theater in der Josefstadt*), Vienna's oldest (1788), whose doors have kept open continuously ever since. Its reopening featured an especially composed overture by none other than Ludwig van Beethoven.

A very different commission was the design of the City Synagogue (*Stadttempel*) in 1824–26 at Seitenstettengasse 2–4. Curiously, it does not look like a synagogue from the outside because Emperor Josef II's Edict of Tolerance (*Toleranzpatent*) (1781) forbade such non-Catholic buildings from betraying their function (see no. 16). This may account for it being the only one of Vienna's many synagogues to escape Nazi torching in 1938, although in part this was due to the building's close proximity to other buildings within the *Innere Stadt*, which would also have caught fire (see no. 58).

Just around the corner, next to the Jerusalemstiege, erected to celebrate 3000 years of that city's history, is the unusual Kornhäusel Tower. Apparently this huge tower house-cum-studio was designed by the architect to act as a refuge from his nagging wife, having a retractable iron staircase from the first floor rather than a conventional doorway at street level.

For more of Kornhäusel's well-proportioned and elegant work catch the blue tram (*Lokalbahn*) from outside the State Opera (*Staatsoper*) and travel to the delightful *Biedermeier* spa town of Baden. Set romantically at the edge of the Vienna woods, many of its public buildings, including the town hall, were designed by Josef Kornhäusel. There is the little-known Kornhäusl-Villa (or Villa Jenamy) too, at the corner of Ottakringer Strasse and Maroltingergasse (16th District), one of Vienna's oldest villas.

When he died Kornhäusel was first buried in the *Biedermeier* Cemetery of St. Marks (see no. 39) but was later reinterred in the Central Cemetery (*Zentralfriedhof*) in Simmering (see no. 63). Kornhäusel outlived the *Biedermeier* era itself by a dozen years, the period having been brought to an abrupt end by the March 1848 Revolution (as a result of which the *Biedermeier* is sometimes referred to as the *Vormärz* or pre-March period). With Paris (and soon Italy and Hungary) in revolution, Viennese students and workers met outside the Lower Austrian Landhaus at Herrengasse 13 to oust the arch-conservative Metternich, free the Press and address Vienna's problem of overcrowding, disease and food shortages. A crowd gathered and shots were fired (despite a plaque of 1571 warning visitors not to fight!) sparking not only a revolution and the resignation of Metternich, but also the meeting of Austria's first democratically elected assembly (see no. 70) and the abdication of Emperor Ferdinand I (1835–48) in favour of his nephew the 18-year old Franz Josef I (1848–1916).

The so-called Kornhäusel Tower on Judengasse

Other places of interest nearby: 12, 13, 15, 16

15 From Julius Meinl to Billy Wilder

1st District (Innere Stadt), Fleischmarkt 7

One of the most enduring, and endearing, Viennese urban myths concerns the city's addiction to coffee (on average over half a litre, per person, per day!). It was for many years recounted how bags of curious green beans were found amongst the abandoned possessions of retreating Turkish troops after their second siege of Vienna in 1683. Thought to be camel fodder they were claimed as a reward by a Polish adventurer called Georg Franz Kolschitzky (1640-94). Using his extensive knowledge of Turkey and Turkish, he had penetrated enemy lines and brought back word of Vienna's impending relief. The reward seemed paltry, but clever Kolschitzky knew he could roast and brew the beans to make coffee – and make a fortune in the process. His statue dressed in Turkish garb and wielding an oriental coffee pot can be seen at the corner of Favoritenstrasse and Kolschitzkygasse in the 4th district of Wieden.

However, whilst it is true that coffee has been served in Vienna since the late-17th century, its beginnings were rather more prosaic. The world's first coffee house appeared in Istanbul in 1554 followed by Europe's first in Venice (1647), then London (1652), Paris (1660) and Hamburg (1677). Not until 1685 did Emperor Leopold I (1658–1705) grant a license to sell coffee and tea in Vienna, to an Armenian trader called Johannes Deodatus (his original premises are marked by a plaque at Rotenturmstrasse 14). Despite this late start, it was the Viennese who elevated coffee drinking into a fine art, creating the thirty or so variations available in the city's myriad coffee houses today. From the original sweet *Türkische* served in its individual copper pot to the frothy milky *Mélange*, there's a coffee, and a coffee house (*Kaffeehaus*), to suit all moods.

A name now synonymous with coffee in Vienna is that of Julius Meinl, purveyor of green and then roasted coffee, since 1862. In 1891 he built a specialised roasting plant on the very site where the Turkish Grand Vizier Kara Mustafa had abandoned his camp back in 1683 (see no. 2). At Fleischmarkt 7 can be seen the company's former office built in 1899, its facade boasting proudly »*Julius Meinl's Kaffee Imports*«. The accompanying reliefs depict somewhat romanticised scenes of coffee being grown, harvested and transported by ship to

Façade of the former Julius Meinl Coffee Imports office on Fleischmarkt

Europe, accompanied by swooping seagulls. The three coats of arms are those of the great trading ports of Hamburg, Trieste and London.

A Meinl Moor on the front of Meinl's Graben shop

By 1939 there were a thousand Meinl stores, all identified by the fez-wearing coffee boy logo (*Meinl Moor*), symbolising quality and excellence. Today Meinl still imports and roasts many types of coffee, which it sells in its bazaar-like gourmet store on the Graben (*or visit www.meinl. com*). A carving of the Meinl Moor can still be seen outside on the corner at number 16, though for some reason he is painted entirely white.

Before leaving the Fleischmarkt offices, notice the plaque in the entrance stating that Billy Wilder (1906–2002) lived here as a schoolboy. He went on to become a director and screenplay writer in America, famous for *The Seven Year Itch*, *Double Indemnity*, *Sunset Boulevard* and, of course, *Some Like it Hot* starring Marilyn Monroe.

Other places of interest nearby: 13, 14, 16, 17

16 Pedestrians Beware!

1st District (Innere Stadt), Fleischmarkt 9

The explorer will not find a greater concentration of oddities in a smaller area anywhere in Vienna than by walking along Fleischmarkt and down Griechengasse. The top end of Fleischmarkt, itself named after the old meat market, boasts the eccentric Kornhäusel Tower (see no. 14) as well as an ornate coffee importer's office (see no. 15). Towards its eastern end is the charming Griechengasse that begins as a narrow sloping passage with flying buttresses overhead. On the wall at the top, actually Fleischmarkt 9, is one of a pair of fascinating tin traffic signs detailing a law from May 8th, 1912 requiring that horse-

A warning to pedestrians at the top of Griechengasse

drawn carriages be preceded by someone on foot, to warn pedestrians of their imminent arrival. The passage is lined with stone bollards, some with iron bands, designed to protect the walls from repeated damage by cartwheels. Thankfully, it is now pedestrianised, and not even the horse-drawn *Fiakers* that brave the busy Ringstrasse would negotiate this precarious thoroughfare.

Griechengasse itself is named after the Greek merchants who settled here in the 18th century to orchestrate Vienna's trade with the Balkans and the Levant. There are two Greek churches here, of which the gilded brick exterior of Holy Trinity at Fleischmarkt 13 can't be missed. It was re-modelled in the Neo-Byzantine style in the 1860s by Theophil Hansen who designed Vienna's Parliament and had worked previously in Athens (also Neo-Byzantine in style is his Christus Church in the old Matzleinsdorf Cemetery on Triester Strasse in the 5th district of Margareten). It is well worth peering inside the colonnaded entrance hall that is always kept dark with only an occasional candle flickering in the gloom. Next-door can still be found the Issakides Greek carpet-merchant's shop. The older Church of St. George (1803) sits on the terrace that opens out below the passage overlooking Hafnersteig. Its construction was permitted by Emperor Josef II (1765-90) whose Edict of Tolerance (*Toleranzpatent*) was proclaimed in 1781 at Fleischmarkt 18. The edict, however, forbade the building from resembling a church externally hence its relative modesty.

At Griechengasse 7 is a 17th century house with a Baroque niched Madonna and Rococo lantern below, as well as Islamic-inscribed wooden panels in its entrance from the 1683 Turkish siege (see no. 2). There is also an interesting old water pump with stone basin and a 13th century medieval watchtower in the courtyard beyond.

Finally, returning to the top of the passage at Fleischmarkt 11/ Griechengasse 9 is the cosy Griechenbeisel Inn in a building that dates back as far as 1447 (see no. 24). Re-named because of the area's Greek presence, one of its ancient vaulted rooms is covered with famous signatures including those of Mozart, Bismarck, Brahms, Prince Eugène of Savoy, Strauss, Beethoven, Richard Wagner, Mark Twain, Johnny Cash, Albert Einstein and original *Tarzan* actor Johnny Weissmueller. Outside is a carving of the famous ballad singer Augustin (*Der Liebe Augustin*) who one drunken night in 1679 fell into a plague pit only to be rescued when passers-by heard his bagpipes! His effigy can also be spotted under a grate in a side passage (near three old Turkish cannonballs) and his name, taken as a symbol of hope, is borne today by the newspaper sold around Vienna by the homeless and unemployed.

Other places of interest nearby: 13, 14, 15, 17

17 Pianos, Wrought Iron and the Renaissance

1st District (Innere Stadt), Bäckerstrasse 7

One of the many joys of discovering Vienna's *Innere Stadt* on foot is stumbling across its many fascinating courtyards (*Innenhof*) and quiet squares, often quite by accident (see no. 29). Most were built during the Baroque and *Biedermeier* periods (17th–19th centuries) but there is one courtyard, at Bäckerstrasse 7 that dates right back to 1587 and the century of the Italian Renaissance. It is especially curious because there is so little architecture from this period to be found in Vienna. The reason for this is thought to have been the huge expense incurred by the building of the city walls following the first Turkish siege in 1529 (see no. 24). Additionally, no Emperor lived permanently in Vienna until after 1683, Maximilian I (1493–1519) spending his money on Innsbruck and Rudolf II (1576–1612) spending his time in Prague, both being places where many wealthy nobles also gravitated together with their potential architectural commissions. The few important Renaissance buildings in Vienna include the Maximilian Palace erected by Emperor Ferdinand I (1556–64) for his son Archduke Maximilian (now stables (*Stallburg*) for the Spanish Riding School) (*Spanische Reitschule*), the Hofburg's Amalientrakt and Schweizertor (the latter still with its original drawbridge mechanism and moat), the graceful cupola atop the Stephansdom's unfinished North Tower, the façade of the Franziskanerkirche (see no. 29) and the Neugebäude hunting palace built for Emperor Maximilian II (1564–76). The latter was a unique pleasure ground whose crenellated garden walls now enclose the crematorium across the road from the Central Cemetery (*Zentralfriedhof*) in Simmering (see no. 63).

Returning to the house in Bäckerstrasse (known as the *Schwanfeldsche Haus*), its somewhat grimy Renaissance entrance portal is given added charm by the lovely old painted glass signboard for Franz Nemetschke's piano shop. Inside, part of the small courtyard retains its Tuscan balustraded balconies, albeit now blocked up, and behind the plain supporting columns are the original stables complete with stone troughs, iron hay basket and even a harness hanging on the back wall. On the opposite side are later balconies with iron railings and lots of trailing greenery adding to the atmosphere. It was here that

Biedermeier portrait artist Friedrich von Amerling (1803–87) lived, famous for his portraits evoking the idealised family life of the bourgeosie, and his collection of decorative wrought iron still hangs here to this day (Amerling also lived in a charming *Biedermeier* courtyard residence at Stiftgasse 8 in the 7th district of Neubau). Other Renaissance houses can be found at Bäckerstrasse 12 and 14, as well as another fine portal just around the corner at Sonnenfelsgasse 15, after which it's probably best to head for Salvatorgasse where a further architectural gem awaits discovery. Here, the late-13th century Chapel of the Saviour (*Salvatorkapelle*) has Gothic vaults inside and outside a stunning and ornate Renaissance portal dating to c.1520. The chapel's founder, Otto Haymo, famously led a conspiracy to liberate Vienna from Habsburg rule after the murder of King Albrecht I (1298–1308) in 1308, an act for which he was executed. His old house,

Balconies in the Renaissance courtyard at Bäckerstrasse 7

nearby at Wipplingerstrasse 8, was subsequently given to the City Council who used it as their Town Hall (*Altes Rathaus*) until it was replaced by the new Town Hall on the Ringstrasse.

Other places of interest nearby: 15, 16, 18, 19

18 Cryptic Cathedral Carvings

1st District (Innere Stadt), St. Stephen's Cathedral
(*Stephansdom*), Stephansplatz

Despite the high level of popular support for the German annexation (*Anschluss*) of Austria in 1938, Austrian resistance against it remained active throughout the war. However, resistance could not be considered as having been organised due to the widespread collaboration of many citizens, and the effective removal by the Nazis of any possible alternative government. Austrians may have felt differently had they known that 140,000 of them would die in concentration camps, a further 600,000 lost in air raids and fighting for the German *Wehrmacht*, not to mention the massive destruction of property marked today by hundreds of metal plaques on the walls of rebuilt apartment blocks (270,000 Viennese lost their homes during the war). The walls of Vienna still bear witness to these terrible times, as for example the quiet back street of Lehárgasse in Mariahilf where the outside of the old court theatre depot (*k.k. Hoftheaterdepot*) is still peppered with gunfire from some unspeakable execution. Despite some partisan activity in remote alpine areas, as well as individual acts of heroism, it was not until spring 1944 that an organised resistance group emerged, with its headquarters sited audaciously under the nose of the Gestapo at Ruprechtsplatz 5 (see no. 13). Their cryptic code name was O5 and it can be seen cut into the wall on the right-hand side of the main entrance to the Stephansdom. The letter O plus 5 (i.e. the fifth letter of the alphabet = E) is OE, that is the first two letters of the word *Oesterreich* (Austria) when spelt without *an umlaut* (two dots) over the letter O.

By April 1945 the Russian Red Army had advanced to the outskirts of Vienna and the O5 were planning a simultaneous coup within the city. Tragically, a junior officer betrayed the group and many of its brave leaders were tortured and publicly hung. It would take another week of bloody street fighting until the last German soldier was eventually flushed from the capital and Austria's Second Republic declared, with Dr. Karl Renner its Chancellor (having already fronted the First Republic back in 1918).

The Museum in the Documentation Centre for Austrian Resistance (*Museum im Dokumentationsarchiv des Österreichischen Widerstandes*) on the ground floor of the Old Town Hall at Wipplingerstrasse 8

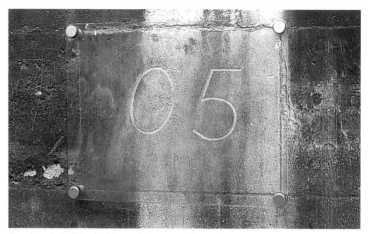

Secret symbol of the Austrian resistance carved near the entrance to the Stephansdom

illustrates the work of the Austrian underground resistance against the Nazi regime, as well as the patriotic front raised against the preceding Austro-fascist government of 1934–38. The centre's massive archive contains details of the 2,700 members of the O5 executed by the Nazis as well as the 65,000 Austrian Jewish victims of the Holocaust *(Shoah)*. The centre's main function today is to strive against neo-Nazi propaganda and the dangers of historical revisionism (e.g. Holocaust denial).

Inside the Stephansdom, in the southern chancel (or Apostles' Choir) near the High Altar, can be found another, more ancient, cryptic carving. On the red marble tomb of the first Habsburg Holy Roman Emperor Friedrich III (1440–93) are cut the vowels of the Roman alphabet – AEIOU. They are said to mean »*Alles Erdreich Ist Österreich Untertan*« (the whole world is subject to Austria), although the fact that Hungarian King Matthias Corvinus drove Friedrich from Vienna in 1485, led many to read them as »*Aller Erst Ist Österreich Verloren*« (in the first place, Austria is lost)! Other interpretations include »*Austria Erit In Orbe Ultima*« (Austria will be the last in the world), »*Aquila Electa Iovis Omnia Vincit*« (the chosen eagle conquers all things) and »*Austria Est Imperare Orbi Universo*« (it is Austria's destiny to rule the whole world). Whatever the meaning, the sepulchre remains the most important imperial tomb north of the Alps. It is worth noting that the cryptogram also appears on the base of the Wiener Neustädter Altar in the nearby Women's Nave, as well as on the ceiling of the Hofburg's Baroque library (*Prunksaal*) begun in 1723.

The Stephansdom holds many other curiosities, such as the roman gravestone incorporated deliberately into the right-hand arch of the main doorway to break its pagan spell (see no. 12) and the two iron standard measures attached to the outside wall to the left of the door (the longer one is the old Viennese *Normalelle* whilst the shorter is the *Leinenelle*). Less explicable are the tiny male and female sex

Old standard measures near the entrance to the Stephansdom

organs carved atop the two columns directly below the clocks on the flanking Pagan Towers (thus named because they resemble minarets). They may be evidence of a pagan fertility shrine having once existed here whose power again needed breaking by being incorporated into the Christian structure. Excavation below the gateway (named the Giant's Portal (*Riesentor*) after mammoth bones were excavated here) revealed ancient graves suggesting that worship and burial long pre-dates the existing cathedral. Inside the main door, immediately on the right-hand side, is the Maria-Pócs Altar, an icon of the Virgin Mary from a Hungarian village that shed tears for the two weeks in 1697 that Prince Eugène of Savoy (1663–1736) waged the decisive Battle of Zenta against the Turks. Meanwhile, in a gated chapel opposite that contains the vault of the Prince himself, can be found a High Gothic crucifix with a beard of real hair said to still be growing! (Another interesting icon is that of Maria Candia, now incorporated into the High Altar of St. Michael's Church (see no. 30). It was donated by a man who prayed for the Virgin Mary's intercession during the 1679 plague – and survived). One final Stephansdom curiosity can be found on the left–hand side of the doorway into the cathedral's unfinished North, or Eagle's Tower (*Adlerturm*). It is a curious iron handle said by some to offer sanctuary in former times to those able to grasp it.

Other places of interest nearby: 19, 20, 21, 22

19 Mozart Passed this Way

1st District (Innere Stadt), the Chapel of the Cross,
outside the northeast wall of St. Stephen's Cathedral
(*Stephansdom*), Stephansplatz

The greatest composer to be associated with Vienna was undoubtedly Salzburg-born Wolfgang Amadeus Mozart (1756–91). This is certainly true in terms of his prodigious output (c.626 individual works) across such a broad range of formats, including operas, symphonies and concertos. Having toured much of Europe by the age of eight, the expression »child prodigy« could have been invented for him. Endless volumes have been written about the composer and even today there's no escaping his image, from confectionery (*Mozartkugeln*) to ticket touts dressed in the flamboyant style he would have recognised.

One mystery surrounding Mozart, whose life has been so thoroughly documented, is why he is the only major composer (other than Vivaldi, see no. 43) whose final resting place is not exactly known. Mozart came to Vienna in 1781 to help celebrate the accession of Emperor Josef II (1765–90) to the throne and decided to stay on. He experienced his most productive years here and occupied fourteen addresses across the city, only one of which (the *Figarohaus* at Domgasse 5) is still standing. In 1782 Mozart married Constanze Weber in the Stephansdom but, despite being musically productive, he became a compulsive gambler losing large sums at billiards, ninepins and cards. That he had money to gamble dispels the myth that he was impoverished, though his income was sporadic and he left Domgasse in 1787 when he was unable to afford the rent.

Mozart's former home on Domgasse seen from Blutgasse

His last home was the Kleines Kaiserhaus at Rauhensteingasse 8 (where he wrote *The Magic Flute* (*Die Zauberflöte*) and now the *Steffl* department store with a fascinating Mozart exhibition on the 4th floor) where in the early hours of 5th December 1791 he died of feverish articular rheumatism. He had been working on his *Requiem* commissioned anonymously by an »unknown messenger« several months before. The mystery patron was later revealed to be the recently widowed Count Franz Walsegg-Stuppach who fully intended to pass the work off as his own.

On December 6th Mozart's body was moved to the Stephansdom where the coffin received benediction in the tiny Chapel of the Cross, outside the northeast wall where it forms a covered exit from the Cathedral crypts below (see no. 30). Due to bad weather it was a sorry little cortège that made its way from the Cathedral to St. Mark's Cemetery (*St. Marxer Friedhof*) (see no. 39) where Mozart's remains, sprinkled with lime to prevent spread of contagion, were wrapped in a sack and placed in a mass grave. History relates how only the gravediggers were present and that the location was subsequently forgotten. Some claim that Mozart could have avoided this ignominious end by a small additional payment, and why this was not forthcoming from family or friends remains a real mystery. His wife's absence from the scene was said to be because she was too upset to attend. However, it should not be forgotten that at this time interment in a mass grave was the norm for all but the very wealthy (by order of Emperor Josef II), and consequently the tending of individual graves was rare. Additionally, funeral services were restricted to the church and mourners rarely made the journey to the cemetery, where the body could only be taken after nightfall. So perhaps it's not such a mystery that Mozart's resting place has been lost, marked only approximately by a broken column symbolizing his unfinished life (grave 179, see front cover). Even poor Constanze searched in vain decades later, seemingly unaware that mass graves were usually cleared every eight to ten years to make space for new ones. A somewhat grander monument erected in 1859 was later removed to the Central Cemetery (*Zentralfriedhof*) in Simmering where it stands next to the graves of Beethoven, Brahms, Schubert and the Strausses.

Other places of interest nearby: 17, 18, 20, 22

The Chapel of the Cross outside the northeast wall of the Stephansdom

20 Carrying the Weight of the World

1st District (Innere Stadt), the Equitable Palais at
Stock-im-Eisen-Platz 3

The *Innere Stadt* contains many city palaces constructed in the Baroque period (mid-17th to mid-18th centuries) when eloquent and exuberant decoration was the fashion. In order to lend strength and power to these buildings the so-called *atlante* (or *telamon*, from the Greek verb to endure or bear) was used. It takes the shape of a colossal male statue designed to support portals and balconies above. The word *atlante* comes from the Greek name Atlas, a god of the archaic pantheon and brother of Prometheus. In Greek legend Atlas sided with the Titans in rebelling against Zeus, the father of the gods. Atlas was defeated and his punishment was to be condemned to support the sky on his shoulders for all eternity.

A fine example of the Baroque use of the Atlas figure is in the portals of the former Bohemian Court Chancellery (*Böhmische Hofkanzlei*) built in 1709–14 at Wipplingerstrasse 7/Judenplatz 11 (see also no. 47). From 1627 the Habsburgs were the rulers of Bohemia (now the Czech Republic) hence this magnificent building designed by the great architect Johann Bernard Fischer von Erlach (1656–1723). The figures themselves are the work of Lorenzo Mattielli, a master of the genre. He is also responsible for the freestanding Atlases supporting the ceiling of the *Sala Terrena* (ground floor room) in Prince Eugène of Savoy's Upper Belvedere Palace (1714–23), designed by that other great Baroque architect Johann Lukas von Hildebrandt (1668–1745).

Atlas figures also appear on the portal of Hildebrandt's Palais Daun-Kinsky (1713–16) at Freyung 4, as well as on the Stadtpalais Liechtenstein opposite the Minoritenkirche. Both architects had a hand in Prince Eugène's Winter Palace at Himmelpfortgasse 3 (1695–1724), in which there is a spectacular Grand Staircase held aloft by four freestanding Atlases, considered part of one of the most magnificent Baroque edifices in all Vienna (not open to the public but the porter will usually allow entry to the inner courtyard). These Atlas figures are probably the work of sculptor Giovanni Giuliani, who like Mattielli was also a master of this architectural device. However, the façade itself is devoid of Atlases due to the narrowness of the street,

Atlas figures supporting the doorway
to the former Palais Erdödy-Fürstenberg on Himmelpfortgasse

although they re-appear on the front of the nearby Palais Erdödy-Fürstenberg.

Inevitably, the architecture of the backwards-looking Historicist period (Ringstrasse Style) of the late-19th century picked up on the Atlas figures, mimicking them in a number of ways (e.g. the doorway of the Van-Swieten-Hof (1896) at Rotenturmstrasse 19 and the old Zentralbad (1887) (see no. 65) at Weihburggasse 20). Most popular was the re-interpretation of the device as a scantily clad female as seen on the pilasters of Julius Meinl's shop at Graben 20, and the overblown examples next-door on Tuchlauben. The former are sometimes referred to as the »Nymphs of Graben« and are said to represent the prostitutes who once plied their trade here! Rather more modest are the females occupying the spandrels on the façade of the famous Musikverein, as well as those in the form of gilded freestanding *caryatids* inside (a device used in Greek temples and named after the priestess of Artemis at Caryae).

Either side of the Parlament on Dr.-Karl-Renner-Ring are two grand porches supported by caryatids echoing those to be found in the *Erechtheion* on the ancient Acropolis of Athens.

Caryatids guarding the entrance to the Equitable Palais on Stock-im-Eisen Platz

Graceful too are the ladies on the portal of the Equitable Palais at Stock-im-Eisen Platz 3. This building, erected in the 1890s to house an American insurance company and as grand as anything on the Ringstrasse, is often overlooked because of its proximity to the Stephansdom. The tiny male figures above the doorway, together with the curious ancient timber in a niche outside, relate to the building's unusual address (see no. 50).

Even the forward-looking Viennese Art Nouveau (*Jugendstil*) couldn't resist the Atlas figure, rendering it in a very stylised manner on the marble-faced façade of Kohlmarkt 9. Now home to Austria's prestigious mapmakers Freytag & Berndt this building by Max Fabiani replaced an earlier house where the composer Frederic Chopin stayed during a visit to Vienna in 1830–31.

Other places of interest nearby: 21, 22, 26, 27

21 The Secret of St. Virgil's Chapel

1st District (Innere Stadt), St. Virgil's Chapel
(*Virgilkapelle*) in Stephansplatz U-Bahn-Station

Most visitors to Vienna walk over an important and curious piece of the city's history without ever realising it. Marked out in pale red stones on the surface of Stephansplatz (and best viewed from the balconies of the nearby Haas Haus) is the outline of the Chapel of St. Mary Magdalene (*Magdalenenkirchlein*). It was built in the 14th

Outline of St. Virgil's Chapel and the Chapel of St. Mary Magdalene in Stephansplatz

century in what was at the time a cemetery surrounding the Stephansdom cathedral, and was used for consecrations and funeral masses until its demolition after a fire in 1781. This destruction in turn caused the abandonment of a concealed subterranean room lying directly below, whose chance re-discovery was only made in 1973 during excavations for the Stephansplatz U-Bahn station.

What came to light after being hidden for nearly 200 years were the mysterious remains of St. Virgil's Chapel. A rectangular room measuring 10.5 metres long and 6 metres wide, its floor lies some 12 metres below the present cathedral square. Ignoring the existing roof vault that was added later, the original walls once soared 1.5 metres above what is now Stephansplatz giving the building an original height of

The mysterious St. Virgil's Chapel below Stephansplatz

13–14 metres. Its walls are 1.5 metres thick and were broken by six recesses (outlined in *white* stones on Stephansplatz), one of which lay where the present subterranean entrance for visitors now lies. They are covered in white plaster painted with red lines to give a crude impression of fine masonry and at the top of each recess is a circled cross. Curiously, the closest parallel for this motif is the Syro-Palestinian region and the art of the early Christian and Byzantine world. Also unusual is the fact that the room only has a clay floor with no evidence of paving and that there is a well with no apparent function. Most mysterious of all however is how the building was actually entered – it can only be assumed by means of a trapdoor in a chapel that existed above the vaulted roof in Stephansplatz.

Although oddly not mentioned in existing 13th century documents, the building has been dated stylistically to the reign of the last Babenberg Duke, Friedrich II (1230–46) (namely by its original vaulting that resembles that of the dateable Michaelerkirche, and the circular cross motif that is reminiscent of the Stephansdom's Late Romanesque rosette in the old West Gallery, built in 1230 but only re-discovered in 1945). It is thought that Friedrich II, eager to elevate Vienna to a Bishopric, commissioned the structure as a potential tomb for St. Koloman, patron saint elect of the new diocese. Koloman was an Irish pilgrim to the Holy Land, revered for his healing powers but hung in error in Lower Austria on suspicion of spying (a lucky stone from the site where he died was incorporated into the Bishop's Portal of the Stephansdom in 1361, though his bones now rest at Melk monastery in the Wachau). After Friedrich's premature death, falling from a horse whilst fighting the Hungarians in 1246, and the accession of the Habsburgs 30 years later since he left no heirs, this tomb plan was abandoned. Later, in the early-14th century, the area's old charnel house (where exhumed bones were stored to make space for new burials) was destroyed through the building of the Stephansdom's chancel. As Friedrich's grand subterranean room now lacked a function its high vaulted roof was removed and a lower one installed and between it and the chapel above a new charnel house was inserted.

The subterranean room then passed to the wealthy Viennese merchant family of Chrannest who used it as a family burial chamber in c.1340. It was they who added several altars, dedicating one of them to St. Virgil after whom the building is named today. After the Chrannest family died out the chamber became the meeting place during the 16th century for the Brotherhood of Merchants, as well as the newly founded Brotherhood of God's Corpse (*Fronleichnamsbruder-schaft*).

By 1378 the chapel above had been extended eastwards by means of a chancel and is thenceforth known as the Chapel of St. Mary Magdalene, illustrated in considerable detail in Jakob Hoefnagel's famous map of Vienna from 1609. The chapel is clearly depicted with its tower and polygonal buttressed chancel to the east. It was the latter that was the seat of the Association of Notaries (*Schreiberzeche*) whose seal bore the image of their patron saint Mary Magdalene. It is interesting to note that the function of the new charnel house was soon replaced by the Stephansdom's far larger subterranean crypts, where thousands of bodies were laid to rest in the period up to 1783 (see no. 30), just two years after the chapel and its hidden chambers had been destroyed.

Other places of interest nearby: 20, 22, 27, 28

22 The Snake's Tongue Poison Detector

1st District (Innere Stadt), the Treasury of the Order
of the Teutonic Knights (*Schatzkammer des
Deutschen Ordens*) on the first floor at Singerstrasse 7
(staircase 1)

In 1190 during the siege of Acre in the Holy Land, the burghers of
Bremen and Lübeck founded the wonderfully named Brethren of the
Teutonic House of St. Mary of Jerusalem. Mercifully abbreviated to
the Order of the Teutonic Knights (or *Deutscher Orden*) it was one of
the three main military-religious orders to emerge from the Crusades.
Despite military defeat at Tannenberg in 1410, and dissolution under
both Napoleon and Hitler, the spiritual branch of the order remains
active as a charitable body, tending the sick and assisting the development of former Communist countries where it maintains a strong
presence.

Its history in Vienna began under the Babenberg dukes when the
knights built a house (*Deutschordenshaus*) in 1222 at Singerstrasse 7,
known at the time as Deutschherrengasse. In the late-14th century
a Gothic church (*Deutschordenskirche*) was incorporated where the
knights' coats of arms and memorial slabs can still be seen. By 1633
its treasury had amassed an exotic collection of objects collected by
the Order's various Grand Masters (*Hochmeister*) and by the late-18th
century the house had assumed its present form.

High dignitaries of the church headed the order for much of its
history and when a *Hochmeister* died his possessions fell to the Order.
An important part of the resulting collection is the precious tableware,
either for practical use or decoration only.

Pride of place must surely go to the *Natternzungenkredenz*, or
snake's tongue salt-cellar, of 1526: a most unusual table decoration by
anyone's reckoning! Dangling from a red coral branch are 13 fossilised
shark's teeth, thought originally to be adders', vipers' or even dragons'
tongues that were believed to exude moisture when placed near poi-
soned food or drink. Only two other examples are known, in Dresden
and in Vienna's Kunsthistorisches Museum (see no. 35). Also curious
are the set of Tiger Shell spoons with curvy silver handles from Goa,
a wavy-bladed Malaysian dagger (*kris*) with Rhino horn handle in the
form of a Buddha and from Persia strange stones, called *bezoars*,

The snakes' tongue poison detector in the Treasury of the Teutonic Knights in Singerstrasse

found in the stomach of the Ibex goat to which supernatural healing powers were once attributed. On show too is the chain of the Order itself, made up of eleven shields each bearing the distinctive black cross emblem, and a stunning bejewelled table clock in which the time, date and planetary movements are measured out by a series of tiny figures.

Before leaving the building be sure to glance at the *Sala Terrena* (ground floor room), a tiny 50-seat concert hall with Venetian-style Baroque frescoes, providing an intimate venue for Mozart concerts. If closed, take a peep at it through the shuttered windows in the equally delightful cobbled courtyard, replete with window boxes, glazed loggias and fragments of sculpture, where both Brahms and Mozart lived briefly.

Other places of interest nearby: 18, 19, 20, 26

23 The World's First Fitted Kitchen

1st District (Innere Stadt), the Austrian Museum for
Applied Arts (*Österreichisches Museum für angewandte
Kunst, MAK*), at Stubenring 5

The Austrian Museum of Applied Arts, abbreviated simply to the MAK,
is Vienna's most ambitious and eclectic museum, presenting eight centuries worth of design, craftwork, *objets d'art* and utilitarian objects.
Individual rooms are devoted to different periods as well as to individual collections, such as Art Nouveau, the *Wiener Werkstätte* (Vienna
Workshops founded in 1903 to produce fabrics, furniture, jewellery,
table-ware and wallpapers similar to the English Arts and Crafts Movement), the 20th Century, Oriental carpets (including the world's only
16th century Egyptian silk *Mameluke* carpet) and furniture. The latter
includes Michael Thonet's 1856-patented, beech bentwood chairs that
were produced in their millions and became popular the world over
(see no. 44).

An exhibit well worth tracking down lies at the end of one of

The celebrated Frankfurt Kitchen in the Museum of Applied Arts on Stubenring

the basement study collections and is known as the Frankfurt Kitchen (*Frankfurter Küche*). It was designed by Margarete Schütte-Lihotzky, Austria's first female student of architecture, who devoted her long life to improving the living conditions of working women throughout Europe. In 1920, whilst still only in her early twenties, she received an award for an allotment design that brought her into contact with the Viennese Modernist architect Adolf Loos (1870–1933), renowned for his extreme functionalism and austere designs. Loos had a considerable impact on design in the inter-war period of Socialist Red Vienna, for example the *Werkbundsiedlung* housing estate (see no. 72), the city's huge new apartment blocks (see no. 82) and ultimately the pared-down ergonomics of the Frankfurt Kitchen itself.

In 1922 Schütte-Lihotzky worked with Loos on Austria's first public housing scheme for the war-disabled and their friendship endured until his death in 1933. The collaboration had a profound impact on her career and led to important developments in the design of houses, *kindergartens* and self-assembly furniture.

During the late 1920s the German city of Frankfurt embarked on a large-scale housing programme and Schütte-Lihotzky was commissioned to help design an inexpensive, functional yet aesthetic apartment. She approached the task scientifically using the American Taylor System to time individual tasks around the home with a stopwatch and to base her design directly on optimal functional requirements. Only in this way would the working woman be able to gain more time for her family and for herself.

As a result of her findings, Schütte-Lihotzky came up with a compact single unit comprising a built-in kitchen (which was only 6.5 metres square and could be mass-produced) separated from a living/dining area by a sliding door. The latter would enable a mother to keep an eye on her children whilst working in the kitchen and through which she could walk effortlessly the three metres from stove to dining table. In order to minimise the surfaces that needed cleaning the kitchen units were placed on concrete plinths and likewise the wall units reached right up to the ceiling. The stove had a special ventilation flue and below the window was a storage cabinet kept cool by an outside opening. Hardwearing and stain-resistant beech wood was used for the work surfaces themselves and there was an ingenious slot through which refuse could be swept into a bin below. Other ultra-sensible devices included a foldaway ironing board, moveable ceiling lamp, oak flour bins to deter mealworms and aluminium pull-out drawers in which to store dry foodstuffs.

The overall compactness of the design impressed the Frankfurt City Council greatly, as a result of which they built c.10,000 apartments between 1926 and 1930, each with the compulsory inclusion of what was now referred to as a »Frankfurt Kitchen«. The costs of the unit were added to the building costs (which overall were reduced through mass-production) and factored into the rent, a solution acceptable to the tenants who did not have to furnish the kitchen. The example to be found in the MAK today is a replica built from Schütte-Lihotzky's memory and serves to remind the onlooker of its technically sophisticated solutions, balanced proportions and subtle colour scheme.

Schütte-Lihotzky's opposition to the annexation of Austria by Nazi Germany and her subsequent alliance with the Communist party led to arrest by the Gestapo and dispatch to a Bavarian prison camp. Thankfully her death sentence imposed in 1940 was lifted. During the ensuing Cold War she received few commissions because of her politics and it was not until 1980 that Vienna eventually recognised her achievements by presenting her with the Vienna City Prize for Architecture and in 1988 with the Austrian Honorary Medal for Science and Art. In 1997 she waltzed with Vienna's Mayor during her special 100th birthday celebrations and in 1998 one of her last commissions was to oversee a housing project designed for women by women.

The indomitable Margarete Schütte-Lihotzky died on January 18th 2000 just short of her 103rd birthday and was buried in the Central Cemetery (*Zentralfriedhof*) in Simmering. Gone she may be but her prototype for the modern fitted kitchen that we now take for granted continues to benefit and inspire the lives of working women (and men!) to this day.

Note: Not far from the MAK, on Marxergasse across the River Wien, can be found the sorry shell of the once-grand Sofien-Saal, a concert hall whose stage was once graced by the Vienna Philharmonic Orchestra. There are plans afoot to restore the ruins as apartments.

Other places of interest nearby: 16, 17, 24, 25

24 One of the Last Bastions

1st District (Innere Stadt), the Palais Coburg at the junction
of the Coburgbastei and Gartenbaupromenade.

The Romans were the first to use Vienna's geography to good effect
in determining the placing of the walls of their fort, *Vindobona* (see
no. 12). After withdrawing from the city in c.400AD these walls together with their associated roads remained, providing the ground
plan for medieval Vienna. The name *Wenia* first appeared in the Salzburg annals of 881AD as part of the Eastern March (*Ostmark*) of
Charlemagne's Franco-German Holy Roman Empire (it is thought to
derive from the Illyro-Celtic word *Verdunja*, meaning woodland stream).

After the empire's collapse, the Saxon King Otto the Great subdued
the German lands and in 976AD his son Otto II bestowed the March
on the Bavarian Margraves of Babenberg under Leopold I (976–94). It
would be their job to protect this eastern frontier, first as margraves
(counts) and later as dukes, and by 996AD the name *Ostarrichi*
(Eastern Realm, the origin of Österreich) is mentioned officially for
the first time. The Babenbergs restored Vienna's trade and culture,
and by the mid-12th century, under Heinrich II (1141–77), had upgraded Austria to an independent dukedom, built a ducal palace on Am
Hof (see no. 3) and given Vienna city status. Using a ransom raised
from the capture by Duke Leopold V (1177–94) of the English King
Richard the Lionheart in 1192 (allegedly at a village inn now occupied
by an apartment block at Erdbergstrasse 41 in Landstrasse), the Babenbergs also built a new city wall in 1195–1250; the silver coins were
produced in a mint founded by Leopold in 1194 at Hoher Markt 4.
Although these fortifications were 4.5 kilometres long, 10 metres high
and 4 metres thick, punctuated by gates (*Tor*) and towers (*Turm*), they
have been largely obliterated by later structures and little remains of
them today other than the occasional piece of walling (e.g. in the Heiligenkreuzerhof, near the third stairwell; the saddle-roofed tower of
the Griechenbeisel inn at Fleischmarkt 11/Griechengasse 9; and the
original Stubentor gate, Vienna's oldest (c.1200), known as the Black
Tower (*Schwarzer Turm*), its outline drawn in black stone on today's
pavement). The rest is marked only by the occasional street name
(e.g. Salztorgasse and Schottentor station) and wall plaque (e.g. the
Katzensteig gate at the bottom of Seitenstettengasse (demolished in
1825); the Stadttor at the Hohe Brücke on Wipplingerstrasse; the

street name of Werdertorgasse; and a mosaic of the Roter Turm (Red Tower) on Rotenturmstrasse).

In 1278 the Habsburg dynasty came to the fore under King Rudolf I (1273–91) and they remained monarchs of Austria for the next 640 years. However, despite Vienna going on to become the capital of a wealthy empire, its by now ancient Babenberg fortifications almost crumbled during the first Turkish siege of 1529 (see no. 2). As a direct result, Em-

A brick in the Mölker Bastei stamped with the Habsburg double-eagle

peror Ferdinand I (1556–64) ordered the construction of Vienna's so-called zigzag wall in their place, as well as the strengthening of the Hofburg (then a castle known as the *Alte Burg* to where he moved his court in 1533). Influenced by the architecture of Italian Renaissance fortresses the massive brick walls, erected between 1531 and 1566, were pierced by eight gateways, with numerous towers as well as stone-clad star-shaped defensive bastions (*Bastei*) jutting out into open ground known as the *glacis*. This no-man's land was 570 metres wide and sloped away from the walls out towards the unprotected suburbs, affording an attacking army little shelter. The huge expense of the walls accounts in part for the paucity of other Renaissance architecture in Vienna (see no. 17).

Though partly breached, the walls survived a second Turkish siege in 1683 and were still more or less intact by the time of the 1848 Revolution (see no. 14). By then however the only threat to Vienna was civil disorder and it was felt that this could be better controlled by building two huge city barracks, connected by a broad street occupying the site of the *glacis* (see no. 51). After all, the revolutionaries of 1848 had used the city walls to protect themselves from approaching imperial troops intent on quelling the unrest.

Thus, on 20th December 1857 by decree of Emperor Franz Josef I (1848–1916), work began on dismantling the Renaissance walls, using the rubble to level the *glacis* and so providing the cramped inner city with some much needed breathing space. The result was the horseshoe-shaped Parisian-style boulevard called the Ringstrasse. Stretching 4 kilometres in length and up to 60 metres in width it is lined with grand cultural and political institutions and remains the Emperor's most significant architectural legacy.

In several places, however, fragments of the old Renaissance walls linger, notably where they continue to provide the foundations for important buildings above. Thus, at the Mölkerbastei named after the Benedictine monastery at Melk that owned land in the city, there is a high brick bastion supporting a row of lovely late-18th century houses called the Pasqualatihaus, after its owner Baron Pasqualati. Here in 1804 and 1813–15, on the 4th floor of number 8, lived Beethoven (1770–1827) in a famously messy apartment where he composed his only opera *Fidelio*. Around the corner is a street called Schottenbastei although no walls remain here.

Similarly, the former Albertina palace and monastery, now the spectacularly renovated Graphic Arts Museum (*Graphische Sammlung*), sits atop an old Hofburg rampart on Hanuschgasse. Most informative of all, however, is the recently restored Coburgbastei, a wall supporting the huge Palais Coburg above, in front of which was once a projecting bastion (*Braunbastei*) whose outer edge can still be seen. Windows at street level allow the passer-by to glimpse at the mighty vaulted casemates (*Kasematten*) running deep within the thickness of the brick walls, once busy with troops and cannon. Inside the building, now a luxury hotel, on the left, is a stunning modern mosaic showing a bird's eye view of Vienna's Renaissance city walls.

Finally, not far away at Stubenbastei, are the foundations of the Renaissance Stubentor gateway and its 22 metre-high adjoining walls revealed during excavation work for the U-3 underground in 1985–87. Its plan has been marked out permanently in white stone at street level and there is a fascinating exhibition in the subway below illustrating

The remains of a projecting bastion in front of the Palais Coburg

the gate's full history from Babenberg times through to its incorporation into the Renaissance wall and final demolition. One further piece of wall is the nearby Dominikanerbastei, clad in white plaster to match the Baroque church it supports above. Nothing at all now remains of the walls along the Danube Canal although there are a few tantalising sculptured fragments from the so-called Gonzagabastei that once stood here, preserved on the U-Bahn platform at Schwedenplatz.

Note: The so-called Äusseres Burgtor next to the Neue Burg is the city wall's only extant gateway although it was actually *inserted* into the wall later in the 1820s to commemorate the Battle of Leipzig at which the Austrians and the Prussians defeated Napoleon. It is flanked by two entrances added by the Austro-fascist party in 1934, their oppressive stylised eagles being one of Vienna's rare examples of truly fascist architecture. From this time onwards, the gate served as Vienna's chief memorial to the fallen soldiers of the First World War.

Other places of interest nearby:
22, 23, 25, 26

An Austro-Fascist eagle on a gateway near the Äusseres Burgtor

25 The Last City Vineyard

1st District (Innere Stadt), Schwarzenbergplatz 2

Tucked into a corner of busy Schwarzenbergplatz, behind a grand stone balustrade, is a most unexpected sight – the last remaining vineyard in central Vienna. It is cared for by the Mayer am Pfarrplatz winery, for purely nostalgic reasons rather than commercial ones. However, they do maintain a *heurige* restaurant in a fine old *Biedermeier* house at Pfarrplatz 2 in Grinzing, where Beethoven lived for a time, and so the little vineyard is no doubt good for advertising.

The tiny vineyard in a corner of Schwarzenbergplatz

It was by order of the Roman Emperor Probus in 280AD that the virgin landscape of the Danube was first planted extensively with vines, although the Celts before them were probably familiar with the grape. Vienna's short hot summers, lingering humid autumns and long cold winters make it ideal white wine country, manifested in its crisp, dry, acidic wines as well as sweet, late-harvest styles. Austria has ten wine regions, mainly in the sunny east, of which the Vienna region is one of the smallest, with c.530 hectares of vineyards located uniquely within the city limits (making it the world's largest wine-growing city). Ninety percent of the grapes, predominantly *Grüner Veltliner*, are pressed for Vienna's typically rustic white wine, with only a minority grown for reds and rosés.

Up until the late-17th century vineyards still covered much of central Vienna. However, with the successful repulsion of the Turks, and the development of the city suburbs in the Baroque period, the vineyards were gradually pushed back to the foothills of the Vienna Woods (*Wienerwald*) north of the city.

Enjoying wine is today as much a part of Viennese culture as art and music, being drunk in cosy taverns (*Beisel*), stylish restaurants and hidden cellars across the city (see no. 5). The ultimate wine experience occurs in the summer when Viennese and visitors alike take off to the vineyards of the outer suburbs (e.g. Grinzing, Sievering, Strebersdorf and Stammersdorf) to visit rustic country taverns known as *Heurigen*. The word *heurige* comes from the word *heuer*, meaning this year, and refers to the most recent vintage from the previous September and October. It was Emperor Josef II (1765–90) who in 1784 lifted the tax on wine, giving vintners the opportunity to sell their wine from their own premises for up to 300 days a year. The grapes had to be grown in the Vienna area and not be supplemented with grapes from elsewhere – and the edict still stands to this day. Only an authentic *heurige* can hang out a pine branch (*Buschenschank*) in March together with the word *Ausg'steckt* (literally hung out) advertising that the wine is now available (ornate stylised metalwork versions of the *Buschen* can also be found around the city). However, it is not until after St. Martin's Day (November 11th) that the wine of the previous year is considered as being properly aged. St. Martin was the first Christian saint not to be martyred and the date of his burial supplanted the earlier pagan feast day of Bacchus, god of wine. In time November 11th also became the traditional feast day for baptising the young wine in many central European wine-growing areas, accompanied in Austria by roast goose so plentiful at this time during the bird's annual autumn migration. It is also possible, for a few short weeks following the harvest, to sample the *early* stages of the new wine, namely in the form of *Most* (unfermented), *Sturm* (early fermented) and *Staubiger* (fermented but still cloudy).

For those interested, Döbling's District Museum (*Bezirksmuseum*) has a section devoted to viniculture in its vaulted cellar (*Weinbaumuseum*), and the Heurige Reinprecht at Cobenzlgasse 22 in the same district boasts the world's largest corkscrew collection.

Of course, as with all good wine regions, there are bad years – and 1450 was just such a year. The vintage was so sour, due to adverse weather conditions, that it was used to slake the lime used in the foundations of the Stephansdom's North Tower producing, it is said, an extraordinarily strong mortar!

Other places of interest nearby: 23, 24, 26, 42

26 Where the *Wurst* is Best!

1st District (Innere Stadt), Wiener Würstelstand
on Kupferschmiedgasse off Kärntnerstrasse

Modern fast food, whilst very convenient in busy modern times, rarely gives the customer a cultural experience to remember, or the opportunity to converse with his fellow man. In Vienna, however, that is exactly what is on offer, from mid-morning until dusk and beyond, on many of the city's street corners. The culinary institution that is the *Würstelstand* (sausage stand), with its colourful retro styling of the 1950s, sliding windows and chrome counter, is a welcome, reassuring and integral part of the modern Viennese cityscape. With 300 or so outlets across the capital this paean to the humble Austrian sausage is

A classic Viennese Würstelstand in Kupferschmiedgasse

undoubtedly Vienna's oldest fast food establishment, with a clientele that transcends all economic and social boundaries. Here, the impoverished student and footsore shopper stand cheek-by-jowl with the company manager, office worker, builder and late-night clubber; male and female, young and old, all enjoying a hearty non-vegetarian snack together. Of the twenty or so different sausages available, each stand

A selection of different Würstel near Schottentor

will sell about half a dozen types at any one time, from the familiar (thin pairs of boiled *Frankfurters* – called *Wieners* in Frankfurt! – and fried *Bratwurst*; the latter when boiled are called *Burenwurst*) to the less well-known (plump, cheese-infused pork *Käsekrainer*, thin spicy Hungarian *Debreziner* and smoked *Tirolerwurst*). Additionally, perspiring gently in its own tiny oven is *Leberkäse* (which translates as liver cheese), a sort of meat loaf that contains neither liver nor cheese and which is served sliced in a sandwich. Occasionally it is made from horsemeat (*Pferdeleberkäse*) and there is a further variation that does include cheese (*Käseleberkäse*). Sausages are traditionally served sliced (*aufg'schnittn*) on a paper tray with a toothpick, together with a roll (*Semmel*) or sliced bread (*Brot*), sweet or sour mustard (*süsser* or *scharfer Senf*) or pickles, and all washed down with a carbonated drink or lager beer. Customers wishing to devour a sausage on the hoof should opt for a sausage hot dog-style, slid inside a baguette suitably lubricated with tomato ketchup and wrapped in a paper serviette.

For a somewhat more refined, but no less Viennese, snacking experience try Trzesniewski's famous buffet at Dorotheergasse 1, where myriad open rye-bread sandwiches are served by uniformed waitresses to standing customers, washed down with a tiny glass (*Pfiff*) of beer. During the increasingly chilly months of autumn and winter Vienna's permanent sausage stands are supplemented by an array of temporary ones selling hot chestnuts (*Maroni*), sliced baked potatoes (*Bratkartoffeln*), hot potato patties with garlic (*Kartoffelpuffer*), *Glühwein* (mulled wine spiced with cloves) and *Punsch* (hot tea, dark rum, orange juice and cinnamon with a shot of wine) – the perfect cure for cold noses and frozen fingers! They are especially prominent in the city's wonderful Christmas street markets (*Christkindlmarkt*) (e.g. Rathausplatz, Freyung, Spittelberg and Schloss Schönbrunn) whose long history can be traced back as far as 1298.

Other places of interest nearby: 20, 22, 27, 30

27 Buildings that Make You Feel Better

1st District (Innere Stadt), Alte Leopoldsapotheke
at Plankengasse 6

With the unique combination of Habsburg grandeur and the legacy of being a major European seat of medical learning, it should come as no surprise to discover that Vienna's high street dispensing chemists (*Apotheke*) are a little different. The following locations should appeal not only to those interested in the history of pharmaceutical retailing, but to anyone who enjoys art and architecture in an unexpected setting.

A perfect starting point is the *Alte Leopoldsapotheke* on Plankengasse, its modest shuttered exterior concealing a veritable treasure house within. Opened in 1803, many of its beautiful shop fittings are still in place. Gleaming black wooden shelves, trimmed with gold urns, rosettes and capitals, carry row-upon-row of white porcelain pots containing therapeutic oils, with brown pots reserved for other extracts. Used until surprisingly recently, and reflecting the fact that most modern drugs are based on plant extracts, the names read like a herbalist's lexicon: crocus, gland lupuli, gelatina animal and paraffin liquid. Similarly, countless wooden drawers below contain further extracts such as Valerian, Marjoram and Gentian. Over the gilded and tiled fireplace that is still in use is an old watercolour advertisement promoting an alpine sanatorium in Semmering. Incredibly, amidst all this history and ephemera a modern and thriving business is carried on with great efficiency.

Similarly appointed, though no longer in use, is the former court pharmacy (*Hofapotheke*) next to the Spanish Riding School, its fine wooden cabinets still in place.

Another old chemist is the *Stadtapotheke zum Goldenen Hirschen* on Kohlmarkt, with its historic sit-down weighing scales, whilst across the Graben at Tuchlauben 9 is the *Apotheke zum Weissen Storch* adorned with a painting and a model of the bird so often associated with childbirth. Around the corner at Bognergasse 5 is the *Engelapotheke* with superb mosaic angels on the front, designed by Oskar Laske, a pupil of Otto Wagner (note also Thomas Moog's original Vienna portrait salon next-door). Beyond the Stephansdom is the *Apotheke zum Römischen Kaiser* at Wollzeile 13, dating to 1760 and brimming with gold fixtures, eagle-topped alcoves and paintings, as is the *Apotheke zum goldenen Reichsapfel* at Singerstrasse 15.

Outside the *Innere Stadt* are some further chemists of note, namely the *Apotheke zum Heiligen Geist* founded in 1551 just outside the Ring at Operngasse 16, and the *Apotheke der Barmherzigen Brüder*, a monastery pharmacy of 1772 at Taborstrasse 16 in Leopoldstadt, with its spectacular painted ceiling. The *Alte Löwenapotheke* at Josef-städter Strasse 25 has a particularly striking exterior with gold-painted

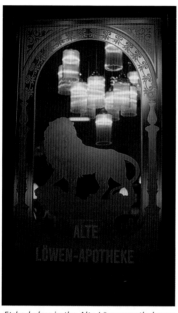

glass signboards, a lion mosaic over a side door and another lion finely etched into the window of the main door. The business was founded in 1782 and in 1816 its owner became the first to introduce gas lighting to Vienna. It caused such a stir that even Emperor Franz I came to have a look! For those interested there is a restored apothecary of 1820 in Alsergrund's Nar-renturm (see no. 54) and a garrison hospital dispensary in the nearby Jose-phinum. A Baroque court apothecary of 1747 is included in the Collection of Religious Folk Art (*Sammlung Reli-giöser Volkskunst*) at Johannesgasse 8 and another example can be visited on request in the St. Elisabeth-Spital at Landstrasser Hauptstrasse 6.

Etched glass in the Alte Löwenapotheke on Josefstädter Strasse

Note: Barbers sometimes acted as doctors and Vienna's oldest barber's shop, which has been in business since 1831, can still be found at Schottengasse 2. On its walls are displayed examples of old curling tongs and other vintage hairdressing implements.

Other places of interest nearby: 20, 21, 26, 28

28 Vienna at your Convenience!

1st District (Innere Stadt), public conveniences near Graben 22

Satirist, writer and social critic Karl Kraus (1874–1936) once wrote that the streets of most European cities are paved with asphalt, whereas those of Vienna are paved with culture. There must be some truth in this because in Vienna even the public conveniences are considered historical monuments! Most noteworthy, on the Graben, is a subterranean lavatory built in 1905 in the Viennese Art Nouveau style

(*Jugendstil*) by Wilhelm Beetz. As such it is the world's oldest existing underground toilet facility! Identified discretely at street level by its elegant green railings and lanterns marked *Herren* and *Damen*, the author can't vouch for the latter, but the gents side is very stylish indeed, replete with brass washstands and door-fittings. On the wall is a copy of an 1883 patent document for

(ABOVE) A signpost to the subterranean public conveniences on Graben

(BELOW) Inside the well-appointed gentlemen's conveniences on Graben

the so-called »oil disinfection system« and flushless odour trap (*Patent-Ölurinoir*) that Beetz himself invented. An imitation of the Graben conveniences can be found on nearby Irisgasse as well as on Hoher Markt.

It was entrepreneur Beetz who at the end of the 19th century had made a contract with Vienna's city council to erect public conveniences at his own cost and to run them for 25 years, after which they would became city property. On many streets he erected his rectangular, roofed Pavilion-type made of pre-fabricated iron walls set on a stone base. Separate entrances led to compartments for both sexes (four for each) as well as a 6-receptacle gents urinal and heated office for the attendant. By 1910 there were 73 in operation, some of which are still standing. A beautifully restored example can be seen on Parkring with lovely coloured glass running around the top and a door boasting first- and second-class facilities! Equally impressive are those in Schönbrunn's Schlosspark, their painted green ironwork mimicking perfectly that of the nearby Great Palm House (see no. 69). A more modest version of this classic Viennese model can be found at the number 43 Neuwaldegg tram terminus in the 17th district of Hernals (also outside Wertheimsteinpark on Döblinger Hauptstrasse in the 19th district of Döbling, in Schönbornpark in the 8th district of Josefstadt and in Türkenschanzpark in the 18th district of Währing). There is a smaller version of this model to be found dotted around Simmering's Central Cemetery (*Zentralfriedhof*) (see no. 63).

Beetz also designed an Octagonal-type urinal comprising iron panels hung on slender columns with delicate grille screens for ventilation. He installed his patented oil disinfection system and flushless odour trap, as well as a guard against freezing in winter. Of 137 such urinals erected by 1910 numerous examples can still be seen, for example in Antonsplatz in the 10th district of Favoriten (also in Rabbiner-Schneerson-Platz in the 2nd district of Leopoldstadt, Gallitzinstrasse in the 16th district of Ottakring close to the cemetery (*Ottakringer Friedhof*) and outside the cemetery of Dornbach (*Dornbacher Friedhof*) in the 17th district of Hernals). At the other end of the scale from such relative splendour is a tiny, antiquated *pissoir* at the side of the Danube Canal, next to the Augartenbrücke. Actually in Wilhelm Kienzl Park, this very modest facility made only of a few aluminium sheets has still been embellished by its designer with a pitched roof, topped off with a row of cheerful stylised metallic flowers.

Finally, in the Opernpassage below the Opernring, is the modern so-called Opera Toilet where for a small fee the visitor can relax to the

An antique octagonal urinal in Antonsplatz

sound of classical music whilst scrutinising nostalgic opera posters decorating the walls – only in Vienna!

The inclusion of the French word *Pissoir* in the Viennese vocabulary has an interesting origin. The early Habsburgs went to great lengths to maintain their Catholic ideals and Spanish court manners and to avoid the rationalist influence of France. However, from the time of ›Empress‹ Maria Theresa (1740–80), the first monarch to speak French, the influence of Paris grew. Notably, the language spoken at court was *Schönbrunner Deutsch*, a nasal upper class mode of speech sprinkled with French expressions. Even today the pavement is occasionally referred to as the *Trottoir*, a milky coffee is a *Mélange* – and of course a gentlemen's urinal is known as a *Pissoir*! Other French words in common Austrian useage include *Coiffeur*, *Brochure* and *Garderobe* (closet).

Other places of interest nearby: 21, 27, 29, 30

29 From Busy Streets to Quiet Courtyards

1st District (Innere Stadt),
the Grosses Michaelerhaus at Kohlmarkt 11

For the traveller exploring the Inner City (*Innere Stadt*) and its immediate surroundings on foot, there's no greater sense of discovery than coming across the numerous courtyards (*Innenhof*) and squares (*Platz*) hidden along Vienna's former medieval back streets (see nos. 17, 22 & 48). Thankfully, the area has been spared unsightly high-rise development due to its UNESCO World Heritage status. Most courtyard houses were constructed during the Baroque and *Biedermeier* periods (17th-19th centuries) and offer the visitor the experience of exchanging bustling streets for peaceful, sometimes leafy havens in only a few paces.

A fine example is the handsome courtyard of the Grosses Michaelerhaus at Kohlmarkt 11, built in 1720 and where the composer Josef Haydn stayed in an unheated attic in 1749 (see the wall plaque on Kohlmarkt). The Court Poet Metastasio died here in 1782 (see the wall plaque on Michaelerplatz) (see no. 30). The courtyard contains a unique row of barrel-vaulted stables as well as graceful wrought iron balconies. The latter are often referred to as *Pawlatschen*, from the Czech word *pavlac* meaning a balconied or galleried courtyard, common in the 19th century tenements of Prague. They were sometimes added later to a courtyard in order to maximise the existing internal living space by creating individual access to each apartment from the balcony outside. The balconies also added a social element to tenement living – as well as somewhere to hang one's clothes out to dry! Examples of hidden courtyards with balconies (as well as elegant glazed loggias) that are worth getting the map out for include Habsburgergasse 5, Bräunerstrasse 3, Augustinerstrasse 12, Weihburggasse 16/21, Singerstrasse 7 (see no. 22), 16 & 22, Grünangergasse 1 and Bäckerstrasse 2 and 7 (see no. 17). Particularly grand courtyards adorn the Palais Wilczek at Herrengasse 5 and the Palais Daun-Kinsky at Freyung 4, the latter with its »Green Man« fountain and curious marble sarcophagus, designed by the present owner in anticipation of his own eventual death!

Interesting examples of courtyards *outside* the *Innere Stadt* can be found at Margaretenplatz 2 and Schlossgasse 21 in the 5th district of

The peaceful courtyard of the Grosses Michaelerhaus off busy Kohlmarkt

Margareten (the latter being one of Vienna's best preserved *Bieder-meier* courtyards) and Neudeggergasse 14 in the 8th district of Josef-stadt.

Sometimes, during later restoration work, buildings and court-yards in the *Innere Stadt* were connected together by passageways producing maze-like *Durchhäuser* (literally through-houses) that seem to transport the visitor from one neighbourhood to another. An enjoy-able example is entered at Blutgasse 9 where a narrow passage leads via a tiny 5-storey balconied light well into the monastic calm of the ancient Fähnrichshof courtyard, and out through the other side to Grünangergasse (it may also be entered from Blutgasse 3). These pas-sageways are sometimes straight (*Durchgang*) connecting two parallel streets, their existence often concealed from the passing pedestrian by wooden gates (see no. 48). Also well worth visiting are three hidden city squares, namely Dr.-Ignaz-Seipel-Platz with its fountains, Old University (*Alte Universität*) founded 1365 and Baroque Jesuit Church;

Quiet Franziskaner-platz and the tiny Kleines Café

the spacious Heiligenkreuzerhof, an unspoilt piece of 18th century Vienna belonging to the Cistercian Abbey of the same name founded outside Vienna in 1133; and Franziskanerplatz containing Vienna's smallest coffee house (*Kleines Café*) and only church with a Renais-sance façade. The latter includes a leafy cloister next-door at number 4 whose exterior wall is dotted with curious roundels that once con-tained portraits of saints.

Other places of interest nearby: 27, 28, 30, 31

30 A Hidden Necropolis

1st District (Innere Stadt), St. Michael's Church
(*Michaelerkirche*) on Michaelerplatz

It could be said that for each of Vienna's historic landmarks above ground, there is another less well-known one concealed deep below it. These subterranean curiosities fall into two groups, namely those uncovered during excavations which date from an earlier period of Vienna's history (e.g. the Romans and early Jews, see nos. 8 &12), and those that were deliberately constructed underground, such as medieval cellars (see no. 5), drains (see nos. 5 & 81) and crypts. To experience the latter, most visitors flock to the labyrinthine Catacombs (*Katakomben*), as the Viennese call subterranean crypts, that run to several levels below the Stephansdom as well as northeastwards out under Stephansplatz. The oldest are those under the cathedral itself in the Ducal Vault that contains the sarcophagus of Duke Rudolf IV (1358–65), the cathedral's founder, as well as 15 other tombs. Also to be found here, stored in lateral niches, are 70 copper urns containing the internal organs of the later Habsburgs, as dictated by Viennese court protocol (their hearts and bodies lie elsewhere; see below). Below the Apostles' Choir is a vault for Vienna's bishops and archbishops, whilst running under the Women's Choir is one for the canons. There is also a mass grave for thousands of victims of the 1713 plague, their bodies simply thrown down shafts that were then sealed up. Convicts and monks would later be given the unenviable task of sorting the bones into some order. In 1530 Emperor Ferdinand I (1521–64) prohibited burial in graveyards within the city walls due to health hazards and by 1735 the cemetery that once surrounded the cathedral had been cleared (see no. 21). Many bodies were re-buried below the cathedral, their redundant headstones incorporated into the outer walls (headstones from another former city cemetery can be found in the walls of a courtyard at Dorotheergasse 17).

When these vaults were full a new crypt was excavated in 1744 below the Stephansplatz itself, consisting of a series of irregular tunnels that eventually extended below all of the north and eastern parts of the old graveyard. They ran as far as a charnel house built in 1470 below the Deutschordenshaus on Singerstrasse (see no. 22) and back under the chancel to meet up with the old Ducal Vault, although the Cathedral's nave, below which run many ancient foundations, was never dug out.

Some 11,000 citizens were buried here during the next 40 years, including the great Baroque architects Johann Bernhard Fischer von Erlach (1656–1723) and Lukas von Hildebrandt (1668–1745). In 1783 when the smell became too much, Emperor Josef II (1765–90) ordered the closure of all crypts within the city limits on health grounds and instigated the opening of suburban cemeteries (see nos. 39 & 52). For years the crypts remained inaccessible until the 1870s when the human remains were finally walled in, creating over 30 chambers filled to the roof with bones.

Unfortunately, in the 1960s parts were rather over-restored, and so for something more authentic (and certainly less crowded) head for St. Michael's Church at the top of Kohlmarkt. The crypt here is smaller and stretches the length and breadth of the Gothic church above it, first documented in 1267, whose salient architectural features were written on the crypt walls long ago to assist orientation in the gloom. The piles of paupers' bones were removed here from the former graveyard that from c.1300, until its closure in 1508 due to its unhealthy proximity to the Palace (*Alte Burg*), occupied Michaelerplatz outside.

The rows of wooden coffins, some of which are painted, represent the well-to-do middle classes and court aristocrats, interred below their church from as early as 1631 in keeping with burial customs prevailing in 17th and 18th century Vienna. Many coffins have collapsed

Rows of wooden coffins in the crypt below the Michaelerkirche

over time, their boards stacked neatly in alcoves by the Salvatorian order that became caretakers of the neglected crypt in 1924. It is worth noting the fine preservation of some of the corpses dating back to the days of Mozart, their clothes, hair and skin preserved by the constantly cool temperature. As happened at the Stephansdom, the crypt was abandoned in 1783 on the order of Emperor Josef II (1765–90), by which time 4000 people from all walks of life had been laid to rest here including Court Poet Pietro Trapassi (known as Metastasio) who lived and died in the house next-door (see no. 29), and from whom Mozart purchased several librettos. Most of the corpses however have long since vanished, their crushed bones accounting for the unnaturally high floor level!

Also curious are the incredible bejewelled skeletons from the real catacombs in Rome that can be found in the Peterskirche just off the Graben, and in the Ruprechtskirche on Ruprechtsplatz. Rare for Vienna, this typically Italian custom involves the clothed remains being placed in glass coffins thus acting as reliquaries for all to see. Another example is that of the martyr St. Bonatus to be found in the Rochuskirche in the 3rd district of Landstrasse.

Outside Vienna there are further jewelled skeletons displayed in the Benedictine monastery of Melk, itself an inspiration for Umberto Eco's medieval murder mystery *The Name of the Rose*, starring Sean Connery as the detective monk Adson of Melk. A further skeleton is the enchantingly bejewelled Valentina in the church of Drosendorf in the Waldviertel region.

Note: Those wishing to pursue further the death rituals of the Habsburgs should visit the Imperial Burial Vaults (*Kaisergruft*) below the Kapuziner Church (Kapuzinerkirche) on Neuer Markt, where 140 of their embalmed bodies lie (dating back to 1633), as well as the Little Heart Vault (*Herzgrüftel*) in the Lorettokapelle of the Augustinerkirche where their hearts are kept in silver urns.

Other places of interest nearby: 27, 29, 31, 32

31 A Shrine to International Language

1st District (Innere Stadt), the International Esperanto Museum (*Internationales Esperantomuseum*) in the Palais Mollard at Herrengasse 9

Incredibly, Vienna can lay claim to being home to about 130 museums and collections, of which the more curious ones are devoted to subjects such as Schnapps, glass snowstorms, shoes, criminal history, unusual cameras, baking, heating and funerals (see no. 41). Amongst these the explorer must not overlook the 23 district museums (*Bezirksmuseen*), tucked away in the suburbs and containing unusual collections devoted to circus clowns (2nd district), the phonogram (6th), brick-making (14th) (see no. 67) and the chimney sweep (4th) (see no. 4).

One unusual collection that lies near the very heart of the

Hofburg, and yet remains one of the *Innere Stadt's* least known, is the Collection of Planned Languages and International Esperanto Museum, or *Internacia Esperanto Muzeo* – in Esperanto! Whilst it may sound somewhat dry, and indeed it does lack the visual punch of many museums, it offers those interested an intriguing glimpse into the world of planned languages. Any visitors making the effort to visit the museum, located in the recently renovated Palais Mollard at Herrengasse 9, will be made extremely welcome by the enthusiastic Esperanto-fluent curators. Esperanto is a *planned* language (not an *artificial* one, as the curators will stress) created in 1887 by Polish optician Dr. Ludvik Zamenhof. Between 1886 and 1895 he lived in Vienna at Florianigasse 8 in the 8th district, now the district court, and his bust can be found in Karlsplatz. Although Esperanto never became the *lingua franca* Zamenhof had hoped for – the word *Esperanto* is from the French verb to hope – it did quickly replace the earlier planned language of *Volapük*. Today it has 3 million speakers, a hundred associations and an active publishing programme.

Esperanto was planned as a very regular language whose vocabulary is two thirds Latin-based (the rest Germanic) with a largely non-European grammar that has only 16 basic rules. Together with having easy-to-remember word stems derived from a list of 900 internationally recognised ones, as well as fewer cases, Esperanto should be as easy (or difficult!) to learn regardless of the student's mother tongue.

The collection was founded by Hugo Steiner in 1927, coming later under the auspices of the Austrian National Library (*Nationalbibliothek*). Today it holds the world's largest archive of inter-linguistic studies, language planning and of the 500 or so other recognised planned languages. Around the walls are fascinating related exhibits such as examples of Esperanto currency, Zamenhof's first book and a recent Esperanto edition of *Asterix the Gaul*. The library even contains a copy of a Klingon-English dictionary as used in the science fiction series *Star Trek*!

Another curious collection residing in the Palais Mollard is the Globe Museum (*Globenmuseum*). Also a part of the National Library, this fascinating collection illustrates the growth of man's knowledge regarding the continents and seas since the 16th century, and also includes celestial globes depicting the constellations of the night sky. It is the only one of its type in the world and contains 207 globes. Austria's oldest globe is here, manufactured in 1536 by Rainer Gemma Frisius, a medical doctor and cosmographer from Louvain in Belgium. Valuable too is the pair of globes (terrestrial and celestial) made in 1541 and 1551 respectively by Gerard Mercator, famous for the Mercator Projection used on maps and globes for centuries thereafter. His terrestrial globe was the first to include the non-right angle curves (known as *loxodromes*) that cut across the meridians and are of importance to navigators. One of the most novel items in the collection must surely be the 19th century inflatable globe complete with its own set of bellows.

Other places of interest nearby: 29, 30, 32, 34

32 The Legend of the Holy Lance

1st District (Innere Stadt), the Imperial Treasury
(*Schatzkammer*) in the Schweizerhof of the Hofburg

At the heart of Vienna's Hofburg (Court Palace) is the Old Palace (*Alte Burg*) where King Ottakkar II of Bohemia built the first fortress in 1275, just prior to the accession of the Habsburgs who would in time make it their imperial palace. Part of the original moat is still visible, as well as a piece of walling (in the passage leading through the Leopold Wing (*Leopoldinischer Trakt*) into Heldenplatz) from the Widmertor gate that once gave access through the old city walls. It is here, in what is today called the Swiss Court (*Schweizerhof*), that the famous Imperial Treasury (*Schatzkammer*) can be found, containing the Habsburgs' crown jewels together with other treasures dating from their time as Holy Roman Emperors between 1452 and 1806.

Arousing especial curiosity are the supposed holy relics whose very ownership was taken as divine endorsement of rightful earthly rule. The power that such objects had over the minds of both ruler and ruled should not be underestimated. The Ecclesiastical Treasury (*Geistliche Schatzkammer*) here contains many such relics displayed in richly ornamented containers dating to the Counter Reformation and the re-establishment of Catholicism. Amongst them is a nail from the crucifixion, against which pilgrims once rubbed their rosaries to gain strength, several thorns from Christ's crown of thorns, at least three fragments of the true cross, a piece of Mary's veil, a fragment of Joseph's cloak in which the child Jesus was wrapped, and Veronica's handkerchief soaked in Christ's blood. Further relics, including St. Stephan's cranium and a fragment of St. Andrew's cross, may be found in the Cathedral Museum (*Dom- und Diözesanmuseum*) in the Zwettlhof (the old cathedral priory) at Stephansplatz 6.

Since medieval people viewed the Holy Roman Empire as a continuation of the Roman Empire itself but under the rule of Christ, the Schatzkammer's Secular Treasury (*Weltliche Schatzkammer*) is also weighted with suitably potent religious relics. These include another fragment of the cross, a splinter from Christ's crib, a piece of the Last Supper tablecloth, a horn of the legendary and miraculous Unicorn (actually that of a Narwhale), and an incredible agate bowl from Constantinople thought once to have been the Holy Grail because

Christ's name (*XRISTO*) appears *within* the grain of the stone. Also on display is St. Stephan's Purse, said to contain blood-soaked earth from the stoning of Christianity's first martyr outside Jerusalem in 35AD, and in whose name Vienna's original Church of St. Stephan is consecrated (Austrians remember St. Stephan on December 26th, known as *Stefanitag*).

Most curious of all is the legendary Holy Lance (*Heilige Lanze*) reputed to have been used by the Roman soldier Longinus to pierce the side of Christ on the cross in order to ensure that he was dead. The usual method was to break the victim's legs but the use of the spear fulfilled Old Testament prophecy that not a bone of the true Messiah would be broken. Following this brief appearance in the Bible (John 19 v.31–37), legend takes over in relating how the spear became the property of St. Maurice and was used by Emperor Constantine the Great to Christianise the Roman Empire in the 4th century. It is then said to have been wielded by Charlemagne to shape the new Holy Roman Empire in the 8th century, finding its way eventually to a Nuremburg church, where it became a revered relic visited by thousands, and finally to the treasury in Vienna. It was here, according to some, that a young Adolf Hitler was inspired to create his Third Reich in the 20th century.

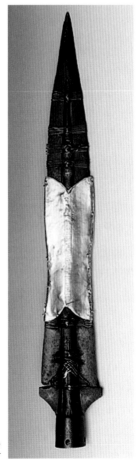

Only recently in 2003 was a thorough scientific and academic analysis of the spear finally undertaken, by an English metallurgist, to separate fact from fiction. It transpires that the spear was broken in antiquity and mended with silver wire whose process of manufacture can be dated clearly to c.600AD. The spear itself is stylistically closest to medieval weapons, not Roman ones, also pointing firmly to a date in the 7th century. That just leaves

The so-called Holy Lance in the Hofburg's Schatzkammer

the curious so-called »nail of the Lord«, suspended within the length of the spear. In reality little more than an iron pin or toggle, x-ray evidence, together with three tiny brass pinheads protruding from its surface, suggests that an actual nail may have long ago been forged deep within it. An inscribed silver sheath was added to the spear in 1084AD in order to strengthen this »nail of the Lord« whereas only much later, in the 14th century, was a gold one added that made reference to the »lance of the Lord«. It must be concluded therefore that the spear is too young to be that of the soldier Longinus, although it cannot be denied that it has gained enormous legendary status with the passing of time.

It is unlikely that the whereabouts of the real spear will ever be known. On the other hand the hidden nail, which would appear to pre-date the spear considerably, remains the real candidate for being a true holy relic of Jesus Christ's brief time on earth. Indeed it is the nail's shadowy existence that could account for the spear's power down through the centuries, setting it quite apart from all other religious relics – a sacred object bound invisibly within a secular one, destined forever to defy man's futile attempts at scientific rationalisation.

Note: The Stephansdom Museum referred to above also contains a painting of Duke Rudolf IV (1358–65), founder of the cathedral and university, painted in c.1360 and thought to be one of the first attempts at modern full-face portraiture in the history of western art. It is often compared to the portrait of the King of France, John the Good (1319–64), hanging in the Louvre. Also worth looking out for are two precious Syrian glass vessels, once believed to have contained earth from Bethlehem stained with »the blood of the Innocents«, as well as the magnificent Persian silk garment used during the burial of Duke Rudolf.

Other places of interest nearby: 30, 31, 33, 34

33 The Emperor's Only Statue

1st District (Innere Stadt), the statue of Emperor Franz Josef I
in the Burggarten, on the Burgring/Opernring

A visit to one of Vienna's numerous back street antique shops (*Alt-waren*) (e.g. Alte Kunst at Plankengasse 7) shows all too clearly how popular Emperor Franz Josef I was with the Austrian people. The shop window is crammed with old postcards, framed portraits and kitsch souvenirs carrying the whiskered image of Europe's longest-serving monarch (1848–1916). His sixty eight year reign marked Austria's longest period of relative stability, though it was born out of the violence of the 1848 Revolution (see no. 14), and was brought about in part by his legendary distrust of change and innovation (see no. 70). He loved the pomp and protocol of old Spanish court cere-monial and yet, in his private life, was a man of modest tastes. Des-cribing himself as a self-employed civil servant, he always rose at 3.30am until the day he died, and gave audience to his citizens twice weekly. He dressed in a simple lieutenant's uniform, ate boiled beef (*Tafelspitz*) almost daily and slept on a single iron bedstead under a camel skin blanket. He had no time for telephones, cars, electricity or even flushing toilets, and preferred hunting to opera. His difficult mar-riage to his wife Elisabeth (*Sisi*) (1837–98) added to his legend in life, as did her assassination in 1898, the romantic suicide of his only son Rudolf with his 17-year old mistress baroness Mary Vetsera at Mayer-ling in 1887, the execution of his brother Maximilian in Mexico in 1867 and the death of his younger brother Karl Ludwig in 1896 after drinking contaminated water from the River Jordan. Somewhat like England's Queen Elizabeth II the Emperor shouldered such tragedies stoically (»Nothing has been spared me in this world!« he once said), continuing to serve and govern his empire as he always had done.

Also English in style was his private Imperial Garden (today's Burggarten) with its restrained design and fountain, tucked behind the Neue Burg. Thrown open to the public in 1919, three years after the Emperor's death, it today contains his only public statue. Incredi-bly, despite his image having once graced the walls of households across the land, no public statue existed in Vienna until this one was erected privately in 1957 on what would have been his birthday, August 18th. This in part reflects his modest character but it also seems that by 1916 the populace were growing tired of Habsburg rule,

The statue of Emperor Franz Josef I in the Burggarten

as well as suffering privations arising from the Great War. It was only a matter of time, and with the conclusion of the war, that the Emperor's successor and great nephew, Emperor Karl I (1916–18), was thrown unceremoniously out of Austria. Forced to renounce any further involvement in Austrian state affairs, though refusing to formally abdicate or renounce his claim to the throne, the last Emperor and his family were forced into Swiss exile in March 1919, transported in a court-green Gräf & Stift limousine that can still be seen in Schloss Schönbrunn's Carriage Museum (see no. 70). The Habsburg era came to an abrupt and ignominious end and Austria's First Republic (a socialist one under Karl Renner) was declared, albeit briefly; grand Vienna, formerly the centre of an empire of 55 million, became suddenly the capital of a small state with six and a half million inhabitants.

Within a few years an association was established to finance a Franz-Josef monument and numerous designs were submitted, including a 30 metre-high »candelabra« at Praterstern dreamt up earlier by renowned architect Otto Wagner. However, it was not until a competition in 1937 that sculptor Hans Andre and architect Clemens Holzmeister were commissioned officially to undertake the work. The annexation of Austria by the Nazis in 1938 put paid to their plans and resulted in a period of mindless iconoclasm. One monument to suffer was a bronze of the Emperor in pensive mood that had adorned the Stadtpark in Wiener Neustadt. It was the work of Josef Tuch and was a copy of an original in stone sculpted by his mentor Johannes Benk in 1904 (for the Infantry Cadet School in Hütteldorfer Strasse). Tuch's work languished in a Liesing scrap yard for the duration of the war until Hans Lauda, President of the Industrial Association, instigated its re-erection in the Burggarten. So it was that some forty years after his death Vienna finally got its statue of Emperor Franz-Josef.

Note: Although the Habsburgs ruled Austria for 640 years, the first ever public statue of one of them, that of the enlightened Emperor Josef II (1765-90), was only unveiled in 1807 in Josefsplatz. Equestrian in style, the statue occupies what was once the enclosed training ground of the Spanish Riding School. It was reform-mad Emperor Josef who so typically opened up the area as a public square (see also nos. 19, 25, 30, 35, 41, 45, 54, 58 & 59!). In deference to the man who had attempted to create a centralised state open to modernisation, Emperor Franz added Josef to his Christian name, hence Franz Josef.

Other places of interest nearby: 30, 32, 34, 35

34 The Myth of Montezuma's Headdress

1st District (Innere Stadt), the Museum of Ethnology
(*Museum für Völkerkunde*) in the Neue Burg on Heldenplatz

Amongst the Benin bronzes, Eskimo anoraks, Easter Island canoe paddles (made for Captain Cook) and Shinto toilet deities of Vienna's

Museum of Ethnology is a single exhibit both curious and controversial. Beautifully lit in a case all of its own is an Aztec headdress, made from 459 shimmering blue and green tail feathers of the male Quetzal bird. It is the world's only surviving feather headdress from pre-Hispanic Mexico and one of only six remaining examples of ancient Mexican feather work. Representations of Aztec deities suggest that such headdresses were considered part of the garments of the gods, and were worn also by priests during temple rituals. During the late-19th and early-20th centuries the Vienna headdress was bundled together with other suitably »exotic-looking« objects that were col-

Detail of a feather headdress in the Museum of Ethnology, wrongly attributed to the Aztec Montezuma

lectively, and quite incorrectly, exhibited as Montezuma's Treasures (see no. 36). Until recently guidebooks were still linking these objects to the Aztec emperor, stating that he gave them as presents to the Spanish conquistador Hernán Cortés, who sent them to his Emperor Charles V (1519–56; the Spanish line of the House of Habsburg ruling Spain as King Charles I), who in turn gave them to his relative Archduke Ferdinand of Tyrol. This has perpetuated a dangerous myth that has unnecessarily fuelled ill-founded nationalistic feelings amongst some Mexicans, in whose minds a potent national symbol has been stolen from their land.

Faced with such understandably passionate feelings the museum undertook careful research to set the record straight. It was discovered that the »presents« given to Cortés during his first meeting with Montezuma (actually *Moctezuma*) on 8th November 1519, were lost irretrievably in the mêlée that followed the Spaniard's unnecessary and fatal imprisonment of the emperor. Existing inventories of an earlier consignment of gifts made prior to the arrival of Cortés make no mention whatsoever of a feather headdress. Thus, the Vienna headdress is unlikely ever to have had any direct connection with Montezuma. Cortés eventually conquered Tenochtitlán (now Mexico City) and in the following decades shiploads of precious Mexican artefacts were sent back to Europe as gifts and trophies. Amongst them were hundreds of delicate feather headdresses, one of which ended up in the art collection of Count Ulrich of Montfort-Tettnang in Upper Swabia, in whose inventory it appears in 1575. In 1590 the Habsburg Archduke Ferdinand of Tyrol purchased the headdress for his famous Chamber of Art and Marvels (*Kunstkammer*) at Ambras Castle near Innsbruck. Later still, the by now well-travelled artefact was acquired by the Habsburgs of Vienna, who displayed it in the city's Lower Belvedere Palace. Some 300 years later, by which time it had become a very rare artefact indeed, the Vienna headdress was »re-discovered« having been stored away in a cupboard and forgotten. It was at this time, due to its documented Habsburg and Ambras connections, that the headdress was linked incorrectly to the Cortés-Montezuma story.

It is this author's view that it is best to regard unique and sensitive artworks such as the Vienna headdress as »cultural refugees«, displayed somewhere other than their place of origin. It is the job of the country fortunate enough to possess them not only to acknowledge their true history but also to protect them for world posterity.

Other places of interest nearby: 32, 33, 35, 36

35 The Beguiling Smile of an Ancient Egyptian

1st District (Innere Stadt), the Art History Museum
(Kunsthistorisches Museum) in Maria-Theresien-Platz
at Burgring 5

Without a doubt one of Vienna's most important museums is the
Kunsthistorisches Museum, housed in a custom-made Ringstrasse
building in the neo-Renaissance style and opened by Emperor Franz
Josef I (1848–1916) in 1891. The art collection is considered the
world's fourth finest and exists thanks to the wealth and artistic inter-
ests of the Habsburg dynasty. It was instigated by Emperor Rudolf II
(1576–1612) and added to by a succession of others (for example
Archduke Leopold Wilhelm during the Baroque period), each with
individual tastes, resulting in a staggering collection of 15th–18th
century Old Masters. Included are works by Titian (court painter to
Emperor Karl V), Bruegel (acquired through family connections in
the Low Countries) and Velásquez (from the Spanish Habsburgs).
›Empress‹ Maria Theresa's son Emperor Josef II (1765–90) was responsible for opening up the Imperial Collection to the public and it still
forms the core of the present museum.

Lured by the picture gallery (*Gemäldegalerie*) and its world famous
images, not to mention the Benvenuto Cellini salt-cellar (*Saliera*)
stolen recently and recovered from a forest in the Waldviertel, few visitors make it to the coin collection (*Münzkabinett*) in which can be
found the curious stone currency of the Micronesian Island of Yap. A
few more visit the Collection of Greek and Roman Antiquities
(*Antikensammlung*) with its fragment of the Parthenon, and the
Collection of Fine Arts (*Kunstkammer*) with its snake's tongue salt-
cellar (see no. 22). However, it is in the Egyptian and Near Eastern
Collection (*Ägyptisch-Orientalische Sammlung*), amongst the pink
granite temple columns from Aswan and the painted mummy cases,
that something very unusual can be found.

Known as the Reserve or Substitute Head (*Ersatzkopf*), this limestone sculpture 27 centimetres high was found by Austrian archaeologists early in the 20th century in a cemetery on the Giza Plain, west of
the great pyramid of Cheops. To be precise it was found in *Mastaba G*,
a *mastaba* being a flat-topped stone or mudbrick structure that marks
the tomb of a wealthy individual or family. A chapel and chamber for

The beautiful Egyptian reserve head in the Kunsthistorisches Museum

statues of the deceased is usually incorporated into the *mastaba* and a vertical shaft leads down into the actual rock-cut burial chamber below. The head has been dated to the 4th Dynasty of the Old Kingdom, that is to say c.2500BC and the reign of the Pharaoh Khufu (known as Cheops by the Greeks), builder of the Great Pyramid itself. Despite the head's incredible antiquity and stylised features, the unknown artist has imbued it with an otherworldly serenity and self-assuredness. Yet unlike most Egyptian funerary sculptures, which archaeologists expect to find in the aboveground statuary chamber of the tomb, the Reserve Head was found buried deliberately in the earth at the entrance to the subterranean burial chamber. As a result its original purpose is hotly disputed, although the consensus amongst experts is that in the period before mummification, the Egyptian soul (or *ka*) could be guaranteed a place in the afterlife by including a surrogate Reserve Head in the tomb. Although some thirty other such heads have been found in ancient Egypt, the Vienna example is by far the most beautiful – and its beguiling and timeless visage may never give up its true purpose. The fact that each of the heads found so far have unique features suggests that they are idealised representations of the tomb owners themselves and as such are amongst the earliest portraits ever made.

The museum's Egyptian collection also contains a clay model of a hippopotamus from the Middle Kingdom (c.2000BC), its blue-glazed body adorned with lotus blossoms and papyrus leaves. The inclusion of such a statue in Middle Kingdom tombs is well documented, as hippopotamus hunting was a royal privilege granted to those citizens who won favour with the pharaoh. Of related interest here is the fascinating Papayrus Collection (Papyrus-Sammlung) in the Neue Burg on Heldenplatz, containing painted mummy masks, Coptic textiles, and even a prescription for pharaonic toothpaste!

Other places of interest nearby: 33, 34, 36, 45

36 The Imperial Cabinet of Natural Curiosities

1st District (Innere Stadt), the Natural History Museum
(*Naturhistorisches Museum*)
in Maria-Theresien-Platz at Burgring 5

To some, Vienna's Natural History Museum is a rather dusty and old-fashioned place, with few of the hi-tech displays that most major museums have installed in recent years. Its cabinets are antiques in themselves and the labelling still refers to long-vanished provinces once part of the old Austro-Hungarian Empire (e.g. Illyria on the eastern Adriatic coast and Galicia, now part of Poland and Ukraine). However, for the explorer interested in the unusual this museum provides a wonderfully rich hunting ground containing a bewildering array of strange objects from the natural world.

Opened in 1889 the building was erected by order of Emperor Franz Josef I (1848–1916), the core of the collection having belonged to Emperor Franz I (1745–65), husband of ›Empress‹ Maria Theresa (1740–80). In 1748 he had bought the world's largest natural history collection from Johann Ritter von Baillou, a Florentine scholar, to which important additions were made over subsequent years as a result of Imperial globetrotting expeditions (especially that of the frigate *Novara*), diplomatic gifts, acquisitions, swaps and bequests. The following items are worth tracking down for obvious reasons, displayed in rooms that themselves have been beautifully decorated to reflect the different collections therein:

Room 1 is an Aladdin's cave of coloured minerals, including a huge split amethyst *geode* at the entrance, and a one-piece crystal obelisk weighing 1,680 kilos. In Room 4 there is a Colombian emerald once wrongly attributed to the Aztec emperor Montezuma (see no. 34). Rather less colourful but no less fascinating is the world's finest collection of meteorites, to be found in Room 5;

Room 7 contains the world's largest fossilised spider, from Argentina's tropical swamps and measuring a frightening 50 centimetres in length, whilst Room 8 has the leg of a 70-ton Ultrasaurus;

Room 10 contains a replica of the first nearly complete Diplodocus skeleton found in Sheep Creek, Wyoming, and sent by American industrialist Andrew Carnegie to Emperor Franz Josef I in 1909; the gallery also contains the world's largest fossilised tortoise;

Room 11 contains the tiny limestone fertility goddess known as the Venus of Willendorf that is 25,000 years old, although the Fanny of Galgenberg, also held by the museum and named after an Austrian ballerina, is 32,000 years old making it the world's oldest figurative sculpture;

Room 20 has a fearsome pair of giant Spider Crabs given as a gift by the *Meiji* Emperor of Japan to Emperor Franz Josef I providing a unique backdrop to the museum's café!;

Room 22 has a unique study collection of Polyps and Medusas rendered in glass by Rudolf Blaschka of Dresden, as well as work by the world's first underwater painter produced in a primitive diving bell off the coast of Ceylon (modern Sri Lanka); it is also home to a bizarre collection of tapeworms including one from the intestines of a Munich doctor that measures 6 feet in length!;

Room 25 contains a Great White Shark whose stomach was found to contain the shoe of a sailor in the Austrian navy;

Room 29 is home to a pair of stuffed eagles shot in 1889 by Crown Prince Rudolf a few days before his suicide at Mayerling;

Room 30 contains the remains of New Zealand's extinct Giant Moa, together with its equally giant egg, whilst Room 31 contains the world's best-preserved remains of the famously extinct Dodo;

Stuffed eagles in the Naturhistorisches Museum shot by Crown Prince Rudolf

The world's most complete skeleton of the extinct Dodo

Finally, sitting in the corner of one of the taxidermy cabinets in Room 39 is Honzo the chimpanzee, brought from Cameroon by Austrian explorer Ernst Zwilling to the zoo at Schönbrunn and infamous for his bad temper and love of beer and cigarettes!

Other places of interest nearby: 32, 34, 35, 45

37 Landstrasse's Little-Known Saint's Fountain

3rd District (Landstrasse), the Karl Borromäus Fountain
(*Borromäusbrunnen*) on Karl-Borromäus-Platz;
take U-3 to Rochusgasse

It is often said that city-dwellers rarely visit places of interest lying on their own doorstep, and that it is visitors who become better acquainted with them. One location that disproves this theory is Vienna's mighty Karlskirche in Karlsplatz, dedicated to Saint Carlo Borromeo (1538–84), which is known to both tourist and inhabitant alike. Also dedicated to the Italian saint is a charming fountain in nearby Landstrasse, again disproving the theory as not even the tourists seem to know of it!

The Karlskirche is Vienna's finest Baroque church, erected by Emperor Karl VI (1711–40) as a result of a vow he made during the plague of 1713. It is difficult not to think that Karl's dedication of the church to Saint Carlo, canonized for his efforts during the 1576 plague of Milan where he was archbishop, was in part because they shared the same name. Consequently both could be glorified by this magnificent building designed by Johann Bernhard Fischer von Erlach (1656–1723). Borromeo's life is illustrated in the ribbon-like reliefs of the two 33 metre-high columns in front of the church that resemble the »double column and scroll« motif of the Spanish Habsburgs, from whom Karl was descended – and from where the dollar sign ($) originated. The saint also appears over the pedimented doorway, as well as in the frescoed dome and over the high altar inside.

A detail of one of the columns outside the Karlskirche

Leaving such grandeur behind, the life of Borromeo can now be taken up in the more modest and intimate setting of Landstrasse's Borromäusplatz. The uniquely beautiful fountain known as the Karl Borromäus Fountain was created in 1909 by sculptor Josef Engelhart (a member of Gustav Klimt's Secession movement) and Slovenian

The little-known Borromäus Fountain in Landstrasse

architect Jože Plečnik, who would later design Vienna's first concrete church (see no. 77). Set in a sunken square surrounded by benches, the fountain takes the form of a simple obelisk surrounded by a clover-shaped basin alive with sculpted frogs and lizards. Beneath a frieze of vine leaves and grapes are dancing cherubs whilst above are three groups of figures acting out the saint's life. This is a curiously peaceful place to while away ten minutes musing on how fortunate one is not to have lived in the days of the plague (see no. 30).

Note: Columns (*Pestsäulen*) celebrating Vienna's numerous deliverances from plague can be found on the Graben (1679), outside Josefstadt's Piaristen-kirche (1713), beside the Maria Geburt Church (1730) in Hietzing and St. Ulrich's Church in Neubau.

Other places of interest nearby: 38

38 A Little Piece of Russia in Vienna

3rd District (Landstrasse), the Russian Orthodox Church (Russische Kirche) at Jaurèsgasse 2; take U-3 to Rochusgasse

For many the only tangible sign of a Russian presence in Vienna is the huge Russian Heroes' Monument (*Russisches Heldendenkmal*) in Schwarzenbergplatz. Soviet troops had wrested the city from the Nazis after bloody street fighting in April 1945 and erected the monument shortly afterwards, on August 19th. Below the statue of a heroically posed unknown Soviet soldier are the names of the fallen together with the words of Stalin. Unfortunately, older Austrians still recall the brutality of their Russian »liberators«, as well as the hardships endured by those living in the Russian controlled zone between 1945 and 1955, when Molotov finally signed the Austrian State Treaty (*Staatsvertrag*).

For a taste of real Russian culture it is much better to head for Vienna's 3rd district of Landstrasse and its little-known Russian Orthodox Church of St. Nicholas. Luigi Giacomelli designed the church in 1893–99 for the Russian embassy, after a plan by St. Petersburg architect Grigorij Iwanowitsch Kotov. If the visitor is fortunate enough to witness a service here they will be rewarded with a glimpse of the incredible candle-lit and gilded interior brimming with painted icons. The air is filled with the fragrance of burning incense, and the

The Russian Orthodox Church of St. Nicholas in Landstrasse

glorious unaccompanied *a capella* singing that has been the central form of worship in Russian churches for a thousand years. The exterior of the church is magical too with walls of white stone and red brick, broken by oriental type arched windows obscured by iron grilles. Below the typically Russian green-domed roof is a beautiful frieze of coloured glazed tiles lending a late-Byzantine feel to the proceedings.

On the subject of tiling it's worth a stroll to nearby Ungargasse where at 59-61 is the Portois & Fix building, erected in 1900 in the Viennese Art Nouveau (*Jugendstil*) style with an abstract façade of tiles in muted shades of green and brown. It was Portois & Fix who were commissioned by the Emperor's wife Elisabeth (*Sisi*) (1837–98) to redecorate her rooms at the Schloss Schönbrunn.

Returning to things Russian, don't forget the tiny Orthodox chapel of remembrance at Simmering's Central Cemetery (*Zentralfriedhof*), just inside Gate 2 on the left-hand side (see no. 63). Constructed in

1894 it is surrounded by the graves of some of Vienna's Russian inhabitants.

Of course being a truly cosmopolitan city, Vienna has numerous other churches erected and used by varying denominations and faiths. These include a splendid Buddhist *Stupa* on the banks of the Danube in the Prater, erected in 1983 to celebrate Austria being the first European country to officially recognise Buddhism, and a mosque with a 32 metre-high minaret (*Islamisches Centrum*) at Hubertusdamm 17, next to the Neue Donau U-Bahn station.

The Russian Orthodox chapel of remembrance in the Central Cemetery

Note: Vienna's Communist newspaper *Volksstimme* was once based at Siebensterngasse 29 in the 7th district of Neubau. Today it is the fashionable Sternbar, named after the Soviet star that still hangs on the wall.

Other places of interest nearby: 37

39 Lost Among
the Lilacs and Birdsong

3rd District (Landstrasse), St. Mark's Cemetery
(*St. Marxer Friedhof*) at Leberstraße 6-8; take Tram 71
from Schwarzenbergplatz (near U-Bahn Karlsplatz U-1/U-2/U-4)

The little St. Mark's Cemetery, now hemmed in on three sides by busy roads, is known mainly for the wintry night in December 1791 when Mozart's body was placed in a mass grave here and subsequently lost (see no. 19). Not surprisingly this fact accounts for the majority of visitors to this leafy oasis, filled with butterflies and birdsong (including the occasional distinctive call of the Nightingale).

St. Mark's, together with Vienna's four other municipal suburban cemeteries, was closed down in 1873, the business of burying the city's dead transferred to the huge new Central Cemetery (*Zentralfriedhof*) opened in Simmering in 1874 (see no. 63). While the other cemeteries were converted into parks in the 1920s (see no. 52), the Cemetery of St. Mark was simply abandoned to nature. Despite some later restoration its mourners in time dwindled away to nothing. This very fact, however, makes a visit here such an unforgettable experience.

Established in 1783 and consequently known also as the *Biedermeier* Cemetery, St. Mark's was the first graveyard to be created outside the *Linienwall* ramparts (today's Gürtel ringroad), following Emperor Josef II's (1765–90) famous Funeral Edict that same year (see no. 30). This dissolved all crypts within the Gürtel on health grounds (burial in graveyards had already been outlawed) dictating they be »relocated to the free and excellently ventilated periphery«. At first, mass burials were the norm (as was the case with Mozart) and it was only later, in the mid-19th century, that family vaults became common.

Peaceful, melancholic and affecting, a series of overgrown tracks lead off the cemetery's main gravel paths, lined with row-upon-row of weathered and crumbling headstones. Crosses, urns and angels jostle for space amongst the overgrown lilacs (their blooms and scent overwhelming in April and May) and ivies, some plants having become so large that they are now engulfing the very tombs they were intended to adorn.

A stroll along the main path up beyond the Mozart grave (number 179, see front cover) and around the cemetery perimeters gives one the feeling of visiting a Graeco-Roman archaeological site. Of the

An abandoned gravestone amongst trees in the Cemetery of St. Mark.

6000 graves themselves there is a plan at the entrance though most of the well-known names, including *Biedermeier* architect Josef Korn-häusel (see no. 14) and Suez Canal engineer Alois Negrelli, are not only little-known outside Austria but were later reinterred in the Central Cemetery (*Zentralfriedhof*) in Simmering (see no. 63). Grave 7 in the 4th row on the right, for example, is the original grave of Josef Strauss (1827–76), second son of Johann Strauss the father, moved later to Grave 44 in group 32A of the Central Cemetery. Look out also for the very unusual sarcophagus-style tomb at the back of the cemetery against the right-hand wall. It is inscribed in English to the memory of a British Brigadier General who was military commissioner to the Austrian army and who died in Vienna in 1854. These days, other than the occasional groundsman sweeping the paths and watering the grass, the Cemetery of St. Mark is peopled more by ghosts from the past than visitors from the present. (Not far from St. Mark's is Vienna's former cattle market (Zentral Viehmarkt) opened in 1883 on Viehmarktgasse, its gate adorned with a pair of mighty stone cows; it has recently been re-developed as a media and technology centre.)

Another *Biedermeier* cemetery can be found in the woods towards the top of Kahlenberger Strasse (*Friedhof Kahlenberg*) in the 19th district of Döbling. Containing only 130 bodies its most famous occupant is probably Karoline Traunwieser who died tragically young aged only 21 and is said to have been the most beautiful girl in Vienna. Also here is the tomb of Carl Josef, Prince de Ligne, an Austrian statesman of Wallonian descent during the Congress of Vienna (1814–15) who died from a cold caught outside his house at Mölker Bastei 10 where he was awaiting his mistress.

Other places of interest nearby: none

40 From the Mortar of Belgrade to the Unknown Soldier

3rd District (Landstrasse), the Museum of Military History (*Heeresgeschichtliches Museum*) im Objekt 18 of the Arsenal off Arsenalstrasse; take Tram D from Schwarzenbergplatz (near U-Bahn Karlsplatz U-1/U-2/U-4) to Südbahnhof and walk through the Schweizergarten

In the wake of Vienna's 1848 Revolution (see no. 14), four vast fortress-like barracks were erected at strategic points around the city (see no. 51). One of these, the so-called Arsenal completed in 1856, was built on a high point south of the Upper Belvedere Palace, in the 3rd district of Landstrasse. Constructed of red brick, it was designed by future Ringstrasse architect Theophil Hansen, together with Ludwig Förster, in a heady synthesis of Byzantine (the dome), Hispano-Moorish (the brickwork and window arches) and late-medieval Italian (neo-Gothic) styles. Emperor Franz Josef I (1848–1916) decreed that a single building of the 31-block Arsenal should be earmarked as Vienna's first purpose-built museum, the Museum of Military History, designed to glorify the Imperial Army. Thus, the museum's interior continues from outside the feeling of a Byzantine church

The main entrance and courtyard to the Landstrasse Arsenal

or Moorish palace, such exoticism providing a peculiarly fitting backdrop to the collection of spoils and trophies from the Turkish Wars to be found on the first floor (see no. 2). These include the Great Seal of Sultan Mustafa II, removed from the neck of his Grand Vizier by Prince Eugène of Savoy (1663–1736) at the Battle of Zenta (1697), so winning back Hungary for the Habsburgs. There is also the huge tent of Grand Vizier Damad Ali Pasha that the Prince acquired at the Battle of Peterwardein (1716). In 1717, a single shot from the Mortar of Belgrade (exhibited nearby) hit a Turkish powder magazine killing 3,000 troops, assisting greatly Eugène's capture of that city, as well as contributing to the eventual securing of Western Europe against the Ottoman threat.

As light relief, in the west wing of the ground floor, look at the incredible array of uniforms worn by the armies of the Crown Lands following the establishment of the Austro-Hungarian Dual Monarchy in 1867. Having suffered numerous defeats in the 19th century the Austrian army won a prize for most elegant outfit at the 1900 Paris Exhibition!

The adjoining First World War section begins with the event that started it all – the assassination of Emperor Franz Josef I's nephew and heir, Archduke Franz Ferdinand, by Bosnian Serb nationalist Gavrilo Princip in Sarajevo on 28th June 1914 (the settee on which the Archduke expired was brought to Vienna in 1997 after the Serbian siege of Sarajevo). It is sobering to compare the tiny bullet-hole in the door of the Archduke's car with the massive destruction wrought by artillery displayed in the following rooms, designed to expedite the war that followed. On the wall is Albin Egger-Lienz's painting *To the Unknown Soldier* whose image of advancing infantry was a symbol of the type of mass warfare that would by 1918 have claimed 8 million lives.

Coincidentally, in the east wing of the ground floor, is the couch on which Austro-fascist Chancellor Dollfuss died after being shot by the Nazis during their abortive coup on July 25th 1934 (he is buried in the picturesque cemetery at Hietzing (*Hietzinger Friedhof*) in the 13th district). Although German annexation of Austria did not follow until 1938, this incident was a part of the grim chain of events that led inevitably to the Second World War in 1939.

Finally, and somewhat surprisingly, there is a section devoted to the naval power of land-locked Austria. Of course in the Habsburg era Austria controlled the Adriatic port of Trieste, although it is still a surprise to learn that the Austro-Hungarian fleet was once the sixth largest in the world. On display is the barnacle-encrusted conning tower of Imperial submarine U20, raised from the seabed, as well as memorabilia relating to submariner Captain Georg von Trapp of *The Sound of Music* fame. There is also a model of the Austrian expedition ship *Admiral Tegethoff* that set out in 1872 to find a northeast passage, via Arctic waters north of Russia, to the Pacific. Icebound the vessel drifted north through the Barents Sea where an archipelago was discovered and named Franz-Josefs-Land. The crew abandoned ship in 1874 and returned to civilisation, an arduous journey illustrated latterly by artist Julius von Payer, whose paintings are on display and who is buried in Simmering's Central Cemetery (*Zentralfriedhof*) (see no. 63). Further memorabilia relating to the expedition may be found at the top of the main stairs in Vienna's Natural History Museum (*Naturhistorisches Museum*).

On leaving the Museum of Military History be sure not to miss Europe's largest collection of gun barrels exhibited in one of the outside pavilions.

Other places of interest nearby: none

The grave of Julius von Payer
at the Central Cemetery (see no. 63)

41 The Undertakers' Museum

4th District (Wieden), the Undertakers' Museum
(*Bestattungsmuseum*) at Goldeggasse 19;
take Tram D from Schwarzenbergplatz
(near U-Bahn Karlsplatz U-1/U-2/U-4) to Schloss Belvedere

In Vienna in the 1900s more than eighty private funeral companies competed for the business of burying the city's citizens in its many grand suburban cemeteries (today occupying 576 hectares). Since 1951 the Municipal Funeral Service alone has been responsible for funerals, and Wieden's fascinating Undertakers' Museum tells the whole story.

Beyond the macabre iron entrance grille, taken from the old Matzleinsdorf Cemetery, are more than 600 artefacts documenting the well-known Viennese interest in death and burial. A visit to Simmering's Central Cemetery (see no. 63) at the weekend, and especially on All Saints' Day (*Allerheiligen*) on November 1st, illustrates all too clearly the attention lavished upon funerals and the subsequent tending of graves. Even today only 18% of the predominantly Catholic Viennese opt for cremation, the rest hoping for a *schöne Leich* (beautiful corpse) and all the pomp that accompanies its burial in the ground.

The Undertaker's Museum contains the elaborate black outfits and regalia worn by both the pallbearers (*Pompfüneberer* from the French *pompes funèbres*) as well as the liveries worn by the hearse-pulling horses. There are also wreathes, sashes, lanterns, torches, black flags and different coloured palls signifying the deceased's profession and former position in life. Somewhat comical is the old packet of undertaker's cigarettes carrying the words *»Rauchen sichert Arbeitsplätze«* (»Smoking protects jobs«). A real curiosity on display is a device whereby a cord attached to the hand of the deceased would ring a bell

*Ornate funeral uniforms
in the Undertakers' Museum*

(LEFT) An eccentric bell system used to ensure people weren't buried alive!

(BELOW) An antique undertaker's hearse

above ground in the event of their returning to life! To avoid such an occurrence, some Viennese (e.g. dramatist Arthur Schnitzler, buried in the old Jewish section of Simmering's Central Cemetery) stipulated in their will that after death they should be stabbed in the heart with a stiletto blade. To this day the city's hospital is still occasionally instructed to administer a lethal injection after death to avoid premature burial.

Another curiosity is the re-useable coffin instigated in 1784 by the enlightened Emperor Josef II (1765–90) in an attempt to save wood and to hasten decomposition. So appalled were the populace at the prospect of being sewn only into linen sacks that their violent protests led to the rescinding of the law within 6 months. Little wonder that a 19th century idea to dispatch the dead at high speed from the *Innere Stadt* out to the Central Cemetery via a subterranean pipeline met with little support! With the coming of the European Union Vienna's funeral business has been once again opened up to market forces. One such private company taking advantage of this calls itself Perikles, after the Greek ›Father of Democracy‹.

Other places of interest nearby: none

42 A Perfect Pair of Pavilions

4th District (Wieden), the Otto Wagner Pavilions on Karlsplatz; take U-1/U-2/U-4 to Karlsplatz

By the 1890s the rapidly growing city of Vienna had been freed from its old city walls, and its suburbs were being rapidly urbanised. In 1893 work began on the construction of the *Stadtbahn*, or Metropolitan Railway, Vienna's first public transport system independent of roads. As with the famous Paris Metro, it was decided that the architectural elements of the system would have a corporate appearance, in tune with the very latest European design ideals.

The architect chosen to supervise the building of the 30 or so stations, bridges, tunnels and other facilities along the proposed 40 kilometre stretch of railway was Otto Wagner (see nos. 70, 74, 75 & 81). He was the perfect choice bearing in mind he would co-found Vienna's Secession Movement in 1897 together with Gustav Klimt. Between them they would pioneer the Viennese Art Nouveau (*Jugendstil*) in which functionality and aesthetics became perfectly fused. Wagner believed fervently that the new railway, which ran predominantly overland, was vital to the creation of a modern city, although his visionary plans for an exclusively underground system went unheeded at the time. Travelling on today's electric U-Bahn, which in 1925 replaced the steam-powered railway of Wagner's day, it is easy to recognise his idiosyncratic style, which rebelled against the dated Historicist (Ringstrasse Style) of the late-19th century. Typical are his use of elegant cut masonry, *Jugendstil* motifs such as sunflower-rosettes and wreathes, stylised lettering and everywhere green metalwork – from balustrades and lanterns to window frames and door grilles. Especially worth visiting are the stations at Stadtpark, Kettenbrücken-

gasse, Hietzing and Rossauer Lände on what is today's U-4 line. Known originally as the Wien Valley Line it followed the course of the Wien River that was culverted, and in part covered,

River, rail and footbridge at Zollamtssteg on Otto Wagner's Metropolitan Railway

at the same time – and in the same style (see no. 83). Look out for the spectacular triple-span viaduct that crosses both river and road at Sechshauser Gürtel and the technically impressive Zollamtssteg footbridge further downstream, where the rail bridge and river run diagonally below it.

One of a pair of Jugendstil former railway pavilions on Karlplatz

The jewel in the crown, however, is the pair of pavilions (1899) facing each other across Karlsplatz. Originally located either side of Akademiestrasse they were designed to provide entrances to the railway, one for each platform, and represent *Jugendstil* architecture at its most refined. Unlike the railway's other stations, which were built traditionally in stone and plaster, the pavilions were made of pre-fabricated, green-painted metal frameworks on which panels of white Carrara marble were suspended. They were then topped with a revolutionary roof of corrugated copper, oxidised to a distinctive green. The *Jugendstil* decoration, in an effort to harmonise the new structures with the nearby Baroque Karlskirche, consists of golden Sunflowers stamped onto the marble with a gold vegetal trim around the roof. The result is still surprisingly successful, its architectural components visible to the onlooker unlike the plastered brick of so many Historicist (Ringstrasse Style) buildings that still fool many into thinking they are real stone. Today, although the pavilions have lost their original function, one of them at least provides access to the U-4 U-Bahn as well as being an exhibition centre, whilst the other is a café.

It should not be forgotten that Wagner also designed the line servicing Vienna's western districts occupying what is now the U-6 line

along the Gürtel ring-road. The stretch between Spittelau and Margaretengürtel follows the path of the old *Linienwall* embankment, built by Prince Eugène in 1704 to protect the vulnerable inner suburbs of the *Vorstädte* (the 3rd–9th districts) from attack. It comprises mainly an elevated track supported by a graceful series of brick-built railway arches (*Stadtbahnbogen*), now infilled with shops, warehouses, cafés and bars. Particularly elegant is the monumental bridge across Währinger Strasse-Fuchsthallergasse together with Wagner's little chapel to St. Johannes Nepomuk, patron saint of bridges. Unfortunately, Wagner's dream of making the Gürtel into another Ringstrasse never came to fruition and his railway is one of the few redeeming architectural features of this now busy thoroughfare.

Returning to Karlsplatz don't miss the charming old, blue-painted tram sign from where an authentic »old timer« tram (post-1903 electrified rather than horse-drawn) runs around the city in the summer months, courtesy of the Tramway Museum (*Strassenbahnmuseum*) at Ludwig-Koessler-Platz in the 3rd district of Landstrasse.

Other places of interest nearby: 25, 43

43 The Composers' Quarter

4th District (Wieden), Wiedner Hauptstrasse 7;
take U-1/U-2/U-4 to Karlsplatz

Vienna is often referred to as the »City of Music« and walking around
the city and its suburbs certainly bears this out. It sometimes feels as
though almost every street bears a plaque to one composer or another, invariably Mozart (1756–91), Beethoven (1770–1827), Schubert
(1797–1828) or Haydn (1732–1809). They are all associated with
Vienna having either been born here, studied here, had patrons here
or else found their first audience here.

Although the guidebooks cover these well-known characters in
great detail, the explorer can still discover an occasional location that
escapes most visitors. An example of this is at Währinger Strasse 26
where an old and ornate marble plaque identifies a former garden
house where Mozart penned his three great symphonies in *E major*,
G minor and *Jupiter* in *C major*. As an antidote to the great composers
it makes for an enjoyable walk to follow in the footsteps of some lesser-known ones in the 4th district of Wieden, south of the famous
Musikverein. Beginning at Wiedner Hauptstrasse 7 can be found the
former *Hotel Goldenes Lamm* (Golden Lamb Hotel), where the Czech
composer Antonín Dvořák (1841–1904) occasionally stayed. He is famous for his symphonies, concertos and chamber music, as well as
his ever-popular *Slavonic Dances*. Around the corner at Karlsgasse 4
is the former home of German-born Johannes Brahms (1833–97) who
liked Vienna's provincial feel, referring to it as »the village«. One-time
Musikverein director, his romantic chamber and piano music appeals
to both laymen and academics alike. His statue adorns nearby Ressel
Park, close to the Technical University (*Technische Universität*) where
the Strauss brothers once studied and where Italian Baroque composer Antonio Vivaldi (1678–1741), the so-called Red Priest, was buried.
It is a little-known fact that the great Venetian came to Vienna late in
his career (for reasons that remain unclear) and died in a room above
the old Kärntnertor gate, next to where the Hotel Sacher now stands.
Vivaldi was buried in a cemetery outside the city walls but, as happened with Mozart (see no. 19), his resting place has been lost, the cemetery being abandoned in 1783 and built over in 1818. Today the
existence of the grave is marked only by a modest plaque put up in
1978.

Farther along Wiedner Hauptstrasse at number 32 is the house where Christoph Willibald Gluck (1714–87) died on 15th November 1787. He is best known for being in charge of ›Empress‹ Maria Theresa's court orchestra and for his opera *Orfeo ed Euridice*, the first to subordinate its music to the dramatic action. Nearby at Waaggasse 1

is a plaque to Finnish composer Jean Sibelius (1865–1957) who lived here during a study trip in 1890–91. As well as gaining inspiration from Bruckner for his tone poem *Kullervo*, which would in time lead to his seven magnificently moving symphonies, Sibelius also failed an audition as violinist for the Vienna Philharmonic Orchestra due to nerves.

Not far away at Mozartgasse 4 is the building where Richard Strauss (1864–1949) lived between 1919 and 1925. Unconnected to Vienna's waltzing Strauss dynasty, he is remembered for his symphonic poems *Also sprach Zarathustra* (*Thus spake Zarathustra*) and *Till Eulenspiegel*, the opera *Der Rosenkavalier* and the moving *Vier Letzte Lieder* (*Four Last Songs*). Finally, at Johann Strauss

Wall plaque to Finnish composer Jean Sibelius at Waaggasse 1

Gasse 4 is the site of the last home of Waltz King Johann Strauss (see no. 57). Although the building was destroyed in the war, the opening bars of his famous *An der Schönen blauen Donau* (*The Blue Danube Waltz*) can be seen inscribed on the wall of number 10 farther up the street. Wieden also contains the last home of Franz Schubert (1797–1828) at Kettenbrückengasse 6 where the young composer succumbed to typhus. Now a museum (*Schubert-Sterbewohnung*) it contains the last letter and silver toothpick of the man responsible for many symphonies, string quartets as well as this author's favourite, the touching song *Ständchen* (*Serenade*), written in 1826 in a garden at Kutschkergasse 44 in the 18th district of Währing and marked by an ornate stone wall plaque.

Other places of interest nearby: 42

44 The Incredible Imperial Furniture Depot

7th District (Neubau), the Imperial Court Furniture Depot
(*Kaiserliches Hofmobiliendepot*) at Mariahilferstrasse 88
& Andreasgasse 7; take U-3 to Zieglergasse

»Bizarre, sensuous, eccentric and precious« is how the official literature describes the myriad objects to be found in the Imperial Court
Furniture Depot. Recently and superbly renovated, this criminally
overlooked museum contains unique and fascinating everyday objects
once used by the Habsburgs, as well a collection of objects reflecting
the continuing development of Viennese furniture-making and interi-
or design.

Founded by ›Empress‹ Maria Theresa (1740–80) in 1747 the Imperial Depot of Court Movables was responsible for the upkeep and
storage of surplus and outmoded furnishings from the numerous
Habsburg properties. It also facilitated the annual move of the imperial household to its various summer and winter residences, in the
days before these were permanently furnished. In 1901 Emperor
Franz Josef I (1848–1916) commissioned the present storage facility
on Mariahilferstrasse and in 1924, several years after the fall of the
monarchy, its doors were opened to an interested Viennese public.

Not to be missed is the incredible Egyptian Room originally installed in the Hofburg in 1810 by the third wife of Emperor Franz II (I)
(1792–1835). Equally stunning is the so-called Heritage – a room crammed with surplus and unwanted candelabra, picture frames, vases
and prayer stools illustrating how tast-
es changed as each new monarch came to the throne. The Habsburg Hall has an intimate collec-tion of objects re-lating to individual

Surplus Habsburg candelabra in the Hofmobiliendepot

personalities such as the weighing scales of Elisabeth (*Sisi*), wife of Emperor Franz Josef I, Crown Prince Rudolf's cradle and Emperor Franz II (I)'s personal garden tools, as well as his Brazilian canaries *Bibi* and *Büberl* – stuffed of course! Also here is the lead coffin in which the executed Emperor Maximilian of Mexico, brother of Emperor Franz Josef I (1848–1916), was returned to Vienna in 1867. Most exotic is Prince Eugène of Savoy's (1663–1736) Indian chintz wall hangings from his hunting lodge in the Marchfeld, whilst in the Emperor Franz Josef Hall can be found Crown Prince Rudolf's oriental Turkish Room with its colourful carpets and divans assembled after his journey to the Orient in 1881. Beyond the Habsburg collections there follows a lovely series of 19th century *Biedermeier* and Historicist alcoves depicting the styles favoured by the bourgeoisie during that century. Look out for the red salon with its tiger skin rug from the 1920s, said to have been a dangerous man-eater shot by Count Louis Esterházy in India and presented to Emperor Franz Josef I as a gift. Thereafter may be found a curious collection of commodes (the predecessor to the flushing lavatory) and spittoons (for spitting chewed tobacco into), as well as the museum's current furniture depot brimming with pieces from the various state holdings. There is also the world's most comprehensive display of chairs including examples of Michael Thonet's mass-produced, beech bentwood chairs, patented in 1856 and exported around the world. Also worth finding is Ernst Plischke's supremely comfortable reclining easy chair in the apartment he designed in 1928 for the ceramic artist Lucy Rie.

The collection concludes with the innocent-looking neo-Rococo table at which the Austrian State Treaty (*Staatsvertrag*) was signed in the Upper Belvedere Palace on May 15th 1955, heralding the final withdrawal from Austria of the four allied powers who had controlled the country since the closing of the Second World War. From this date onwards, Austria would be free, independent and neutral.

Other places of interest nearby: 45, 46, 76

45 The Smallest Shop in Vienna

7th District (Neubau), shop at the corner of Burggasse and Breite Gasse; take U-2/U-3 to Volkstheater

In a city known for the grandeur of its architecture it comes as something of a surprise to discover one of the capital's familiar flag-draped information plaques adorning a building other than a palace or church. However, just inside the 7th district of Neubau, close to the fascinating Spittelberg Pedestrian area (see no. 48), there is a plaque marking the little-known »Smallest House in Vienna«. Built on the corner of Burggasse and Breite Gasse in 1872 it is now the premises of watchmaker Friedrich Schmollgruber. The exterior of the building is suitably adorned with a charming array of decorations related to timekeeping. On the corner, for instance, is a clock in the form of a huge pocket watch held aloft by skeletal hands-of-

Schmollgruber's tiny watchmaker's shop on the corner of Breite Gasse

time from which sprout metallic leaves. Similarly, the gable-end has a pair of moon-and-planet clocks, and even the chimneystack is adorned with a blackened weather vane below the quaint chimney caps revolving in the wind. Look out also for the painted longcase clock on the wall of Schmollgruber's goldsmiths next-door. Beyond the watchmaker's sturdy metal doors is a tiny trading area only 14 square metres in size, smaller even than those of the clockmakers behind the Kirche am Hof (see no. 7).

Vienna can also boast another retailing superlative in the shape of the first and oldest button shop (*Knopfniederlage*) founded by A. Frimmel in 1844 on Freisingergasse, just off Graben. Although recently converted to a chocolatier it still retains many of its original fixtures and fittings, its walls still lined with hundreds of boxes containing every conceivable type of button imaginable and within a setting more suited to a palace than a shop. A superbly painted glass signboard still graces the outside of the premises.

Returning to Burggasse there can be found a cultural complex nearby known as the Museums Quartier, opened in 2001 in the grounds of the former Court Stables (*Hofstallungen*). The latter were built in 1725 to a design by the great Baroque architect Johann Bernhard Fischer von Erlach (1656–1723) and his son Josef Emanuel. This accounts for the lively horses' heads sculpted over several of the doorways that once led to the draught-horse stables, and the several hundred carriages that were pulled right up to the dissolution of the monarchy in 1918.

Note: Vienna has many more unusual shops, including the Zauber-Klingel magic shop at Führichgasse 4 (1st District), founded in 1876; the Modell-Hüte hat shop at Herrengasse 6; E. Massl's lampshade shop at Stallburg-Gasse 2; Böhle's delicatessen at Wollzeile 30, with its enormous selection of bottled beers; the smoked meat specialist (*Geselchtes Fleisch*) on Postgasse; and the wonderfully old-fashioned Engelhof Bon-Bon shop at Neubaugasse 18.

Other places of interest nearby: 35, 36, 46, 48

46 The Creation of the Croissant

7th District (Neubau), former shop at the corner of Burggasse and Sigmundsgasse; take U-2/U-3 to Volkstheater

Although Vienna is famed for its delicious pastries and cakes, notably *Apfelstrudel* and *Sachertorte*, available in the many coffee houses and cake shops (*Konditorei*), the less grandiose products of the humble baker should not be overlooked. Many bakers (*Bäckerei*) produce the full range of Viennese breads, namely 14 different rolls, buns and croissants, six kinds of black bread and three kinds of white, including the basic wheat and rye loaf known as *Hausbrot* (house bread).

A traditional Viennese bakery well worth a visit is Grimm's at Kurrentgasse 10 in the *Innere Stadt* – worth it just for a look in the window! The old-style bakeries often had lovely black glass signboards on which the different breads were listed proudly in gold paint (e.g. Neustiftgasse 23 and Johannesgasse 23, the latter including a painting of the loaves and rolls themselves). Painted glass shop signs, once commonplace in Vienna, are now increasingly rare and considered historic works of art in themselves (e.g. *Carl Zapletal's Moderne Fotografie* studio at Josefstädter Strasse 73 and the Italian-French fruiterer around the corner at Lange Gasse 20-22; see also text nos. 17 and 27).

An old baker's advertisement painted on glass on Neustiftgasse

The sign on a former bakery on Burggasse makes mention of poppy seeds (*Mohn*), cream cheese (*Topfen*) and croissants (*Beugel*). It is an overlooked fact that Vienna could justifiably be taken as the home not only of the croissant but also the bagel. The latter is Jewish in origin but became popular after a Jewish baker presented one to King John III of Poland (Jan Sobieski) who helped repel the Turks during their second siege of Vienna in 1683 (see no. 2). From the same period came the croissant, its crescent shape said to resemble the half-crescent moon seen on Turkish flags. It found its way to France when ›Empress‹ Maria Theresa's daughter Marie Antoinette married the future King Louis XVI.

A baker's advertisement on the corner of Burggasse and Sigmundsgasse

In the *Innere Stadt,* at Grünangergasse 8, is a doorway with bread rolls, croissant and pretzels carved above it belonging to the so-called Kipferlhaus. *Kipferl* is another German word for croissant and legend states that it was here that the first one was baked in 1683.

Also of interest, in the 8th district of Josefstadt at Lange Gasse 34, can be found one of Vienna's oldest bakeries that produced bread continuously from 1701 to 1963. Located inside a Baroque house built in 1697 and known today as the Alte Backstube it is now a café and still contains the original equipment installed 300 years ago, as well as a museum reflecting the craft of Vienna's guild of bakers. Finally, in neighbouring Neubau, there is another historic former bakery at Neustiftgasse 47. Built in 1903 the façade of the Bäckerei Karl Obenaus carries a lively series of reliefs depicting farmers harvesting and bakers baking.

Note: The only church outside Vienna's old city walls to survive the second Turkish siege of 1683 was the Servitenkirche at Servitengasse 9. As well as boasting some splendid Baroque stucco work, and being the city's first church with an oval nave, it is also home to the chapel of the Servite St. Peregrine, remembered for giving bread to the poor. So-called Peregrine bread rolls have been sold in Vienna, from 6th April to 6th May, ever since a local baker honoured the saint by making similar donations to the needy.

Other places of interest nearby: 35, 45, 48

47 The Latest
»Best View in Town«

7th District (Neubau), the Büchereien Wien library on
Urban-Loritz-Platz; take U-6 to Burggasse-Stadthalle

Despite being situated on predominantly level ground, Vienna has
long offered the visitor some striking panoramas of the city. A climb
up 343 steps to the watchman's room of the Stephansdom's southern
tower (*Südturm*) for instance (itself best seen from the balconies of
the nearby Haas-Haus or the Skybar on the top floor of the Steffl store
at Kärntner Strasse 19) affords a wonderful overview of the rooftops
of the *Innere Stadt*. A similar vista, albeit a lower level one seen from
outside the Ringstrasse, is available from the gardens of the Upper
Belvedere Palace as well as the rooftop café of the Gerngross department store on Mariahilfer Strasse. The eastern districts of the city can
be seen from the gondolas of the Ferris wheel (*Riesenrad*) in the
Volksprater (see no. 59), whereas the western suburbs may be viewed
from Penzing's loftily situated Kirche am Steinhof (see no. 75). A trio
of lookout towers on Vienna's western hilltops also provide some
breathtaking views of this area (see no. 78). A brisk walk up to Schloss
Schönbrunn's *Gloriette* (itself the focal point of a wonderful night time
view from Hütteldorfer Strasse) similarly provides a magnificent westwards overview, as well as northwards to the Kahlenberg and Leo-
poldsberg on the edge of the Vienna Woods (*Wienerwald*). From the
latter two natural vantage points may be seen the peaks of the distant
Rax and Schneeberg at the southwestern edge of the Vienna Basin, as
well as the Hungarian Plains and Carpathian Mountains far away to
the east. For Danube river scenery head for the 252 metre-high Danube
Tower (*Donauturm*) whose viewing terrace offers a panorama from
Klosterneuburg to the Hainburg Mountains.

A new viewing point may now be added to this list, namely the innovative new library straddling the Burggasse-Stadthalle U-Bahn station. Called the Büchereien Wien it contains 240,000 books, 60,000
audiovisual items, 130 computers and 150 studying booths. The library is the work of urban architect Ernst Mayr, once a self-confessed
»second tier architect«, whose anonymously submitted design was
selected out of 120 submissions from across the EU. A highlight for
visitors is the broad stone staircase, made up of 100 stone steps, which

Looking north towards the Vienna Woods from the Büchereien Wien

climbs up the building's exterior to a rooftop café and public terrace. Although the view over to the *Innere Stadt* is obscured, the numerous viewing balconies afford an interesting vista both south down the Gürtel ringroad to the Favoriten water tower (see no. 67), as well as north to the astronomical observatory in Sternwartepark (see no. 78), with Kahlenberg and the Vienna Woods beyond. The building makes for a perfect combination of learning and leisure!

For an absolute contrast, but a no less interesting one, visit the *Prunksaal* (Grand Hall) of the National Library on Josefsplatz in the Hofburg, at 77 metres in length the largest Baroque library in Europe. Commissioned as the court library by Emperor Karl VI (1711–40), it was designed by Johann Bernhard Fischer von Erlach in 1723 and contains 200,000 leather-bound volumes, including the private collection of Prince Eugène of Savoy (1663–1736). On the roof is a great jumble of statuary dominated by Minerva, goddess of wisdom, flanked by two Atlas figures supporting two gilded globes and a clutch of scientific instruments (see no. 20). With its marble columns, gilded bookcases, statuary and frescoed dome one couldn't find a better example of how Viennese architecture has changed from Baroque to modern times.

Note: Taking in the glorious view from Schloss Schönbrunn's *Gloriette* might be a good time to imagine how the scene might have looked back in 1945 when the buildings of Vienna were suffering considerable damage from allied bombing raids. So successful was the post-war clean-up operation and subsequent re-building projects, helped greatly by the Marshall Plan, that it is difficult today to see where buildings have been patched up. It would be hard to imagine that the left-hand side of the *Gloriette* itself was entirely destroyed were it not for the original bomb-damaged masonry on show below a nearby tree. It is interesting to note that the site of the *Gloriette*, itself built as a triumphal arch celebrating the victory of Maria Theresa's army over Frederick II of Prussia in 1757, was originally to be occupied by a palace to rival Versailles: alas it was never realised.

Other places of interest nearby: 45, 46

48 Stepping Back in Time

8th District (Josefstadt), Lange Gasse 29; take U-2/U-3
to Rathaus and walk up Josefstädter Strasse

This particular location needs little accompanying text since its charm lies in the immediate impact it has on the explorer opening the anonymous wooden gate at Lange Gasse 29. Indeed, visitors must only afford themselves a fleeting glimpse of what lies beyond, for this is no tourist attraction but rather a place where normal Viennese citizens have lived for the last 250 years. Situated in the district of Josefstadt, named after Emperor Josef II (1765–90), this is one of Vienna's smallest yet most charming courtyards, created originally for servants and workers in the 18th century. The modest, single-storey terraces have a unique charm of their own, with washing out to dry and children's toys strewn about amongst the pot plants. Lange Gasse 29 offers the fortunate visitor an intimate glimpse of a Viennese way of life that has scarcely changed in centuries.

Next, the explorer should head south into the neighbouring 7th district of Neubau and the Spittelberg Pedestrian Area, once an island on a Danube tributary where victims of the 1679 plague were quarantined. Here there is an original working class quarter of tenements restored recently to their 18th and 19th century condition and complimenting well the terraces in Josefstadt. A stroll along the narrow cobbled streets reveals a fine ensemble of buildings, such as Spittelberggasse 9 with its *trompe l'oeil* painted windows, the Baroque houses at 18 and 20, and the pretty *Biedermeier* building at Gutenberggasse 29. It is hard to believe that this stylish area was for years a notorious »Red Light« district where 58

*A charming hidden courtyard
at Langegasse 29 in Josefstadt*

of the 138 houses were taverns, filled with musicians, prostitutes, textile workers, tramps and, one night in 1778, even Emperor Josef II himself! To this day the Gasthaus *Witwe Bolte* carries an inscription that states, »Through this door in the arch, Emperor Josef II fled«. It is harder still to think that in 1809 the troops of Napoleon were camped here (see no. 61) as were the Turkish army in 1683 (see no. 2). Indeed the fine Renaissance house at Ulrichsplatz 5 probably only survives today because it was close to where the Grand Vizier Kara Mustafa himself was camped (see the gilded Turkish horseman in a niche on the corner of Kellermanngasse).

A further architectural curiosity in this area is the little-known early-19th century *Biedermeier* passage running through the Sünn-Hof at Landstrasser Hauptstrasse 28. It is wonderfully preserved for its entire length and now contains shops and cafés that spill out onto the street in summer. Such a passageway running between two parallel streets, and which is unique to Vienna, is known as a *Durchgang*. Another lively example of a *Durchgang* is in the Hirschenhof connecting Windmühlgasse 20 with Mariahilfer Strasse 45 in the 6th district of Mariahilf. A wall plaque records that the famous Viennese *Biedermeier* playwright Ferdinand Raimund (1790–1836) lived here – though it doesn't record that he committed suicide after being bitten by what he thought was a rabid dog. A little artier in feel is the *Durchgang* connecting Lerchenfelder Strasse 13 with Neustiftgasse 16 (7th district of Neubau), its stepped and high-vaulted whitewashed archways lending an almost Spanish feel. A pristine example in the same district, untainted by retail de-

A Durchgang between Lerchenfelder Strasse and Neustiftgasse

velopment, can be found in the Adlerhof between Burggasse 51 and Siebensterngasse 46. Finally, a narrow *Durchgang* in the *Innere Stadt*, filled with shops and restaurants, runs between Lugeck 5 and Wollzeile 5. It is famous for the Figlmüller restaurant that prides itself on serving Vienna's largest *Wiener Schnitzel*!

Other places of interest nearby: 45, 46, 50

49 Grass Raincoats and One-Legged Milking Stools

8th District (Josefstadt), the Austrian Museum of Folk Art (*Österreichisches Museum für Volkskunde*) in the Schönborn Palace at Laudongasse 15–19; take Tram 43/44 from Schottentor U-Bahn and then one stop on Tram 5

Founded in 1895, and housed since 1917 in the imposing setting of the former summer palace of Friedrich Karl Schönborn-Buchheim (assistant chancellor of the Empire), the Austrian Museum of Folk Art is an unexpected collection reflecting everyday life in the Austrian provinces. It is home to a charming and colourful array of objects from the 16th-19th centuries, of which the following caught this writer's eye:

Room 1 contains a painted figurehead, from a sleigh (c.1750), known as the *Bird of Self-Recognition* that depicts quite literally a Baroque figure of speech meaning to analyse oneself; here also are intricately painted Easter eggs (c.1900, though still exchanged today) from former Crown lands such as Moravia (now the Czech Republic) and Galicia (now part of Poland and Ukraine);

Room 2 has a wonderful Slovenian/Croatian grass rain cloak common in southern Alpine regions until the 20th century, as well as straw winter shoes and a birch fungus cap;

Room 3 holds some cheerful painted Tyrolian window boxes (c.1895) made by mountain guides, farm hands and shoemakers that were sometimes given as love tokens;

Room 8 contains a one-legged Tyrolian milking stool of the type preferred in central Alpine areas over the more usual three-legged models;

Room 10 has a magnificent elongated iron weathervane (c.1860) depicting the various crafts and techniques of a village blacksmith;

Room 11 holds an ingenious Moravian trap designed to catch three mice in one night;

Room 13 has a curious wooden beehive carved with the Habsburg double eagle, also from Moravia (now the Czech Republic);

Room 16 contains cups used by the Imperial house to wash the feet of 24 old and poor men and women on Maundy Thursday; pictures of Emperor Franz Josef I (1848–1916) and his wife Elisabeth carrying out this surprising custom (relating to the fact that the Emperor was also King of Jerusalem) may be found in the Court Silver and

A magnificent oven in the shape of a peasant lady in the Austrian Folk Museum

Porcelain Collection (*Hofsilber- und Tafelkammer*) in the Hofburg's Michaelertrakt;

Finally, Room 17 is home to a splendid glazed ceramic oven in the form of a rotund peasant lady whose huge inflated skirt ensured the maximum radiation of heat from within! She stood originally in the Korninger Inn in Münzbach bei Perg, Upper Austria and was always referred to as *Annamirl* by the locals. Be sure not to miss *Annamirl* again on leaving the museum where she can be seen adorning a superbly crafted old wrought-iron street sign on the corner of the building.

Other places of interest nearby: 48, 50

Note: Another former palace, similar to that of the Schönborn-Buchheims in that it is now surrounded by modern buildings, can be found at the junction of Schaumburgergasse and Rainergasse in the 4th district of Wieden. Built originally for Count Thomas Starhemberg it was used from 1841 by the Schönburg-Hartensteins. Now unloved and abandoned, its rooftop statues looking down on a garden filled with mistletoe-heavy trees, suburban Vienna rarely gets more romantic.

50 The Little Visited Locksmiths' Square

8th District (Josefstadt) monument in Schlosserplatzl
at junction of Tulpengasse and Wickenburggasse;
take U-2/U-3 to Rathaus

There is a small geographic area occupying the space between Stephansplatz, Graben and Kärntnerstrasse with the unusual name of Stock-im-Eisen Platz. Meaning literally »Stick in Iron Square« it relates to the nail-studded piece of timber that can be seen behind glass on the corner of the grand Equitable Palais building at number 3 (see no. 20). The lively group of figures over its doorway throws some light on this curiosity for it depicts a group of young men hammering nails into a log. Viennese tradition stretching back to 1533 relates that a larch tree was felled here in c.1440 and declared by locksmiths to be a symbol of their guild. Thereafter, it became the custom for apprentice and journeying locksmiths to hammer a nail into the trunk for good luck and a safe passage home. By the 19th century the trunk had acquired

A wrought iron key signifying a locksmith on Schlosserplatzl

such legendary status that even Hans Christian Andersen wrote of it, believing the myth that it was a remnant of the primeval forest that once covered central Vienna. It is even said that labourers excavating the Stephansplatz U-Bahn station in 1973 knocked the occasional nail into the ancient trunk for good measure.

At this point the explorer should escape the relentless bustle of Stephansplatz and head for the quiet and little-visited Schlosserplatzl (Little Locksmiths' Square) behind the Town Hall (*Rathaus*). Here, in the centre of a rose-filled square is a contemporary *Stock-im-Eisen*, complete with hundreds of nails knocked into it. This was undertaken in 1988 to celebrate the 700th anniversary of the Vienna Guild of Locksmiths. Their offices can be found in the fine balconied building along one side of the square, bearing pertinent carvings on its door as well as a huge wrought iron key hanging on the corner. Scenes from the locksmiths' story, together with other Viennese legends, can be found painted inside the arcade fronting the Vogelweidhof (1926) at Wurzbachgasse 2–8, a Red Vienna apartment block in the 15th district of Rudolfsheim-Fünfhaus (see no. 82).

Other places of interest nearby: 48, 49

The little-known locksmiths' monument behind the Rathaus

51 Mighty Barracks and the First Skyscraper

9th District (Alsergrund), the Rossauer Barracks
(*Rossauer Kaserne*) on Maria-Theresien-Strasse; take Tram D
to Maria-Theresien-Strasse; not open to the Public

With the demolition of the old city walls (see no. 24) and the construction of the Ringstrasse, Vienna gained a magnificent city boulevard to be proud of. Its finest buildings tend to lie between the twin spires of the Votivkirche at Schottentor and the City Opera (*Staatsoper*) on Opernring. However, as an alternative to such well-documented grandeur, it is worth exploring the lesser-known buildings that terminate the horseshoe-shaped Ringstrasse, where it reaches the Danube Canal.

Downstream for instance, on Stubenring, is the bombastic former War Ministry (*Kriegsministerium*), Otto Wagner's Modernist Postal Savings Bank (*Postsparkasse*) with its façade of grey marble slabs suspended on 17,000 metal rivets, and on the canal side itself, the Urania people's observatory (see no. 78). By way of a contrast, and lying upstream, are two totally different buildings. The first, the so-called Rossauer Barracks (meaning Horse Forest Barracks) that occupies much of nearby Maria-Theresien-Strasse, is a mighty barracks whose turreted façade is best viewed from the opposite side of the canal. Its name refers to the woodland village that originally stood here where waggoners once watered their horses. Erected in the 1860s it was mirrored originally by a second barracks where the Postsparkasse now stands in Georg-Coch-Platz on Stubenring. Both barracks were connected by the broad Ringstrasse, along which cannon and troops could move quickly, and were erected to quell any further civil unrest following the 1848 Revolution (a further barracks, known as the Arsenal, was built on a hill beyond the Upper Belvedere Palace; see nos. 14 and 40).

The Rossauer Kaserne is described as being in the Mock English Tudor (or Windsor) style, and is somewhat reminiscent of an overblown Hampton Court. An enduring urban myth concerning the barracks is that its towers were added later, to house the latrines that the architect absent-mindedly forgot to include in his original plan!

Another good vantage point to take in the enormity of the building (today home to Vienna's police force) is from Deutschmeisterplatz. Here a monument topped by a flag-wielding bronze soldier celebrates the legendary Viennese regiment whose headquarters the barracks once were (note: the dead of both this regiment and others are remembered in a series of wall plaques, as well as an altar made from old artillery shells and a 4-metre high artillerymens' candle, in the former garrison church, the Votivkirche (see no. 79), up the road at Schottentor).

Looking towards the Rossauer Barracks from Deutschmeisterplatz

A short walk across Schottenring reveals a very different building in the shape of the stylish Ringturm. Designed by Erich Boltenstern and erected in 1955 it is the only real tower block in Vienna's *Innere Stadt*. It rises 73 metres into the air and on its roof is a 20 metre-high mast, down the sides of which are 117 red, white and green light bulbs. For those interested in weather forecasting there is an information board on the Hütteldorf-bound platform of the nearby Schottenring U-bahn station that explains how varying combinations of these flashing lights at night can give the weather for the following day (red flashing upwards or downwards = temperature change; green flashing upwards or downwards = weather change; constant green = no change; flashing red = storms; flashing white = ice).

Finally, at Schottenring 20, there is the former stock exchange (*Börse*) built by one of the major Ringstrasse architects, Danish-born Theophil Hansen, after whom the subdued red of the building's stylish brickwork is called (*Hansenrot*). Over the road at Schottenring 7–9 is a plaque marking the former site of the Ringtheater that burned down in 1881 killing 386 people. It was as a result of this disaster that the doors of many shops and other public buildings had by law to open *outwards* into the street and not inwards – something still found to this day.

Other places of interest nearby: 1, 53, 54

52 The Forgotten Jewish Cemetery

9th District (Alsergrund), the Rossau Jewish Cemetery
(*Friedhof Rossau*) behind the retirement home at
Seegasse 9–11; take Tram D to Porzellangasse.
The cemetery may be visited at any reasonable time by
informing a member off staff in the foyer and then
proceeding to the viewing balcony at the back of the building

Jewish people have long had a sizeable and important presence in Vienna, both in the *Innere Stadt* (see no. 8) and in the 2nd district of Leopoldstadt (see no. 58). For a thousand years they have lived here, numbering 180,000 by 1910, though this number was reduced drastically in the Second World War during the worst of the city's numerous anti-Semitic episodes.

In 1874 the huge Central Cemetery (*Zentralfriedhof*) in Simmering was laid out and for the first time Jews were buried alongside Catholics and Protestants, though admittedly in distinct zones. Prior to this the Jews had their own cemeteries several of which survive, albeit under somewhat controversial circumstances. Vienna's oldest Jewish cemetery, and indeed one of Europe's oldest, is the Rossau Cemetery in the 9th district of Alsergrund. Its 900 original headstones date as far

Broken headstones in one of Europe's oldest Jewish cemeteries on Seegasse

back as 1450 and continue up to 1783 when the cemetery was finally closed, along with other burial grounds within the *Linienwall* (today's Gürtel ringroad), for health reasons by Emperor Josef II (1765–90). Today it languishes somewhat behind a modern retirement home, itself built on the site of an old Jewish hospital that was demolished in 1972. Amongst the tall grass, and even taller trees, are the 280 headstones that were identified and re-erected after the Nazi desecrations of 1938 (see no. 13). However, many remain cracked and dislodged, and it was not until 1984 that the cemetery was consecrated.

A notable grave is that of banker Samuel Oppenheimer of Heidelberg (1630–1703), one of the first so-called Court Jews to be protected by Imperial Letter and enticed back to Vienna after the expulsions of 1699 under Emperor Leopold I (1658–1705) (see no. 58). Most significantly he organised the financing of Prince Eugène of Savoy's (1663–1736) campaigns against the Turks in the 1680s, as well as the wars with the French, though the Habsburgs never settled their debts with him forcing the Oppenheimer dynasty into eventual bankruptcy. Nearby is the grave of his son-in-law Samson Wertheimer (1658–1724) who was financial administrator to no less than three successive emperors.

After the cemetery's eventual closure, Jewish burials were made in a new graveyard appended to Währing's municipal cemetery (*Währinger Friedhof*) opened in 1783 on Semperstrasse just outside the Währinger Gürtel. As with other suburban cemeteries it was largely cleared and made into a park in the 1920s, having been made redundant by the new Central Cemetery (*Zentralfriedhof*) opened in Simmering in 1874 (see no. 63). However, the Jewish part remains to this day, albeit overgrown and unkempt. Surrounded by high walls and presently closed for security reasons, its half-buried and toppled stones, many of whose name plaques were torn off long ago, recall Prague's old Jewish cemetery (note also the charming winged egg-timer carved over the entrance at Schrottenbachgasse 3). Amongst the 10,000 closely packed graves from the late-18th to 19th centuries (visible from over the park wall at the back) are those of influential bankers, industrialists and railway engineers. Notables include the Fürth family from Bohemia who built what is now the American Consulate, Israel Hönig von Hönigsberg, the first Jewish Imperial official to be ennobled, the Epstein family who were also ennobled by the Emperor (hence the coat of arms on their tomb), and Bernhard Pollack, art collector, whose tomb was later dug out by optimistic treasure hunters in the mistaken belief that it would be filled with valuables.

The cemetery was commandeered by the Nazis in 1941 in order to excavate part of it as a fire reservoir and it fell to the area's already traumatised Jewish community to exhume as many bodies as possible. As if that weren't enough, many of the skulls and other bones were then spirited away to the Natural History Museum for insensitive and unecessary measurement and cataloguing. Just over 200 skeletons would eventually be returned in 1947 for the few remaining Jews to re-bury in what was left of their now vandalised cemetery.

Although this historic site, arguably Europe's most important Jewish cemetery, has been ear-marked for future restoration, its current lamentable condition, like that of Friedhof Rossau, is due in part to the fact that the families of those interred simply no longer exist – exterminated or expelled by the Nazis during the Second World War. That, together with the feeling that somehow the important contribution made by Viennese Jewry to the economic and artistic development of Vienna has yet to be either fully understood or wholly acknowledged.

These explanations are graphically reinforced when one visits the old Jewish section, inside Gate 1, of Simmering's Central Cemetery (*Zentralfriedhof*), its bullet-strafed and tumbling headstones, once as grand as anything in the well-maintained Catholic section next-door, now abandoned to the ravages of untamed vegetation and subsidence (see no. 63). Even the graves of novelist Arthur Schnitzler (Group 6, Row 0, Grave 4), Jacob and Amalia Freud (Group 50, Row 4, Grave 53), and the Austrian branch of the powerful Rothschild family (Group 6, Row 29, Grave 49/051) look unkempt, the only evidence of visitors being the rows of tiny pebbles (Memory Stones) left behind. Nowhere is the tragic destiny of Vienna's pre-war Jewish community better emphasised.

Note: Another Viennese Jewish cemetery can be found at Ruthnergasse 28 in the 21st District of Floridsdorf. Its rows of headstones give details not only of what those interred did in life (e.g. a chief inspector of the local railway; a rabbi, as signified by a carved pair of hands) and what their particular talents were (e.g. a cedar tree representing great wisdom), but also how they died (e.g. a grave from 1928 carrying a carving of a motorcycle).

Other places of interest nearby: 51, 53, 56

53 Meet Me at the Strudlhof Steps

9th District (Alsergrund), the Strudlhof Steps
(*Strudlhofstiege*) on Strudlhofgasse;
take Tram D to Porzellangasse

Between Liechtensteinstrasse and Währinger Strasse, in the heart of the 9th district of Alsergrund, is a rather curious flight of stone steps. Known as the Strudlhof Steps they were designed in 1910 by the architect Johann Theodor Jäger. Their purpose was to connect the former water meadows of Liechtensteinstrasse, along which a Danube tributary once ran, with Strudlhofgasse above, the two areas lying at different levels due to a geological fault. The steps are actually named after Peter von Strudl (1660-1714), founder of the Academy of Fine Arts (*Akademie der bildenden Künste*), which was housed originally in the Strudlhof before moving to today's Schillerplatz. Strudl was also responsible, together with his brother Paul (who sculpted the effigy of Emperor Leopold I on the Graben Plague Column (*Pestsäule*), for the statues in the Hofburg's Baroque library (*Prunksaal*).

The Strudlhof Steps are a lovely example of the Viennese Art Nouveau (*Jugendstil*) with sweeping curves, green balustrades, standard lamps, and a brass fish head spouting water from a mosaic backdrop. Looking especially seductive at night, it is little wonder that they inspired local writer Franz Karl Heimito von Doderer. Born in Weidlingau bei Wien in 1896, Doderer was the sixth and final child of a wealthy Viennese architect and building contractor, related by marriage to leading Ringstrasse architect Heinrich von Ferstel. Biographies show the young Doderer dressed as an archer at his parents' country home, the Riegelhof, in Prein in the Rax mountains southwest of Vienna. In the First World War Doderer was a cavalry officer but spent 1916–20 in a Russian prisoner of war camp in Siberia. It was during these years that he decided his life's calling was ultimately to be a writer. After the war he studied history and psychology and wrote various essays, poems and other pieces for Viennese newspapers. Finally, in December 1941 he made the first notes for his lengthy novel *The Strudlhof Steps* (*Die Strudlhofstiege, oder Melzer und die Tiefe der Jahre*): less wisely he joined the Nazi party, though this was less about ideology and more about gaining access to the Association of Writers. In 1942 he went to the Russian front winding up again as

The Strudlhof Steps in Alsergrund looking from the direction of Liechtensteinstrasse

a prisoner of war, this time in Norway.

After the Second World War, although initially banned from working in publishing because of his brief Nazi affiliation, Doderer sought spiritual refuge in Catholicism and was soon working again, as a freelance writer. However, it was not until 1951 that publication of *The Strudlhof Steps* brought him sudden and lasting success. Overnight

Doderer became Vienna's most famous post-war writer and following publication in 1956 of his other great novel *The Demons* (*Die Dämonen*) he received the Austrian State Prize for Literature. The reason he still remains largely unknown outside Austria is in part because the translated versions of his books are rarely kept in print. However, it is also because the world he so effectively described was a uniquely Viennese one that had little meaning to those outside it.

The Strudlhof Steps transports the reader back to *fin de siécle* Vienna as seen through the eyes of schoolboy René Stangeler (Doderer himself). He observes how his parents, sisters, houseguests and other middle class characters commute between the oppressive heat of the Viennese summer and the cool, refined rusticity of the Rax, Schneeberg and Semmering mountains. The various strands of the story all eventually come together at the steps themselves.

Doderer continues the theme in *The Demons* set in the 1920s and penned in his favourite tavern *Zur Stadt Paris* (now sadly closed) at the corner of Josefstädter Strasse and Lenaugasse. This time, however, behind the charming tea parties and tennis there runs insecurity, political instability and sexual dissoluteness as Vienna slides towards the civil war of 1934. Both books have a gripping storyline running in tandem with a series of philosophical reflections that attempt to understand the mannered, melancholic and hedonistic Viennese soul.

Doderer died in 1966 and is buried, along with Gustav Mahler, in the cemetery at Grinzing (*Grinzinger Friedhof*) in the 19th district of Döbling. The author's ephemera, including pictures and furniture from his study, can be found in Alsergrund's District Museum (*Bezirksmuseum*) at Währinger Strasse 43. Doderer himself lived along the road at number 50 and often frequented the Café Brioni near the Franz-Josefs-Bahnhof.

A surprisingly similar flight of *Jugendstil* stairs known as the Fillgrader steps (1905-07), though less ornate and lacking any literary connections, may be found at Fillgradergasse off Mariahilfer Strasse. They were designed by Max Hegell to help transport the pedestrian from the Wien river (now culverted) up to Mariahilfer Strasse.

Note: At Strudelhofgasse 9 stands the Palais Strudelhof, once home to Austrian Foreign Minister Graf Berchtold, where in July 1914 he drafted the ultimatum to Serbia, which in turn led to the First World War.

Other places of interest nearby: 51, 52, 54, 55

54　The Fools' Tower

9th District (Alsergrund), the Fools' Tower
(*Narrenturm*) in courtyard 13 of the
Altes Allgemeines Krankenhaus off Sensengasse;
take Tram 40/41/42 from U-Bahn station Schottentor (U-2)

The 9th district of Alsergrund is home to Vienna's New General Hospital (*Neues Allgemeines Krankenhaus* or *AKH*) that is famous for being Europe's largest. Nearby, on the suitably named Spitalgasse, is its even more famous predecessor the Old General Hospital (*Altes Allgemeines Krankenhaus*), founded by the enlightened Emperor Josef II (1765–90) in 1784. In its day the hospital was one of the world's most modern and boasted 2000 beds. Many world famous doctors and surgeons passed through its doors including psychiatrist Julius Wagner-Jauregg (1857–1940), a 1927 Nobel Prize for Medicine winner for his *Discovery of the Therapeutic Importance of the Malaria Vaccination in Progressive Paralysis*.

The hospital's old courtyards are now a busy university campus, although one of them retains a curiosity known as the Narrenturm, or Fools' Tower. Constructed in 1784 to a design by court architect Isidor Canevale, the cylindrical tower was designed as a purpose-built asylum and represents the first time that the so-called »insane« were housed and treated, rather than being publicly displayed and humiliated. It has five floors each with 28 centrally heated cells running off

The Narrenturm, or Fools' Tower, in the grounds of the Old General Hospital

a central courtyard, the better to supervise the patients. The tower was nicknamed the *Guglhupf* after a famous Austrian cake of a similar shape! However, not all the tower's occupants were suffering legitimate mental infirmity as highlighted by the case of Count Seilern, disciplined by the Kaiser for committing his son on the grounds that the boy refused to marry the girl chosen for him by his father.

Disused after 1866 the *Narrenturm* is now home to the Federal Museum of Pathological Anatomy (*Pathologisch-anatomisches Bundesmuseum*) and contains an educational if somewhat grisly collection of c.4000 specimens (many abnormalities and deformities) preserved in formaldehyde (including the world's finest display of kidney and gallstones). The collection, founded in 1796 and housed originally in the dissection ward of the Old General Hospital, was supplied from 600 hospital corpses a year as well as court-ordered autopsies. The museum also contains over 2,000 replicas of diseased body parts made out of paraffin wax and, on the ground floor, a reconstruction of Dr. Robert Koch's 1882 discovery of the tuberculosis bacillus.

Alsergrund has numerous other medical associations being home to many university departments, doctors and of course the original practice of Sigmund Freud (see no. 84). Additionally there is the Josephinum at Währinger Strasse 25 opened in 1785 to house the Institute of the Military Academy of Medicine and Surgery, founded by Emperor Josef II (1765–90) for the training of field surgeons and army doctors. Since 1920 the Institute for the History of Medicine has had a museum here (*Museum des Institutes für Geschichte der Medizin*) that includes a unique collection of life-size anatomical study models (*Wachspräparate-Sammlung*). They were commissioned by the Emperor in 1780, following a visit to Florence, from the Florentine physiologist Felice Fontana and the Tuscan anatomist Paolo Mascagni. For added realism the figures were modelled out of Ukrainian beeswax!

Note: In Courtyard 6 of the Old General Hospital can be found a tiny prayer house once used by Jewish patients and later descrated by the Nazis. After the war it was used as an electrical transformer house but has now been restored as a memorial.

Other places of interest nearby: 49, 51, 53, 55

55 007 in Vienna

9th District (Alsergrund), the sweet shop at
Währinger Strasse 65 opposite Volksoper;
take Tram 40/41/42 from U-Bahn station Schottentor (U-2)

The film *A View to a Kill* was the 14th in the long running and lucrative James Bond series, based on the spy novels of Ian Fleming. However, by all accounts the film relied more on its gadgetry and special effects than the panache and daring-do of its ageing star Roger Moore. Wisely Moore sipped his last Vodka Martini and retired to a life devoted to charity work and a well-earned knighthood. Amongst those considered for his replacement were established »action men« Mel Gibson, Tom Selleck and Don Johnson. Somewhat surprisingly it was the relatively unknown Timothy Dalton who clinched the part. Born in March 1946 in Colwyn Bay, North Wales he had played a variety of roles in films as diverse as *The Lion in Winter*, *Flash Gordon* and *The Doctor and the Devils*. Not being a typecast actor allowed Dalton to

play Bond his own way – dark and introspectively. His first outing was based on Fleming's short story *The Living Daylights* that had appeared in *The Sunday Times* on 4th February 1962. Directed by John Glen the film premiered at the Odeon in London's Leicester Square on 27th June 1987, attended by Prince Charles and his then wife Diana. The Vienna premiere (titled *Der Hauch des Todes*, or *Breath of Death*) followed on August 13th at the Gartenbau Kino.

This was of special interest to Bond's Austrian audience because much of the first half of the film uses Vienna as a backdrop, both officially and unofficially. The plot dictates that Bond is sent to Bratislava in the old Czechoslovakia to protect a valuable defecting Russian agent and to eliminate a

The sweet shop window at Währinger Strasse 65 displaying photographs of James Bond

Vienna as Bratislava: looking across Währinger Strasse towards the Volksoper

KGB sniper he knows will be waiting there to thwart the escape. The Russian, Koskov, is in a concert hall (unofficially Vienna's Volksoper on Währinger Strasse) and Bond takes up position above a nearby bookshop, actually a wonderfully traditional sweet shop at Währinger Strasse 65, whose window to this day carries photographs of a saturnine-looking Dalton in *de rigueur* tuxedo and bow tie.

Not surprisingly for a 007 movie, the sniper Bond lines up through the sight of his high-powered rifle turns out to be the beautiful Kara (played by Maryam d'Abo) – and of course he deliberately misses his target! Koskov is grabbed and dispatched speedily to the safety of the West via a gas pipeline, in a scene that begins at Vienna's Steinsporenbrücke over the Danube (still dressed up to mimic the Eastern Bloc) and ends at an old gasworks (see no. 64), now *officially* in Vienna. Bond and Kara, needless to say already involved romantically, remain in »Bratislava« for several street scenes shot along

Vienna's number 42 tram route, suitably disguised with Skoda cars and Czechoslovakian shop signs (these include the former Währing tram depot, now a supermarket, and Kara's apartment on Antonigasse). The pair eventually escape in Bond's Aston Martin and finally cross the border into snowbound Austria using Kara's cello as a sledge! After some fairly schmaltzy scenes visiting Vienna's Schönbrunn palace by horse-drawn *Fiaker* and riding gondola 10 of the Ferris wheel (*Riesenrad*) in the Volksprater (see no. 59) the film shifts location to Oxfordshire (Stonor Park to be exact), Tangiers and then finally Afghanistan.

Curiously, few of the Bond biographies, nor indeed many of the city's guidebooks for that matter, make any mention of Vienna as a film location and indeed few visitors are even aware that 007 was ever here. Coincidentally, during the writing of this book a season of Bond films was screened at the aforementioned Gartenbaukino, and again the accompanying promotional material failed to make any reference to the fact that Vienna had provided much of the backdrop for *The Living Daylights*.

James Bond returned to the screen in 1988/89 in *Licence to Kill* but by then Dalton was already feeling typecast and wisely moved on to theatre and television work as well as the occasional motion picture. In this writer's mind Timothy Dalton remains the only Bond to have got close to portraying the secret agent that author Fleming had in mind – with all his vulnerabilities and contradictions; he just had the misfortune of coming along at a time when Bond was somewhat out of fashion. Six years later and the baton would be taken up with greater commercial success by the less sombre Pierce Brosnan (for the film *Goldeneye*), who notably had been considered as a replacement for Roger Moore, but was at the time contracted to his television series *Remington Steele*.

Other places of interest nearby: 53, 54

56 The Reich's Monstrous Monuments

2nd District (Leopoldstadt), the Flak towers
(*Flaktürme*) in the Augarten;
take Tram 31 from U-Bahn Schottenring (U-2/U-4)

On March 15th 1938 200,000 Viennese gathered in the Hofburg's Heldenplatz (Heroes' Square) to celebrate the annexation (*Anschluss*) of Austria with the so-called »Fatherland« of Germany, something many had wanted since the end of the First World War. Adolf Hitler himself appeared on the balcony of the Neue Burg from where he proclaimed: »As Führer and Chancellor of the German nation and the German Reich I hereby announce to German history that my homeland has entered the German Reich.« Afterwards Hitler took an aeroplane directly back to Germany – and the rest as they say is history (see nos. 13, 18 and 58). Within a few years the grand Heldenplatz itself would be ploughed up to plant vegetables in an attempt to feed the city's bewildered population already suffering the privations of Hitler's faltering »thousand year Reich«.

In the meantime Vienna's existing and at times bombastic imperial architecture seems to have suited the city's new occupiers and nothing of note was added to the architectural canon. However, on 9th September 1942 Hitler decreed that, like Berlin and Hamburg, central Vienna should be protected by several huge anti-aircraft towers (*Flaktürme*), three pairs of which would form a defensive triangle centred on the Stephansdom. Consequently in 1943/4 German troops commenced construction of one pair in the Augarten, thus defacing Austria's

oldest surviving Baroque garden laid out in 1712, another in Arenbergpark in the 3rd district of Landstrasse and a third straddling Mariahilferstrasse (Esterházypark and Stiftskaserne courtyard) in the 6th district of Mariahilf. The towers were built

A Second World War communications tower in Arenbergpark, Landstrasse

of almost indestructible reinforced concrete 2.5-3.5 metres thick and were self-contained with their own water and power supplies, military hospital and filtered air system in case of gas attack. Each pair comprised a large, heavily-gunned attack tower (*Gefechtsturm*) as well as a smaller communications tower (*Leitturm*). The former is either a square fortress-style tower, as in Arenbergpark (9-storeys, 41.6 metres high and 57 metres square) or a circular tower, actually 16-sided, as in the Augarten and Stiftskaserne courtyard (12-storeys, 50.6 metres high and 43 metres in diameter). The heaviest artillery (105–128mm guns) was on the roof with lighter armaments (20–30mm) on the projecting balconies below. The communication towers, from where anti-aircraft operations would be orchestrated, were all rectangular in shape (9-storeys, 39-51.4 metres high and 24 by 39 metres in plan). They were more lightly armed with communication facilities and searchlights on the roof. By the end of the war the towers had only just been made operational and were also serving as air raid shelters for the local populace, protecting up to 30,000 people in each. In the event of a successful war the towers' designer, motorway architect Professor Friedrich Tamms, had designs on his drawing board to clad them in slabs of black marble on which the names of dead German soldiers would be chisel-

led in gold leaf. The towers would thus become combined monuments to victory and the dead (rendering them curiously similar to Ravenna's Roman Mausoleum of Theoderich as well as the Castel del Monte in Apulia).

Plans were even found in a Berlin architect's office for the bulldozing of Jewish Leopoldstadt and the erection of a vast Nazi Forum. In reality, Leopoldstadt is a thriving community once more and the

An attack tower in the Augarten, Leopoldstadt

flak towers have become immoveable reminders of the darkest chapter of Vienna's history (despite Russian attempts to dynamite the Augarten's attack tower after the war: an act subsequently and erroneously ascribed to a group of Viennese schoolboys igniting a forgotten weapons dump!).

Hitler famously described Vienna as being like a pearl for which he would provide a suitable setting: by the end of the war that setting comprised only ruined buildings, his abandoned *flak* towers bearing silent witness to their creator's madness. Subsequently, only the communication tower in Esterházypark has found a comprehensive new use, namely the fascinating House of the Sea (*Haus des Meeres*). The exterior of the tower also doubles as a climbing-wall (*Kletterwand am Flakturm*) offering 25 different routes, the vertical face and projecting balcony mimicking perfectly an overhanging alpine rock face reaching up to 34 metres high. A conservatory (or biotope) containing a miniature rain forest filled with monkeys and birds has been bolted onto one side and is entered by a door cut with much effort through the 2.5 metre-thick reinforced German concrete, the latter ensuring a constant temperature for the aquaria and vivaria within. A viewing platform is now open on top of the Haus des Meeres flak tower.

Stable temperatures have also prompted the Austrian Museum of Applied Arts (MAK) (see no. 23) to use the attack tower in Arenbergpark as an archival depository and seasonal exhibition space, known as the Contemporary Art Tower (CAT).

Note: a former air-raid shelter at the base of the communication tower in Esterházypark now contains the Museum of Medieval Legal History: the History of Torture (*Museum für Mittelalterliche Rechtsgeschichte: Die Geschichte der Folter*).

Other places of interest nearby: 51, 52

57 On Waltz Street

2nd District (Leopoldstadt), the Johann Strauss Museum
(*Johann-Strauss-Museum*) at Praterstrasse 54;
take U-1 to Nestroyplatz

In 1863 when Johann Strauss the Younger (1825–99) came to live at Praterstrasse 54 he was already a household name. The address suited him being a majestic and cosmopolitan boulevard that sliced through the cosmopolitan district of Leopoldstadt, from the edge of the *Innere Stadt* out to the Prater. His father Johann Strauss the Elder (1804–49), composer of *The Radetzky March*, was long dead and so too the painful rivalry between the two of them. Strauss surpassed his father's fame, taking the mantle of Waltz King and touring Europe, Russia and even America.

A wall plaque marking the apartment where Johann Strauss wrote
The Blue Danube Waltz

It was in the apartment on Praterstrasse, now an excellent museum, that he composed Vienna's unofficial anthem *An der Schönen blauen Donau* (*The Blue Danube Waltz, opus 314*). Originally scored for the Vienna Male Voice Choir, it was performed as such to a nonplussed audience in 1867 in the former Diana Rooms at Obere Donaustrasse 95. However, shortly afterwards it was performed in Paris with an orchestra and immediately became a worldwide favourite. Today, the piece always features in the Vienna Philharmonic Orchestra's popular televised New Year's Day concert from the Golden Hall of the Musikverein. Strauss finally left Praterstrasse in 1878 and died in 1899 having composed several hundred waltzes, including *Geschichten aus dem Wienerwald* (*Tales from the Vienna Woods*), and operettas, notably *Die Fledermaus* (*The Bat*). His last home at Johann-Strauss-Gasse 4 in Wieden was unfortu-nately destroyed in the Second World War (see no. 43) although on the wall of an apartment at number 10 can be seen the ope-ning bars of his famous Danube Waltz.

Music from The Blue Danube Waltz on a wall near Strauss's last home in Wieden

Over the years Praterstrasse was also home to numerous other scholars, artists and doc-tors. Film music pioneer Max Steiner (1888–1971) for instance was born at number 72 and worked at the Volksprater before moving to Broadway and Hollywood. His 300 film credits include *Casablanca*, *Gone With the Wind*, *King Kong* and *Treasure of the Sierra Madre*. Note the Venetian-style *Dogenhof* next-door at number 70, based on the *Cá d'Oro* palace on Venice's Grand Canal, and part of an attempt to build an Italian quarter in Vienna. Number 44 was the surgery of Alfred Adler, the founder of Individual Psychology, whilst at number 31 was the former Carltheater where Johann Nestroy (1801–62) was dramatist and director (his statue is outside number 19). Finally, at number 22 is the modest room where novelist, dramatist and 1981 Nobel Prize winner Elias Canetti (1905–94) spent his school days, whilst number 16 is the birthplace of novelist and playwright Arthur Schnitzler (1862–1931), whose *Traumnovelle* (*Dream Story*) set origi-nally in *fin de siècle* Vienna, was used by Stanley Kubrick as the basis for his last film *Eyes Wide Shut*, starring Tom Cruise and Nicole Kidman.

Other places of interest nearby: 58, 59

58 Memories of »Mazzes Island«

2nd District (Leopoldstadt), the former Greator
Leopoldstadt Temple (*Leopoldstädter Tempel*)
at Tempelgasse 3–5; take U-1 to Nestroyplatz

Vienna's 2nd district of Leopoldstadt, across the Danube Canal, has always been a point of disembarkation for those arriving from lands to the north and east. It was on low-lying marshy ground here, subject to regular flooding, that in 1625 Emperor Ferdinand II (1619–37) established a walled Jewish ghetto known as the *Unterer Werd*. From an Old German expression meaning Lower Island, the area is encompassed by today's Taborstrasse, Obere Augartenstrasse, Malzgasse, Schiffgasse and Krummbaumgasse. It replaced the original medieval ghetto of the *Innere Stadt* (see no. 8) and soon began to flourish. However, in 1699 with the Catholic Counter Reformation in full swing, Emperor Leopold I (1658–1705) banished the ghetto's 3000 Jews and resettled the area with his own artisans. He was egged on by both Christian Viennese burghers, as well as his bigoted Spanish wife Margarita Teresa, who blamed her numerous miscarriages on the Jews. Leopold re-named the area Leopoldstadt and replaced the synagogue at Grosse Pfarrgasse 15 with his own church, the Leopoldkirche.

Needless to say the expulsion weakened both imperial and city finances and in time the Jews filtered back, encouraged by the enlightened Emperor Josef II's (1765–90) Edict of Tolerance (*Toleranzpatent*) (1781) permitting them to establish communities outside the *Innere Stadt* (see no. 52). They arrived from Bohemia and Moravia (now the Czech Republic), Galicia (now part of Poland and Ukraine) and Hungary, opening shops and coffee houses in the area's warren of back streets. Eventually, successful middle class Jews were occupying large houses on Praterstrasse and the area gained the nickname of »Mazzes Island«, after the unleavened Passover bread made in Jewish bakeries. After the 1848 Revolution Jews were allowed to choose their place of residence and total legal emancipation followed in 1867 under Emperor Franz Josef I (1848–1916). As a result, a huge influx of Jews arrived from the east and their self-assurance was soon expressed in wonderful buildings such as the Temple of the Sephardic Jews in Zircusgasse (1837) and Leopold Förster's Great Temple on Tempelgasse (1858), Vienna's largest synagogue. In 1938 both structures would be

Mighty columns marking the former site and size of the Great Temple synagogue on Tempelgasse, Leopoldstadt

destroyed by the Nazis (see nos. 13 and 52), although one wing of the Great Temple (known also as the Leopoldstadt Temple) remains, together with four huge white columns erected in 1997 to give an impression of its former dimensions. The fascinating potter's studio opposite contains a unique ceramic model of the synagogue as it once appeared, and a mosaic on a wall at the end of the road reinforces the impression.

After the First World War the number of Jews peaked at 200,000 (10% of Vienna's population) of which half lived in Leopoldstadt, whilst the well-to-do moved out to the 1st and 9th districts. The contribution of Viennese Jewry at this time to politics, business, science and the arts is unquestionable, with names such as Freud, Schnitzler, Wittgenstein, Canetti, Schönberg and Mahler amongst them. However, it wasn't long before anti-Semitism reared its ugly head once again, notably under Dr. Karl Lueger, city mayor and founder of the Christian Social Party, with the Jews being made scapegoat for declining economic fortunes.

Following the 1938 annexation (*Anschluss*) of Austria by Germany most of Vienna's 185,000 Jews were exiled or exterminated, their religious buildings defiled and their businesses »Aryanised«, in other words expropriated, by the Nazis (see no. 13); many Jews were deported from the former Aspangbahnhof railway station in Landstrasse, now called the Platz der Opfer Deportation. The sensitive and informed visitor should spare a thought for the lost Jews of Vienna, especially when sipping a coffee in the Café Mozart, buying a sandwich at an Anker bakery, drinking an Ottakringer beer (see no. 78), purchasing medicine at the Engel Apotheke or riding on the Ferris wheel (*Riesenrad*) (see no. 59) – all were once Jewish enterprises, most of whose owners would not survive the war. Thankfully, Jewish life is today reasserting itself yet again with a modest population of c.7000, a dozen synagogues across the city and Leopoldstadt once more the focus of the indomitable Jewish spirit. Little wonder however that their presence is near invisible, with Kosher shops (e.g. Ainhorn's traditional butchers at Grosse Stadtgutgasse 7) marked only by tiny prayer scrolls nailed diagonally to the doorframe and armed security guards outside their synagogues.

Other places of interest nearby: 57, 59

59 Strongmen, Giants and the Tattooed Lady

2nd District (Leopoldstadt), the Prater Museum
at Oswald-Thomas-Platz 1, next to the Planetarium
and Riesenrad Ferris wheel in the Volksprater;
take U-1 to Praterstern (U1)

The 2nd district of Leopoldstadt, lying just beyond the Danube Canal, is well worth visiting for its Jewish history (see no. 58) and for the Prater, the enormous city park famous for its woods (*Grüner Prater*), miniature railway (*Liliputbahn*) and fairground (*Volksprater*). It is also known for its old flat racing and trotting courses (the *Freudenau Rennbahn* and *Krieau Trabrennbahn* respectively), the former boasting some fine old stable blacks, the latter laying claim to Europe's first steel and concrete *Jugendstil* grandstand; built in 1912 it was the first such structure to receive listed status in Europe.

The Prater (from the Spanish *Prado* meaning open plain) was originally a royal hunting ground opened to the public in 1766 by Emperor Josef II (1765–90). It appealed immediately to all classes who to this day still enjoy promenading along its chestnut-lined promenade (*Hauptallee*) to the octagonal *Lusthaus*, a hunting lodge that once sat in the middle of a lake (don't miss the chapel hidden in trees down towards the Danube with its charming woodland Stations of the Cross). Of Vienna's many smaller museums the Prater Museum, dedicated to the colourful history of the fairground, is certainly one of the most interesting and unusual. Here, in a single room crammed with artefacts and images from its golden age, is a model of the world famous Ferris wheel, or *Riesenrad*. It is curious because it contains the original complement of 30 red cabins, half of which were not replaced on the real thing following severe fire damage during the last days of the Second World War. Its Jewish owner Eduard Steiner died in the concentration camp at Auschwitz in

A model of the world-famous Riesenrad Ferris wheel in the Prater Museum

southern Poland. The *Riesenrad* (meaning huge wheel) is 64.75 metres high and was the work of British engineer Walter B. Bassett, based on other wheels he had designed in Paris and Blackpool, England (both long since demolished). It was erected in 1897 on the occasion of the Golden Jubilee of Emperor Franz Josef I (1848 – 1916). The wheel gained lasting celluloid fame when Orson Welles made his famous »cuckoo clock« speech under it in the 1949 thriller *The Third Man* (see no. 1). Later, in 1987, the wheel would also provide a location for the James Bond film *The Living Daylights* (see no. 55), as well as *Before Sunrise* in 1994.

On the walls of the museum are evocative nostalgic photographs of moustachioed strong men, posters for *Lionel the Lion Man* and *Sylvia the Tattooed Lady*, as well as pictures of tall men, fat ladies and the little people employed to inhabit the miniature town of *Liliput-stadt*. There is also a garishly painted, dragon-shaped carriage from the wonderfully named *Lindwurmgrottenbahn* (Dragon's grotto railway) as well as numerous fragments from other old rides and sideshows now long since dismantled or else destroyed in the war. Indeed, it was only due to the efforts of local historian Hans Pemmer, who collected many of the exhibits personally and presented them to the City of Vienna, that the museum exists at all.

An original wooden Helter Skelter in the Volksprater

An especially interesting section is devoted to the 1873 World Exposition that was held on the nearby showground (*Messegelände*), as well as the charming *Venice in Vienna* exhibition with its full-size replica canals, gondolas and pretty waterfront *palazzi*. All that remains of the latter are the poignant old posters, photographs and the street name *Venediger Au*, meaning Venetian meadow or island.

Today, the fairground is still a noisy, colourful and atmospheric place that manages to mix successfully the modern »white knuckle« rides with the old-fashioned ghost trains, rifle

Colourful modern amusements in the Volksprater

ranges, strength contests, an original wooden Helter Skelter (*Toboggan*) and even a carousel from 1887 using real ponies that thunder around to the sound of a pipe organ (*Wiener Pony-Carousel*). The only thing really missing these days are the old puppet booths after one of whose comic characters, the Punch-like Hanswurst, the *Volksprater* takes its alternative name of *Wurstelprater*.

Far more modest, though no less authentic, is Vienna's other fairground, known as the Böhmische Prater on Laaerbergstrasse in the 10th district of Favoriten. Founded in the 1880s and named after the Bohemian migrants who came here to work in the local brick-works (see no. 67), it is home to several historic fairground rides as well as the Otto Geissler collection of street organs. In the time of Emperor Josef II (1765–90) the rising ground here was used as a lookout point (known more recently as *Monte Laa*) and indeed it still provides a good vista of Vienna today.

Other places of interest nearby: 57, 58

60 Mysterious Mexikoplatz

2nd District (Leopoldstadt), Mexikoplatz; take U-1 to
Vorgartenstrasse; alternatively take the round-trip by boat
leaving during summer time from Schwedenbrücke with
optional disembarkation at Mexikoplatz

One way to see the sights of Vienna that does not involve using the
busy Ringstrasse is to take a circular boat trip down the Danube Canal
and up the Danube proper. The view may not be as grand, but the
traveller will get to see a handful of unusual places missed by most.
These include the Freudenau and Nussdorf locks (see no. 83), the
UNO-City and Donauturm (see no. 47), the luxury Danube Hilton
hotel built inside an old granary, the Millennium Tower (Europe's
fourth highest office block), Friedensreich Hundertwasser's colourful
Spittelau incinerator, the mighty Rossauer Kaserne barracks (see no. 51)
and numerous converted fishing cabins on the riverbank, which still
retain their distinctive suspended square fishing nets.

Also visible will be the striking red-tiled towers of the Church of

*The Church of St. Francis of Assisi,
or Jubilee Church, in Mexikoplatz*

St. Francis of Assisi. Known also
as the Jubilee Church, it dominates Mexikoplatz and was constructed to mark the Golden
Jubilee of Emperor Franz Josef I
(1848–1916) in 1898. The design,
which was the result of a competition won by architect Victor
Luntz, is realised in the so-called
Rhine Romanesque style. In the
same year the Emperor's wife
Elisabeth (*Sisi*) (1837–98) was
assassinated, by Italian anarchist
Luccheni, whilst boarding a stea-
mer on Lake Geneva. A chapel to
her memory (*Elisabethkapelle*)
was incorporated into the church
plan using the left transept. It is

based on the Palatine chapel of Aix-la-Chapelle Cathedral and given a Byzantine flourish by the use of gold mosaics.

Nearby is the famous Reichsbrücke that crosses the Danube to the 22nd district of Donaustadt. It was across this bridge in April 1945 that retreating German troops fled to the west bank in the face of advancing Russian forces, and indeed for some time after it was called the Bridge of the Red Army. The relentless pursuit of German troops by the Russians all the way to the *Innere Stadt* accounts for the lack of pre-war architecture in both the 2nd district of Leopoldstadt and especially along the banks of the Danube Canal, having been bombed into oblivion (1,178 buildings were destroyed in Leopoldstadt during this short time, twice as many as had been lost through earlier allied air raids). Even on April 12th 1945, hours before the liberation of the city, an SS detachment murdered nine Jews in a cellar at Förstergasse 7.

In August 1976 the bridge mysteriously and quite unexpectedly collapsed (with one fatality) and was subsequently rebuilt. This is all the more curious because it was the only bridge over the Danube to have been left standing after the war – presumably unseen damage below the waterline finally took its toll (one of the bridges destroyed in the war was the Floridsdorfer Brücke not far upstream, two original piers from which can still be seen in the water together with the original west bank bridgehead).

Equally curious is why Mexikoplatz is so named although some claim it commemorates Maximilian, brother of Emperor Franz Josef I, who was executed by republican revolutionaries in Mexico in 1867, following his abortive attempt at carving out a Habsburg outpost there. It seems more likely, certainly according to an inscribed stone in Mexikoplatz today, that the name acknowledges the little-known fact that it was only Mexico (together with the Soviet Union) that lodged an international protest against Hitler's annexation (*Anschluss*) of Austria with Germany in 1938.

Whatever the reason, over the years travellers from former Eastern Bloc countries have tended to congregate in Mexikoplatz and it retains the lively feel of an eastern bazaar, with shops selling cheap watches, vodka and textiles. Passengers disembarking from the large Danube passenger ships that now moor on the river nearby have enhanced this vibrant ethnic mix further.

Other places of interest nearby: none

61 Napoleon and the Lion of Aspern

22nd District (Donaustadt), Napoleon's Headquarter (*Napoleons Hauptquartier*); take U-1 to Kaisermühlen VIC and then Bus 91 A to Ölhafen, turn left off Lobgrundstrasse and follow signs from Napoleonstrasse

The first half of Emperor Franz II (I)'s reign (1792–1835) was dominated by Napoleon's declaration of war on Europe. Following Habsburg military defeats in 1797 and 1800, French troops were only kept out of Vienna by ceding territories to them in Italy and the Netherlands. However, on November 13th 1805 Napoleon eventually entered the city and occupied the Schönbrunn palace where his golden eagles still adorn the main gates to this day. To cap it all, in 1806 he established the Confederation of the Rhine (*Rheinbund*) forcing Emperor Franz II (1792–1806) to relinquish his title of Holy Roman Emperor, a Habsburg hereditary title since 1438 (see no. 3), reducing him to Emperor Franz I (1804–35) of Austria. In time the Austrian army regrouped under the Emperor's brother Archduke Karl and proclaimed a War of Liberation. As a result, in spring 1809, Napoleon again marched on Vienna and reoccupied the Schönbrunn. Ten days later, however, he suffered his first major defeat, at the Battle of Aspern in the dense river forests of the Lobau, on the east bank of the Danube. Austrian troops had strategically withdrawn here launching a surprise attack in which 20,000 French troops were killed, making a hero of Archduke Karl in the process. His equestrian statue can still be seen in the Heldenplatz (Heroes' Square), together with that of Prince Eugène of Savoy (1663–1736), ironically a Frenchman, who had routed the Turks a century before.

It makes for a fascinating walk to explore what remains of the unspoilt wooded region of the Lobau, the sound of musket fire replaced today with birdsong, wildflowers and an estimated 5,000 species of living creatures. Signposted off Napoleonstrasse can be found the former locations of Napoleon's headquarters (*Hauptquartier*), powder magazine (*Pulvermagazin*) and cemetery (*Franzosenfriedhof*), each marked by an inscribed stone obelisk. In Aspern itself, at Asperner Heldenplatz 9, there is a museum devoted to the battle, as well as a magnificent stone lion by sculptor Anton Dominik Fernkorn (who also produced

Stone obelisk marking the site of Napoleon's headquarters in the Lobau

Napoleonic cannonball embedded in the wall of a house at Praterstrasse 19

the statue of Archduke Karl in the Heldenplatz; both lion and statue appear in miniature on the sculptor's headstone in Vienna's Central Cemetery in Simmering). It commemorates the 50th anniversary of the battle and the 23,000 Austrian troops who died. At Haidgasse 8 in Leopoldstadt is the *Zum Sieg* (The Victory) tavern whose name recalls the battle whilst at Praterstrasse 19 there is a building with an 1809 cannonball embedded in it.

Bloodied but unbowed Napoleon soundly defeated the Austrians six weeks later at the Battle of Wagram. As a result, Austrian Chancellor Prince Clemens von Metternich adopted a policy of rapprochement, including the marriage of the Emperor's daughter Archduchess Maria Louisa to Napoleon. Vienna thus escaped further trouble and eventually became the setting for the Congress of Vienna in 1814 following Napoleon's defeat at the Battle of Leipzig and exile to Elba. Austria regained much of its lost territory and enjoyed 33 years of peace in the ensuing *Biedermeier* period (shattered ultimately by the 1848 Revolution; see no. 14).

Left behind in Vienna was the French emperor's only son, Franz Karl Josef (known as *L'Aiglon* or the eaglet), languishing in the Schloss Schönbrunn, his only companion a crested lark that can be seen preserved in the bedroom where he died – and where his father Napoleon once slept in triumph. The poor child's eagle-adorned cradle and carriage (*phaeton*) are still in Vienna (in the Hofburg's Schatzkammer and in Schönbrunn's Wagenburg respectively).

Also connected with Napoleon is an Italian mosaic copy of Da Vinci's *Last Supper* in the Minoritenkirche that he commissioned in Milan as a replacement for the original that he intended to remove to Paris. Weighing 20 tons it was unfinished at the time of his final defeat at Waterloo (1815) and bought later by Emperor Franz I (1804–35).

Also commissioned by Napoleon, but not erected until the 1820s, was the Doric Theseustempel in the Volksgarten, intended to house Antonio Canova's statue *Theseus and the Minotaur* that can now be found in the stairwell of the Kunsthistorisches Museum. The building is a replica of the Theseion in the agora of ancient Athens.

Note: mosaic devotees should not miss the superb Venetian-style work at Kärntner Strasse 16 undertaken in 1896 by Eduard Veith (and restored in the 1950s) that depicts the five continents. The oriental scenes on the right-hand side are particularly effective.

Other places of interest nearby: none

62 The Cemetery of the Nameless Ones

11th District (Simmering), the Cemetery of the Nameless
(*Friedhof der Namenlosen*) at Alberner Hafen;
take Tram 71 from U-Bahn Simmering (U-3) to terminus
at Kaiserebersdorfer Strasse, then Bus 76A or walk

Of all Vienna's 55 cemeteries, both large and small (see nos. 39, 52 &
63), one of the most poignant must surely be the Cemetery of the
Nameless Ones. It lies on the bank of the Albern Dock beyond some
huge grain warehouses and is protected from flooding by the earthen
rampart of a flood protection bank (*Hochwasserschutzdamm*) erected
in the early 1930s. Lying just outside the city limits the cemetery is
somewhat difficult to get to and is consequently little visited, other
than the first Sunday after All Saints' Day (November 1st) when some
Viennese lay flowers here. Another reason that few visitors are encountered is that of the 104 corpses laid to rest here between 1900 and
1940, the majority are those of unidentified people, assumed to have
drowned in the river nearby. Their corpses were washed ashore by the

Unknown graves in the Cemetery of the Nameless at the Albern docks

current at the confluence of the Danube Canal and Danube proper. Forty-four persons were later identified but the final resting places of most are embellished only with a clump of mournful purple iris and a simple cross inscribed with the word *Namenlos* (Nameless). The occasional flickering candle and bunch of flowers lends a touching dignity to this melancholic place otherwise marked only by a small Chapel of the Resurrection added in 1935. Between 1840 and 1900 the cemetery had a predecessor on the riverbank itself although its 487 bodies were never exhumed and the site has now been lost to the river forest (a signpost marks the spot). With the construction of the nearby Albern grain dock in 1939 the river currents were themselves altered so that the Danube no longer brings its dead to the Cemetery of the Nameless. Despite this, each All Saint's Day sees the fishermen of Albern build a raft decorated with wreathes bearing a plaque reading »For the victims of the Danube« in German, Slovakian and Hungarian. Accompanied by a mournfully playing band the raft is pushed out into the river from where it will drift slowly downstream to Bratislava, Esztergom, Budapest and beyond.

Other places of interest nearby: none

The grave of a nameless person drowned in the Danube

63 One of Europe's Greatest Cemeteries

11th District (Simmering), the Central Cemetery
(*Zentralfriedhof*) on Simmeringer Hauptstrasse;
take Tram 71/72 from U-Bahn Simmering (U-3)
and alight at Haupttor/Tor 2 (Main Gate/Gate 2)

In the second half of the 19th century, as Vienna's burgeoning population expanded beyond the old city walls and inner suburbs, the suburban cemeteries laid out by order of Emperor Josef II (1765–90) (see no. 30) quickly became inadequate, especially following the cholera epidemic of 1873. As a result, the Central Cemetery opened on All Saints' Day (*Allerheiligen*), November 1st 1874 in the outlying southern district of Simmering. Replacing the existing five municipal suburban cemeteries, which were mostly cleared and turned into parks (see nos. 39 & 52), it was designed to service an Imperial capital of 4 million inhabitants.

Now Europe's second largest cemetery and covering an area of 241 hectares, it contains three million dead – twice Vienna's present population. Its three main gates warrant a tram stop each and the cemetery even has a team of early morning hunters employed to shoot the rabbits that nibble freshly placed wreathes! The cemetery is used by all creeds and nationalities, albeit often in distinct zones, and in addition there are the 500 Graves of Honour (*Ehrengräber*) reserved for Vienna's outstanding artists, scientists, musicians and other noteworthies. Several of these were relocated here from other cemeteries in order to endear the new, and somewhat remote, cemetery to the populace (see no. 39). Two such personalities, moved in 1889, were the composers Beethoven (1770–1827) and Schubert (1797–1828) whose original and rather forlorn headstones can still be found in the old Währing local cemetery (closed in 1873, abandoned in 1888 and now the Schubertpark) at the junction of Währinger Strasse and Teschnergasse. It is hard to imagine that 20,000 mourners once gathered here to see Beethoven laid to rest.

Today, visitors come to the Central Cemetery for a number of reasons: the musicians' monuments (Group 32A); the overgrown old Jewish cemetery inside Gate 1 desecrated by the Nazis in 1938; the poignant fields of war crosses towards the back of the cemetery; the Islamic graves facing Mecca (Groups 25 and 27A); the Russian

Orthodox cemetery (see no. 38); a Buddhist *Stupa*; the grave of Hans Hölzl, better known as Austrian pop singer Falco (Group 40); and the incredible floral tributes, lanterns (see page 221) and other paraphernalia that still accompany modern Viennese funerals (see no. 41). However, when faced with 316,000 graves it is easy to overlook those of the less famous but equally interesting citizens of Vienna. What

Typically elaborate late-19th century gravestone in the Central Cemetery in Simmering

follows is just a small selection of such graves that can be found in reasonably close proximity inside the Main Gate (Gate 2):

1) Along the inside of the cemetery wall on the left-hand side – Group O (Graves of Honour) row 1/12, Ida Pfeiffer (1797–1858), indomitable lady traveller who visited the Holy Land, Madagascar, South America, Iceland, China and India alone and wrote successfully of her exploits; also row 1/67, Dr. Josef Edler von Kühn (1833–1913), founder of the original Soup Kitchen for the needy that found popularity across Europe and the USA despite a lack of public funding; and row 1/101, Siegfried Marcus (1831–98), the all but forgotten inventor of the electrically-ignited petrol engine (see no. 73);

Group 22B nos. 1–9, close to a point half way along Group O, the grave of nine aviators killed in 1914 when the Körting Military Airship II exploded after colliding with an aeroplane;

2) In the left-hand Old Arcade straight ahead from the Main Gate – first alcove, August Zang (1807–1888), mining magnate whose headstone depicts a miniature mine entrance complete with lantern-carrying dwarves;

3) To the left of the left-hand Old Arcade – Group 31B row 13/8, Godwin Brumowski (1889–1936), Austria-Hungary's most successful First World War pilot who died in a plane crash over Amsterdam airport;

4) To the right of the right-hand Old Arcade – Group 12E row 2/22, Franz Mannsbarth (1877–1950), Austrian balloonist and builder of Austria's first airship;

5) On the right-hand side of the main path beyond the Old Arcades – Group 14A no. 45A, Josef Kornhäusel, architect (see no. 14);

Group 15E row 16/21, Andreas Keller (1797–1877), saved the life of Archduke Ferdinand, later Emperor Ferdinand I (1835–48), from an assassination attempt at Helenental near Baden;

Group 16A row 7/23, Dr. Ludwig Köchel (1800–1877), creator of the *Köchel Index* by which Mozart's works are still identified today;

Group 16B row 5/19, Georg Klimt (1867–1931), a brother of the famous artist Gustav Klimt, who specialised in embossed copper plaques and reliefs;

Group 17B row 1/10, Ludwig Bösendorfer (1835–1919), world-class piano manufacturer who exhibited successfully at the world exhibitions in London (1862), Vienna (1873) and Paris (1900) and whose customers included Franz Liszt, Leonard Bernstein and many major ruling houses;

6) On the left-hand side of the main path beyond the Old Arcades – Group 32A no. 23, Alois Negrelli (1799–1858), engineer responsible for the initial planning of the Suez Canal as well as other important waterways and railways in the Austrian crown lands and beyond; also no. 37, Professor Julius von Payer (1842–1915), alpine researcher and artist on the Austro-Hungarian Arctic Expedition of 1872–74 that discovered and named Franz-Josefs-Land, an archipelago in the Barents Sea, during a failed attempt to find a navigable northeast passage through to the Pacific(see no. 40);

Group 32C no. 18, Professor Julius Wagner-Jauregg (1857–1940), a 1927 Nobel Prize winner (see no. 54); also no. 33, five Austrian victims of an avalanche on the 7,640 m high Dhaulagiri mountain during an expedition to the Nepal Himalaya in 1969, their headstone embellished suitably with 5 ice picks; and no. 54, Curd Jürgens (1915–1982), successful stage actor and international film star including several Hollywood productions;

Group 33F row 1/1, Dominik Bauer

Grave to Austrian climbers lost in the Nepal Himalaya

The graves of Russian soldiers who died during the liberation of Vienna in April 1945

(1841–1904), the cemetery's first grave-digger;

7) Finally, on the far left-hand side beyond the above – Group 37 row 4/121 and 122, Albine Pecha, nurse, and Dr. Hermann Müller, doctor, who both died in 1898 having been infected accidentally by plague bacteria brought back from India for research purposes.

No trip to the Central Cemetery would be complete without a visit to the truly atmospheric Schloss Concordia, identified by a huge carved figure of Christ immediately opposite Gate 1. This ramshackle turreted old restaurant and café is at its most magical in winter when patrons from all walks of life sit at modest tables illuminated exclusively by candlelight. Highly recommended is the bizarrely shaped *Superschnitzel* whose consumption amidst such faded grandeur is sometimes accompanied by piano music, creating a unique atmosphere of theatrical melancholy.

Note: A similarly romantic venue is offered by the candlelit Salettl café nestled amidst a group of trees heavy with mistletoe at Hartäckerstrasse 80, opposite the entrance to the cemetery in Döbling (*Döblinger Friedhof*). The octagonal building was designed by Friedrich Pindt, a student of the architect Otto Wagner (see no. 42).

Other places of interest nearby: none

64 Gasometer City

11th District (Simmering), Gasometers 1–4 on Guglgasse;
take U-3 to Gasometer

Until 1899 the responsibility for supplying the city of Vienna with its gas lay in powerful and private hands. However, it was in this year that the Simmering Gas Works (built 1896–99) opened for business, the appearance of its four huge gas storage containers (referred to incorrectly as gasometers) signalling the start of a municipal gas supply to all Vienna. Each gasometer was 67 metres high and 65 metres wide (big enough to hold the famous *Riesenrad* Ferris wheel), with a capacity of c.90,000 cubic metres inside the telescopic iron container within. This would rise and fall accordingly as the flammable gas was either added (generated from hard coal) or consumed via a 700 kilometre-long network of pipes fanning out across the city. The gas containers were made airtight at the base by means of a huge pool of water 12 metres in depth. On the outside of the containers can still be seen the huge circular gauges (or gasometers, as they are correctly termed) that showed the pressure and level of the gas inside. Needless to say, the gauges are surmounted by the Habsburg double-eagle motif.

Although the Simmering works could supply 110 million cubic metres of gas annually, to 100,000 meter-holders, the gasometers would ultimately not be able to keep pace with increasing demand from the ever-growing city. Their combined storage capacity was only equal to half a day's require-

The former Simmering Gas Works re-born as a housing and retail complex

ment of gas. After being upgraded several times to reflect technological advances, gas production ceased in 1969 and the gasometers were finally de-commissioned in 1986.

Thankfully their decorative, 55 metre-high brick-built outer casings, each made from 46 million bricks, together with their undoubted historic significance prevented their demolition. Instead, in 2001,

Detail of the apartment blocks built inside Gasometer A by Jean Nouvel

having made a brief appearance in the James Bond film *The Living Daylights* (see no. 55), they were each ingeniously and successfully re-invented by four internationally renowned architects (Jean Nouvel, Manfred Wehdorn, Wilhelm Holzbauer and the Coop Himmel-b[l]au group). Now boasting its own U-Bahn station (outside which is an enormous preserved gas valve), Gasometer City encompasses the four structures each uniquely transformed and linked together by elevated walkways, containing a large shopping centre, offices, 615 apartments with 1,500 inhabitants and a media centre, as well as the Vienna City and County Archives (*Wiener Stadt- und Landesarchiv*). The only things missing are some of the 44,000 old-fashioned public street lamps that the gasometers were supplying by 1914.

Luckily for those interested in such curiosities a few remaining examples can still be found dotted around the city. Best of all is the beautifully restored and working bracket lamp outside the *Wien Energie* office at Josefstädter Strasse 10–12, one of the few examples of the city's many lion's head brackets to still carry its glass bowl (see also Marchettigasse 8 in the 6th district of Mariahilf). Also of interest is a tall curving standard lamp of 1890 outside the Café Weimar on Severingasse in Alsergrund (see also Am Hof), as well as Vienna's last standard lamp (shut down in 1962) outside Hietzing's District Museum (*Bezirksmuseum*) at Am Platz 2.

Also in Hietzing is another lighting-related curiosity, namely a plaque on the Parkhotel Schönbrunn to Thomas Alva Edison. He was the inventor of the light bulb who stayed in the hotel in 1911 whilst supervising the installation of electric lighting in the Habsburg's summer palace opposite.

Of course, in the days before the introduction of gas and electricity, some streets in Vienna would have been lit by traditional lanterns, a splendid example of which may be seen at Schönlaterngasse 6 (Beautiful Lantern Street) in the *Innere Stadt* (see no. 6).

Note: It is interesting to note that one of the three housing associations responsible for the Gasometer housing complex has also been responsible for the creation of several other unusual locations in Vienna. GESIBA (*Gemeinwirtschaftliche Siedlungs- und Baustoffanstalt*) was founded originally in 1921 as the Non-Profit-Making Estates and Building Materials Association, providing cheap materials and loans to co-operatives and residents' associations during the period of Socialist Red Vienna. By the mid-1920s they were creating groundbreaking residential developments of their own, the most important of which was the unique *Werkbundsiedlung* housing estate in Hietzing (see no. 72). In the 1970s they were involved in the creation of the incredible Alt-Erlaa estate (see no. 82) and just recently the successful regeneration of the endangered Baroque/*Biedermeier* district of Spittelberg (see no. 48).

Other places of interest nearby: none

65 The Socialist Swimming Pool

10th District (Favoriten), the Amalienbad swimming pool
at Reumannplatz 23; take U-1 to Reumannplatz

The combination of long hot summers and easy access to the peaceful waters of the Old and New Danubes (see no. 83) means that swimming is something of a national pastime in Vienna. For those wishing to go *al fresco* there is the historic bathing island of Gänsehäufel on the Old Danube (*Alte Donau*), with its tree-fringed beaches and areas reserved for certain public workers, hence signs to the Tram Drivers' Baths (*Strassenbahnerbad*)!; also the elegant Krapfenwaldbad in the foothills of the Vienna Woods (*Wienerwald*) in the 19th district, with its Mediterranean pines, original wooden changing rooms (1914) and stupendous views back over Vienna; and likewise the Schafbergbad in the 18th district, which also combines bathing with lovely vistas. For those happier under cover there is the historic Jörgerbad in the 17th district of Hernals, completed in 1912 with stained glass windows depicting goldfish and charming wave-pattern tiling in the foyer.

However, the *pièce de resistance* of Viennese swimming pools must surely be the Amalienbad, which illustrates how Vienna's Socialist government of the 1920s could not only provide facilities for the people, but could do so in considerable style. Otto Nadel and Karl Schmalhofer, who at the time were employees of the city's architectural department, designed the building. When opened in 1926 it was one of the largest of its kind in Europe and had a capacity of 1,300 people. Amalienbad is also considered to be one of the finest architectural

*Art Deco elegance
in the Amalienbad
in Favoriten*

achievements of Socialist Red Vienna (see no. 82). The main pool is 33 metres long with a curving glass roof that, until reconstruction following heavy bomb damage sustained during the Second World War, could be slid open to the sky. Most significantly the interior was not left plain, rather it was embellished in the popular Art Deco style of the day. Nowhere is this more apparent than in the use of colourful mosaics, both practical and aesthetic, in the main pool, sauna and foyer, for which Amalienbad is famous. The square in which the baths were erected is called Reumannplatz after Jakob Reumann, labour leader and Vienna's first Socialist Mayor, well known for his struggles with the City Council in order to improve workers' conditions.

On the subject of swimming pools it is interesting to note that the only pool within the *Innere Stadt* is to be found in the modern Vienna Marriott hotel. However, that was not always the case as lurking behind an innocent-looking doorway at Weihburggasse 20 is the abandoned Central Bath (*Zentralbad*), the first and only public baths built in the first district (unfortunately not open to the public). It lies over a natural spring producing 200,000 litres of water a day that once flowed into a suite of beautifully tiled Moorish-style baths occupying a series of colonnaded subterranean halls. In the yard beyond is an underground furnace room illuminated by a glass roof.

Note: that other great pleasure palace of the people, namely the cinema, is also well represented in Vienna though, like its historic counterpart the swimming pool, it too suffered terrible damage during the Second World War. Definitely worth looking out for is the Metro Kino at Johannesgasse 4 in the *Innere Stadt*, a beautiful *belle époque* (1900) cinema run by Austria's Film Archive with an especially cosy wood-panelled auditorium replete with chandelier and fine plastered ceiling. Also of interest is the Breitenseer Lichtspiele at Breitenseer Strasse 21 in the 14th district of Penzing. Opened in 1909 in a Viennese Art Nouveau (*Jugendstil*) building it is the city's, and possibly the world's, oldest operational cinema, its 186 original wooden seats still in place. Note too the vintage 1954 Filmcasino at Margaretenstrasse 78 (Margareten), with its mirrored neon-lit facade, seductively curved foyer and intimate bar area, as well as the 194-seat Bellaria Kino on Museumstrasse, which not only shows nostalgic films from its own archives but was itself the subject of an award-winning documentary called *Bellaria - As Long as We Live!*

Other places of interest nearby: none

66 The Spinner at the Cross

10th District (Favoriten), the Spinner at the Cross monument (*Spinnerin am Kreuz*) in front of the George-Washington-Hof at junction of Triester Strasse 52 und Windtenstrasse; take Tram 65 from U-Bahn Karlsplatz (U-1/U-2/U-4)

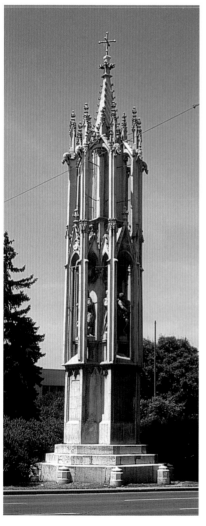

The elaborate Gothic wayside cross known as the Spinnerin am Kreuz

One of the main thoroughfares south out of Vienna has for centuries been Triester Strasse, reminding the traveller of the former Habsburg port on the northern Adriatic coast (where the giant insurance company *Assicurazioni Generali* was founded in 1831, according to a wall plaque at Graben 12). Part way down on the roadside, and looking not unlike a discarded fragment from the Stephansdom, is a beautiful, 16 metre-high, late-Gothic monument. Dating to 1452 it is in actual fact a wayside cross and shrine marking the then southernmost boundary of Vienna's inner suburbs, and consequently of its safe area. It was also on this prominent spot, known as the Wienerberg, that until 1868 public executions took place. The monument's canopied sculptures include the Crucifixion and the placing of the crown of thorns on Christ's head.

In addition to these known facts there are two legends connected with the monument that are worth relating here. The first concerns its designer, Johann Puchsbaum, who was also architect of the Stephansdom's unfinished north, or Eagle's, tower (*Adlerturm*). Cost cutting in the face of the fast approaching first Turkish siege of 1529 explains why work on the tower stopped. Legend however tells us that Puchsbaum fell in love with the master stonemason's daughter, Mary, whom he would only be permitted to marry if he completed the north tower within a year. Realising quickly that this would be impossible he made a pact with the devil to help complete the work, in return promising never to utter holy names again. Needless to say when Mary appeared one day and poor Puchsbaum called her name from the scaffold where he was working it gave way under him. Having inadvertently disobeyed the devil's demands he plunged to his death, leaving the tower unfinished to this day. A further example of Puchbaum's work is the beautiful Gothic Sacred Heart *baldachin* (canopied altar) to be found against the north wall of the Stephansdom.

The second legend relates to the monument's contemporary name of *Spinnerin am Kreuz* (Spinner at the Cross). It is said that a faithful wife spent years here waiting for her husband's return from the Crusades, biding her time by spinning wool. In those days only a wooden post stood here (first mentioned as early as 1296) and the woman vowed that she would use the money raised from her labours to erect a stone cross should her husband return safely – which he eventually did! A 1920s mural illustrating the legend can be found further down the road on the opposite side. Indeed, so beloved is this Viennese tale of enduring love in the face of adversity that it decorates several other buildings across the city, for example the entranceway at Opernring 4.

Other places of interest nearby: 67

67 A Wonderful Water Tower

10th District (Favoriten), the Water Tower
(*Wasserturm*) at Windtenstrasse 3 off Triester Strasse;
take Tram 65 from U-Bahn Karlsplatz (U-1/U-2/U-4)

During the course of the 19th century Vienna witnessed the Industrial Revolution, the taming of the Danube (see no. 81), the razing of the old city walls (see no. 24) and a doubling in its population. By 1890 there were c.1.4 million inhabitants and the Favoriten pumping station was built to supply water to this burgeoning population. Designed by Franz Borkowitz in 1889 it was part of a municipal scheme to bring alpine spring water to the capital from the Rax and Schneeberg mountains 75 kilometres southwest of Vienna (see no. 10). This accounts for the street name of nearby Raxstrasse. By 1900 there were 1.7 million people in the city increasing to an all-time high of more than 2 million by 1910. The necessary creation of other more effective water facilities around the city (including a new pipeline all the way from the province of Styria) meant inevitably that the by now increasingly inadequate Favoriten complex would be wound down.

Of the seven original structures that made up the station only the tower remains – but what a tower it is! Rising 67 metres into the air it can be seen from miles around (see no. 47), due in part to it being situated on high ground so that gravity could assist the water flow. Made of red brick it has an air of military strength about it and indeed as »cultural property« (according to a plaque outside) is protected by the Hague Convention in the event of war! As so often in Vienna, the tower is wonderfully grand for a building with such a mundane purpose. Its yellow and red brick walls have stone corbels and leaded lights incorporated into them, all topped off with a roof of polychrome tiles and a church-like onion-shaped dome. Over its huge wooden doors are the words »*Wasserwerk der Stadt Wien*« inscribed in gold.

Today the tower has been restored superbly and the interior, with its upward spiralling metal ramp, houses occasional temporary exhibitions. Most noteworthy is the original pumping equipment that can still be seen in its original state.

Also of interest in the context of Vienna's water supply is a charming old water tower from the reign of Emperor Ferdinand I (1835–48) built in 1836 in the 18th district of Währing. It was designed to take water pumped from the Danube Canal and to distribute it with the

*The ornate
Favoriten water tower*

help of gravity to the growing suburbs (*Vorstädte*). In order to achieve the latter the tower, like its successor in Favoriten, was deliberately set atop a hillock, in Anton-Baumann-Park on Klettenhofergasse.

Note: Continuing out along Triester Strasse is the Wienerberg whose deposits of Pannonian clay marl (*called Tegel*) were first extracted for brick-making during the reign of ›Empress‹ Maria Theresa (1740–80). Once the largest brickworks in Europe it is now the Wienerfeld recreation area containing pools that were originally clay pits. Together with workings farther east on the Laaer Berg (see no. 59) it has been estimated that the brickworks of Southern Vienna produced over 50 million cubic metres of bricks, especially during the great building era of the so-called Ringstrasse or *Gründerzeit* (Founding Period) of 1860–1900. This is not surprising once one realises that most of the city's buildings from this time are of brick cleverly disguised with moulded render to look like stone. A museum dedicated to the history of brick-making in Vienna (*Wiener Ziegelmuseum*) exists as part of the Penzing District Museum at Penzinger Strasse 59.

Other places of interest nearby: 66

68 Schönbrunn's Beautiful Spring

13th District (Hietzing), the Beautiful Spring
(*Schöner Brunnen*) off the Obeliskenallee (to the left of the
Römische Ruine) in the Schlosspark at Schloss Schönbrunn;
take U-4 to Schönbrunn and enter via Meidlinger Tor

The spectacular Schlosspark of the Habsburgs' summer palace at Schönbrunn, open to the public since 1799, is a must for all interested in garden history. Despite the formal vistas and terraces so beloved of Baroque landscape gardeners working in the French idiom, the many tall clipped hedges conceal intimate pathways leading to an abundance of hidden follies and oddities. Armed with the official guidebook the explorer will discover sham Roman ruins, a reproduction of ›Empress‹ Maria Theresa's maze (*Irrgarten*) and labyrinth, an obelisk carved with scenes from Habsburg history, the beautiful Great Palm House (see no. 69) and statues of Apollo, Hannibal and a vestal virgin, to name but a few. If there is time, a foray into the neighbouring zoo (*Tiergarten*), itself the world's oldest (1752), will reveal a charming timber-framed Tyrolian farmhouse, opposite which is Crown Prince Rudolf's original wooden play hut now looking somewhat forlorn.

However, it should not be forgotten the reason why Schönbrunn is so called. To find the answer one must escape the crowds and head to the southeastern part of the garden, between the Obeliskenallee and the Ruinenallee, where a narrow hedged walk leads to the original *Schöne Brunnen* (Beautiful Spring). Legend relates that it was Emperor Maximilian II (1564–76), whilst out hunting, who was first impressed by the delicious waters of a natural spring he came across. As a result he purchased an old mill on the nearby River Wien and converted it into a hunting lodge. Emperor Matthias (1612–19) »rediscovered« the spring for himself in 1612 whilst also on a hunting foray (his monogram can still be seen carved onto a plaque on the right-hand wall of the present well-house). Such was the quality of the water emanating from the spring that by 1642 a pleasure palace (*Lustschloss*), built here for Emperor Ferdinand II's (1619–37) widow Eleonora Gonzaga, had been named *Schönbrunn* after it. Although this palace was destroyed and the well damaged during the second Turkish siege of 1683, a new imperial summer palace was soon commissioned from Baroque architect Johann Bernhard Fischer von Erlach

(ABOVE) Maria Theresa's pavilion for the original Schöne Brunnen

(LEFT) Sculpture of the nymph Egeria inside the pavilion

(finished in 1713). In the spring of 1758 a well-house was erected over the spring by court gardener Adrian van Stekhoven. Eventually it fell to ›Empress‹ Maria Theresa (1740–80) to modify the palace into the building we see today, now painted in its iconic mustardy yellow (*Schönbrunnergelb*) though originally coloured white or pink. It was also by her order, in 1771, that the present grotto pavilion was built over the well to a design by court architect Isidor Canevale. Behind the mock stalactite and shell encrusted walls is the graceful reclining nymph Egeria, dispensing the sweet water from her vase into a giant scallop shell. From the time of its discovery onwards, water from the Schöne Brunnen was prized highly by the Imperial household. Until an Alpine spring water supply to Vienna was instigated in the late-19th century (see no. 10) the Habsburg court drew all its water from this source. They had every drop transported to the Hofburg by mule and on long journeys even took it with them in sealed metal boxes!

Other places of interest nearby: 69, 70, 73

69 The Most Graceful of Greenhouses

13th District (Hietzing), the Palm House
(*Palmenhaus*) in the Schlosspark at Schloss Schönbrunn;
take U-4 to Hietzing and enter via Hietzinger Tor

A considerable part of the western side of the park at Schloss Schönbrunn, the Habsburgs' summer palace, is occupied by Vienna's famous
zoo (*Tiergarten*). It is built on the site of Emperor Franz I's (1745–65)
royal menagerie established in 1752 thus making it the oldest zoo in
the world. As the husband of ›Empress‹ Maria Theresa (1740–80),
Franz used his wealth and power to indulge magnificently his personal interest in the natural world, bringing about the creation of the
city's superb Natural History Museum (*Naturhistorisches Museum*)
(see no. 36). He was also a very keen botanist and gardener financing expeditions to Africa and the West Indies to collect rare species
and bring them back to Vienna. In 1860 Emperor Franz Josef I's
(1848–1916) brother Maximilian (later and briefly Emperor of
Mexico) commissioned a circumnavigation of the globe. The many
resulting additions to Emperor Franz I's imperial botanical collection
prompted the idea of building a mighty glasshouse in the Schlosspark
at Schönbrunn, and the architect Franz Xaver Segenschmid was commissioned to design it. After visiting notable existing glasshouses in
London (Kew Gardens), Glasgow and Brussels, work on his massive
wrought iron and glass structure began. Opened on 19th June 1882 by
Emperor Franz Josef himself, the Great Palm House (*Palmenhaus*) is
113 metres long with no less than 45,000 panes of glass. It is made up
of three pavilions, each containing plants from a different climatic
zone. The 28 metre-high central pavilion is home to a temperate collection of plants that includes a pair of hundred year old palms, whilst
the cold north pavilion has species that include Himalayan plants.
The humid southern pavilion contains tropical rainforest plants from
equatorial regions.

Although no longer the largest glasshouse in Europe it is surely
the most beautiful. The proportions of its convex and concave lines
account for its elegant appearance in spite of the massive construction
techniques employed. Unfortunately, in February 1945 three bombs
fell through the roof and many of the plants froze to death. The structure was subsequently repaired and reopened in 1953 but forced to

The Great Palm House in the park at Schloss Schönbrunn

close again, this time due to serious rust damage caused by the relentless action of humidity on the ironwork. Using the very latest technology, including the installation of dirt-resistant glass, the Palm House has again been restored and is once more open to visitors eager to look inside this most graceful of greenhouses.

The only major group of exotic plants missing from the Palm House are desert plants, but these can now be found in the nearby and recently opened Desert House (*Wüstenhaus*). It contains an artificial cactus-filled desert landscape inhabited by colourful gecko lizards basking in the sun and tiny elephant shrews scurrying around amongst the rocks and succulents. The building itself, dating from 1904, was originally used for over-wintering certain plants from the Great Palm House.

Just as historic as Schönbrunn's Palm House, though considerably smaller, is the former Imperial conservatory that overlooks the Burggarten behind the Neue Burg, once the Emperor's private garden (see no. 33). It was designed by the architect Friedrich Ohmann in 1901 in the Viennese Art Nouveau (*Jugendstil*) style and today contains a free-flying tropical butterfly collection (*Schmetterlinghaus*) as well as a very stylish, palm-filled café (*Palmenhaus*).

Other places of interest nearby: 68, 70, 73

70 The Emperor's Private Railway Station

13th District (Hietzing), the Court Pavilion
(*Hofpavillon*) on Schönbrunner Schlossstrasse;
take U-4 to Hietzing

The family history of the Habsburgs, as with that of most European dynasties, is peppered with tales of excess and eccentricity. If this weren't the case they would certainly not be of such interest to the visitor today. With their sprawling empire and ever growing capital, the Habsburgs seriously indulged themselves when it came to the matter of transport. The Imperial Carriage Museum (*Wagenburg*), for instance, housed in the former Winter Riding School at Schloss Schönbrunn contains a red leather litter (a type of sedan chair carried on poles by a mule either end) embellished with 11,000 gold-plated nails that was used solely to transport the Archduke of Austria's hat! Comical too is the sausage-shaped hunting sledge (*Wurstwagen*) of Prince Leopold of Bourbon-Salerno (a son-in-law of Emperor Franz I) with its swivel seat enabling him to follow his target without having to walk! Also here is the gilded scallop-shell carriage of ›Empress‹ Maria Theresa (1740–80) in which in 1743 she personally led seven other ladies in a *quadrille* in the splendour of the Hofburg's Winter Riding School (*Winterreitschule*). They were celebrating the withdrawal of Bavarian and French troops from Bohemia (a hundred years later the same building would be the setting for Austria's first democratically elected assembly in the wake of the 1848 Revolution, and by which the peasantry were emancipated; see no. 14). Similar in style is Maria Theresa's golden racing sleigh, used often in the courtyards of the Hofburg on snow imported specially from the suburbs!

Most outrageous of all, however, is the gold-plated coronation carriage used at the coronation of Emperor Josef II (1765–90). Weighing 4,000kg and tall enough to enable its occupants to stand up straight, it has windows of finest, bevel-edged Venetian glass and a series of painted side panels depicting the virtues of the ruler – a veritable palace on wheels! As if this weren't plush enough, it was pulled by eight white horses with red velvet harnesses embroidered with gold, topped off with ostrich feathers. Equally extravagant, in the nearby Museum of Technology (*Technisches Museum*) (see no. 73), is the luxurious saloon carriage used by Emperor Franz Josef I's wife

Elisabeth (*Sisi*) when travelling by rail. It was built in 1873 and fitted out with the finest upholstery, furniture and candelabra.

Best of all, however, and also to be found in Hietzing is the one-off Imperial and Royal Court Pavilion that straddles the platforms of today's U-Bahn station. It was designed in 1898-99 by the famous architect Otto Wagner, together with his pupil Leopold Bauer as well as Josef Maria Olbrich, later the creator of the Secession building on Karlsplatz. The sole purpose of this miniature palace in the Viennese Art Nouveau (*Jugendstil*) style was to provide private access for Emperor Franz Josef I (1848–1916) to his own imperial train (*Kaiserzug*) on Vienna's metropolitan railway (*Stadtbahn*). This had only recently been designed and laid out by Wagner (see no. 42), who took the opportunity to ingratiate himself with the Emperor by designing the Hofpavillon for use by the royal family during their summer stays at nearby Schönbrunn.

The private railway station built at Schönbrunn for the Habsburg royal family

The station is entered through a graceful iron canopy topped with little golden crowns, below which arriving imperial carriages could find shelter. Inside is a single domed octagonal waiting room on the wall of which is a specially commissioned painting depicting a bird's eye view of the new railway itself. It was intended »to shorten the seconds spent waiting by the monarch with the sight of a work of art«! Incorporated into the finely crafted wood panelling and other fixtures can be seen designs based on the Emperor's late wife Elisabeth's favourite flower, the split-leaved Philodendron.

Unfortunately for Wagner, despite all the effort and grandeur he lavished on this little building, the Emperor only seems to have used the station at most twice, a fact which has been put down to his famous distrust of all things modern (see no. 33).

Other places of interest nearby: 68, 69, 73

71 Klimt's Last Studio

13th District (Hietzing), the Klimt Villa at
Feldmühlgasse 15a/Wittegasse; take U-4 to Unter St. Veit
Since 2007 the villa is operated by the Belvedere Museum
and will be re-open in 2008 as a memorial and research centre.

When visiting the art galleries of Vienna, or many of the city's gift shops for that matter, the name of artist Gustav Klimt (1862–1918) will be encountered again and again. Son of an immigrant gold engraver from Bohemia (now the Czech Republic), Klimt began his career in the 1880s, along with his brother Ernst, by decorating the grand buildings springing up along the Ringstrasse (notably the ceilings of the Burgtheater's two side pavilions, enabling the Court to remain aloof from the public, and the stairwell spandrels of the Kunsthistorisches Museum). In 1897, however, having withdrawn from public life following the death of both Ernst and his father, he re-orientated himself artistically by co-founding the Association of Austrian Fine Arts – Secession. This was a progressive movement of like-minded artists and architects who believed fervently that the backwards-looking Historicist tradition, typified by the overblown buildings of the Ringstrasse, was holding Vienna back in the arts. This was especially apparent when compared with Paris where Impressionism and Symbolism had been causing a sensation. Within a few short years the Secession had created the fully-fledged Viennese version of European Art Nouveau, known as *Jugendstil* (see nos. 42, 53, 70 & 75), in which art and architecture, aesthetics and function, were fused seamlessly together. In 1903 a group related to the Secession, but devoted to applied arts such as fabrics and wallpapers, was founded. Called the Wiener Werkstätte, this increasingly commercial organisation created a rift in the overall membership of the group leading to the eventual break up of the Secession.

Klimt meanwhile had left the group in 1905 to develop further his increasingly idiosyncratic style of painting, financed by his wealthy patrons. A measure of how far the artist had moved on from his early works can be gauged by the uproar caused when his three murals for the strait-laced New University on the Ringstrasse were unveiled – Klimt returned his fee and removed them! Viewed in retrospect Klimt's incredible originality and versatility is all too obvious – his glittering golden period culminating in *The Kiss*, the sumptuous portraits of society women, the impressionist landscapes of Lakes Attersee and

Garda, and his later works influenced by Japanese art and the bold primary colours of the artist Matisse.

It was during this latter phase, whilst working simultaneously on two works *The Bride* and *Lady with Fan* in his studio in Hietzing, that Klimt suffered a fatal stroke as he prepared for his daily walk. He died of pneumonia shortly after on February 6th 1918 aged just 56. Klimt was buried in the cemetery at Hietzing (*Hietzinger Friedhof*) close to his fellow Secessionists Otto Wagner and Koloman Moser who died the same year, as well as Jean-Baptiste Cléry, the last servant of Louis XVI who had married ›Empress‹ Maria Theresa's daughter, Marie Antoinette.

It has long been known that Klimt's birthplace at Linzer Strasse 247 was demolished in 1966 and that his earlier studios at Sandwirtgasse 8 (1883–92) and in a garden pavilion at Josefstädter Strasse 21 (1892–1912) were also no longer standing. Likewise it was thought that his last studio, in Hietzing, had been obliterated in 1923 by the construction of a neo-Baroque villa on the same site. However, as a result of a local citizen's initiative in 1998, the original plans for Klimt's last studio were re-discovered revealing the exciting fact that its walls still existed, encased within the fabric of the later villa.

The grave of Gustav Klimt in the cemetery at Hietzing

The so-called Klimt Villa in Hietzing incorporating Klimt's last studio on the ground floor

As a result the modest studio where Klimt worked from 1912 on-wards (now referred to erroneously as the Klimt Villa) has undergone modest restoration by the Gustav Klimt Memorial Society and can again be experienced by his many admirers. With its whitewashed walls and black-painted window frames it once stood in the midst of a large garden full of vividly flowering vegetation, tended by Klimt himself and thought to be depicted in his painting *Orchard with Roses* (1912). It is to be hoped that in time the flower garden and orchard familiar to Klimt will blossom once again.

Note: Klimt's paintings and drawings can be seen in the Upper Belvedere Palace (including *The Kiss*), the Leopold Museum in the MuseumsQuartier, the Vienna Museum and the Secession building in Karlsplatz, the Graphic Arts collection of the Albertina and Hietzing's District Museum. The Josefstadt District Museum at Schmidgasse 18 also contains an exhibit devoted to Klimt since he once lived and worked nearby. Little-known are two fine reproductions of Klimt's original works to be found hanging on the walls of the Café Griensteidl in Michaelerplatz, next to the Hofburg.

Other places of interest nearby: none

72 A Unique Housing Estate

13th District (Hietzing), the Werkbundsiedlung
Housing Estate at Woinovichgasse/Veitingergasse
off Jagdschlossgasse); take U-4 to Hietzing
and then Tram 60 to Jagdschlossgasse

Due to its proximity to the Habsburgs' summer residence at Schön-brunn, the 13th district of Hietzing rapidly became a desirable address as Vienna's suburbs were developed during the 19th century. A the-matic tour in itself can be made of the area's many fine villas (though not open to the public) built during the *Biedermeier* (e.g. the former home of actress, and mistress to Emperor Franz Josef I, Katharina Schratt at Gloriettegasse 9), *Jugendstil* (e.g. Friedrich Ohmann's wrought iron-fronted Villa Schopp at Gloriettegasse 21; Villa Langer at Beck-gasse 30 by Slovenian architect Jože Plečnik; the Mietvilla at Stoesslgasse 2 by Ferdinand Meissner; and Schlossberggasse 14 by Otto Wagner's son) and Modernist periods (e.g. the Classicistic Villa Skywa-Primavesi designed by Josef Hoffman in 1915 at Gloriettegasse 14–16; and the surprising Gingerbread House (*Lebkuchenhaus*), clad in brown figurative majolica tiles, from the same architect at Watt-manngasse 29). There are also no less than five villas by Modernist architect Adolf Loos, famous for his austere functionalism (Villa Scheu at Larochegasse 3, Villa Strasse at Kupelwiesergasse 28, the barrel-vaulted Villa Steiner at St-Veit-Gasse 10, Villa Rufer at Schliess-manngasse 11 and Villa Horner at Nothartgasse 7).

However, there is also something else in Hietzing that will delight any explorer interested in architecture. From the tram stop at Jagd-schlossgasse it makes for a pleasant walk to travel up the street of that name, passing at number 36 the old hunting lodge after which it is called. At the top on the right is the so-called *Werkbundsiedlung*, a model housing estate of 70 houses that couldn't differ more from Hietzing's traditional villas.

Founded in Germany in 1907 the Werkbund was somewhat simi-lar to England's Arts and Crafts Movement, though it was not opposed to reaping the financial rewards made possible by mass-production. In 1930–32 Vienna's Socialist city council organised a Werkbund Housing Exhibition based on one held successfully in Stuttgart in 1927. A group of international Modernist architects were each invited to design and build an affordable, two-bedroom family house in a small space. It was hoped the homes would provide an innovative alternative to the vast housing blocks erected in the 1920s (see no. 82). Set side-by-side, so that their qualities could be judged comparatively, the houses were the work of Vienna's own Adolf Loos, Margarete Schütte-Lihotzky (see no. 23) and Josef Hoffmann, Frenchman André Lurçat, American Richard Neutra and Dutchman Gerrit Rietveld, among others. Meant only to be temporary the geometric, Bauhaus-style houses, which still appear modern today, were bought up and rented out by the city council in 1934 having proved too expensive for prospective purchasers.

Although four were lost in the Second World War the rest are still lived in and were renovated in the 1980s. A small information centre at Woinovichgasse 32, itself designed by the exhibition's director Josef Frank, contains plans and cut-away models as well as a fascinating panoramic photograph of the site in 1932, uncluttered by the tall trees and later buildings that have now concealed the estate from

Modernist housing by André Lurçat at the Werkbundsiedlung housing estate in Hietzing

view.

By way of a complete contrast, visit the Margaretenhof housing estate, with its traditional street lanterns, cobblestones and profusion of Historicist details, at the junction of Pilgramgasse and Margaretenstrasse, in the 5th district of Margareten.

Other places of interest nearby: none

73 A Milestone in the Manufacture of Steel

14th District (Penzing), the Technical Museum
(*Technisches Museum*) at Mariahilfer Strasse 212;
take U-4 to Schönbrunn and walk up through
the Auer-Welsbach-Park

Anyone remotely interested in things technical, such as mining and industry, energy and transport, and even the development of musical instruments, should make every effort to visit Vienna's superb Museum of Technology. Amongst the thousands of fascinating objects, many of which reflect Austria's contribution to the development of modern technology, is the so-called *Marcuswagen*, an early automobile created in 1888 by Vienna-based German-Jewish inventor Siegfried Marcus (wall plaques at Mondscheingasse 4 in the 7th district of Neubau and Mariahilfer Strasse 107 in the 6th district of Mariahilf mark the former sites of his workshops). In 1870 Marcus is thought to have been the first to successfully combine petrol, as fuel, with electric ignition, thus creating the internal combustion engine. Unfortunately, it was the now famous Benz and Daimler who took the petrol car into full-scale production; meanwhile the name of Siegfried Marcus was all but expunged 50 years later by the Nazis. Thankfully his prototype car, of which only one was ever made, was bricked up in the museum's cellar for safekeeping during the Second World War and thus preserved for posterity.

The country that lays claim to being the cradle of the European Industrial Revolution is Great Britain, especially in the development of iron and steel production; however there is one relatively recent process that originated in Austria. In the late-19th century the heartland of Austria's mining, iron and steel industries was the province of Upper Styria. It was here in 1881 that the Austrian-Alpine Coal & Mining Company was created with its headquarters in Donawitz. Following a forced merger in 1938 with the Hermann Göring Works in Linz, the group came eventually to be known as VOEST-ALPINE AG. Assisted by investment made possible by the Marshall Plan after the Second World War VOEST became central to Austria's nationalised industry and has to this day continued to carve out new markets for itself, despite the Europe-wide collapse of heavy industry.

Dominating the Museum of Technology's Heavy Industry Hall is a

Vessel 1 from VOEST's Linz factory in the Technisches Museum

vast metal crucible from VOEST's Linz factory known as Vessel 1, and it was in it that the first commercial production of steel by the so-called Basic Oxygen Process (BOP) occurred in late 1952. Developed by VOEST the process enables large quantities of molten pig iron to be refined quickly into steel by the high-speed injection of pure oxygen. In this way up to 300 tons of iron can be blown into steel in little more than twenty minutes. The importance of the discovery of this technique is illustrated by the fact that two thirds of the world's steel is today smelted using what has become known as the Linz-Donawitz (or LD) process. Vessel 1 was one of a pair of crucibles commissioned specially for the job from the Gutehoffnung plant at Oberhausen in Germany's Ruhr Valley. It towers over a nearby Bessemer Converter of 1866 on whose basic principles, developed by Henry Bessemer in the English steel town of Sheffield in 1855, the revolutionary process was based.

Other places of interest nearby: 68, 69, 70

74 The Villas of Otto Wagner

14th District (Penzing), Wagner Villas I and II at
the junction of Bujattigasse and Hüttelbergstrasse;
take Tram 49 from U-Bahn Volkstheater (U-2/U-3)
to terminus at Hütteldorf-Bujattigasse

The Viennese architect Otto Wagner (1841–1918) is often associated with Gustav Klimt's Secession movement of 1897, in which like-minded artists and architects rebelled against what they saw as the backwards-looking and restricting Historicist style, as typified by the buildings of the Ringstrasse. Out of the Secession grew the Viennese version of Art Nouveau (*Jugendstil*), in which both Klimt (see no. 71) and Wagner made a lasting name for themselves (see nos. 42, 70 & 75).

It is interesting, however, to note that both men learned their trade in the very Historicist (Ringstrasse Style) school they were soon to detest. Wagner's conversion to *Jugendstil*, and in time to Modernism, can be illustrated very clearly at several sites across the city. A prime example is on the Graben where he is responsible for two closely situated buildings, namely the Historicist Graben-Hof (1876) at numbers 14–15 and the later, less formal-looking Ankerhaus (1894) at number 10. The latter is a much lighter affair, its modern iron girder construction left deliberately visible and topped off with Wagner's own stylish roof studio, occupied later by the artist Friedensreich Hundertwasser. Similarly, at Rennweg 3 in the 3rd district of Landstrasse, Wagner's own townhouse (1891) still seems decidedly old fashioned, despite its trademark projecting cornice, when compared with the austere Modernist façade of his last home on the first floor at Döblergasse 4 (1912) in the 7th district of Neubau, where he lived and worked until his death in 1918. The façade of the latter is broken only by minimal decoration of blue tiles and aluminium. Even Wagner's two famous apartments overlooking the Naschmarkt at Linke Wienzeile 38-40 (1899), with their mass of floral *Jugendstil* motifs appear somewhat busy when compared to his Modernist work. Most at odds, however, are his two villas on Hüttelbergstrasse in the 14th district of Penzing, designed at either ends of his career. Villa Wagner I at number 26 was built in 1888 as his summer residence and takes the form of a grand Italianate villa with classical colonnaded portico. Sold in 1911 it was saved from ruin in 1972 by the *Fantastic Realism* artist Ernst Fuchs who converted the building into his own private museum

Villa Wagner I, now the Ernst Fuchs Private Foundation, at Hüttelbergstrasse 26 in Penzing

(Ernst-Fuchs-Privatstiftung) (plans are afoot to extend the collection out into the extensive garden by Autumn 2006). It was Fuchs who added the fertility goddess at the front, as well as the coloured cornice and fountain house nearby. In stark contrast, next-door at number 28, is the Villa Wagner II where Wagner moved in 1913 (not open to the public). Its austere Modernist exterior of whitewashed concrete and aluminium is relieved only by a glass mosaic over the door (by Koloman Moser) and a few blue tiles, the latter echoing his Döblergasse house, as well as a building (*Schützenhaus*) he designed on the Danube Canal (see no. 83). Yet despite his relentless move towards Modernism Wagner ended up being buried in a traditional Historicist-style tomb in the cemetery at Hietzing (*Hietzinger Friedhof*), where Klimt is also buried, designed by himself many years before his eventual death in 1918. In architectural terms Otto Wagner had come full circle.

Other places of interest nearby: none

75 Respite and Peace Under a Golden Dome

14th District (Penzing), the Steinhof Church
(*Kirche Am Steinhof*) at Otto-Wagner-Spital, Baumgartner
Höhe 1; take Bus 48A from U-Bahn Volkstheater (U-2/U-3)

The architect Otto Wagner (1841–1918) was responsible for some of Vienna's most idiosyncratic architecture, including villas (see no. 74), railway stations (see nos. 42 & 70), river weirs (see no. 83) and a bank (see no. 51). He excelled at presenting functional features in whatever decorative style happened to be in vogue at the time. In *fin de siècle* Vienna this tended to be Wagner's own version of European Art Nouveau, known as *Jugendstil*. His very last commissioned work was a magnificent church, curious for being Vienna's only such building to be rendered entirely in the *Jugendstil* idiom. Standing on a high point and reigning over the terraced pavilions of the Lower Austria Psychiatric Hospital and Nursing Home, Wagner's Church of St. Leopold (known also as the Steinhof Church after an old field name) was constructed between 1904 and 1907. Since it forms but one element of the overall hospital plan, itself dictated by the geography of the Gallitzin Hill on which it is built, the church unusually faces north instead

Otto Wagner's Kirche am Steinhof high on the Gallitzinberg

of the more usual east. With functionality never far from his thoughts Wagner used this imposed aspect to maximise the natural therapeutic light flooding into the building. This made it quite unlike traditional churches whose east-west alignment so often resulted in the dark and mysterious candle-lit interiors favoured by the Viennese.

As Vienna's first truly modern church, and possibly the world's first example of ecclesiastical functionalism, Wagner employed several new construction techniques, such as the bolting of thin marble slabs onto the brick-built superstructure. However, its striking copper dome, nicknamed the *Limoniberg* (Lemon Mountain) because of the way it glints in the sun, still harks back to the traditional onion-shaped towers of Baroque churches. The interior of the church is also typically functional being an open cube, rather than a long hall cluttered with columns, affording each member of the congregation a clear view. Designed first and foremost with the hospital's infirm patients in mind, Wagner ensured that the pews had no sharp edges and were laid out so as to be easy to supervise. Similarly, the floor is sloping to facilitate cleaning and the stoups had running water to prevent spread of infection. He even designed special robes for the priests and envisaged the church as a place of worship for all creeds. The only real decoration inside this calm contemplative place is the gilded altar canopy and Kolo Moser's stained-glass windows through which daylight can stream and lift the troubled souls within.

On returning back down the hill look out for the memorial to the mentally ill victims of the Nazis as well as Otto Wagner's oft-overlooked Viennese Art Nouveau theatre (*Jugendstiltheater*) that also makes up part of the overall hospital complex.

It is worth bearing in mind too that the winter visitor to the Kirche am Steinhof may be privy to one of the wonders of the natural world. At dusk each night from late October 140,000 rooks fly from their foraging grounds 30 kilometres away to, amongst other locations, the tall trees of Baumgartner Höhe, where they spend the night in possibly the largest rook dormitory in Europe. Each winter they migrate from Eastern Europe to the warmer climes of Central Europe, and Vienna seems to be a favourite destination.

Not far north of the Kirche am Steinhof, on Savoyenstrasse, is the Schloss Wilhelminenberg, a summer residence built in 1785 by Russian ambassador Gallitzin after whom the hill on which the church and hospital lie is named. Its landscaped park contains a fine classical garden temple.

Other places of interest nearby: none

76 Vienna's Lost Railway Stations

15th District (Rudolfsheim-Fünfhaus), the Westbahnhof
railway station on Neubaugürtel; take U-3 to Westbahnhof

Up until the Second World War Vienna could boast six grand and imposing mainline railway stations, built in the late-19th century to connect the capital with the farthest reaches of its sprawling empire. Needless to say, these vital transport facilities became strategic targets during allied bombing raids and were consequently reduced to ruins. Books of nostalgic photographs and old picture postcards are all that remain to give the visitor an impression of these lost palaces of travel.

Although they have been replaced by purely functional structures of concrete and glass, the observant explorer may still find a few tangible remains of the old buildings, built in the eclectic style of the time known as Historicist (Ringstrasse Style). At the Westbahnhof for example, rebuilt in 1952, there is in the lower ticket hall a battered, life-size statue of Emperor Franz Josef I's wife Elisabeth (*Sisi*) (1837–98). Carved from Carrara marble the statue is the work of sculptor Hans Gasser and once adorned the front of the original turreted station building (built 1858) that gave access to the so-called Empress Elisabeth Western Railway, servicing northwest and southwest Europe. Sisi herself would travel from here to the Habsburg retreat at Bad Ischl, known as the Kaiservilla, as well as to her Bavarian homeland. After the war the statue was believed lost until 1982 when it was re-discovered in a federal warehouse, restored and returned to the foyer of the reconstructed Westbahnhof on 13th March 1985. It is from today's

A statue of Empress Elisabeth (Sisi) that once adorned the old Westbahnhof

Westbahnhof that trains depart to Salzburg and western Austria, and to north and west Europe, including Germany, Switzerland, Benelux and Northern France. Whilst at the station look out also for the wall plaque just inside the main door in memory of »150 Austrians from all walks of life« dispatched from here on April 1st 1938 to the infamous concentration camp of Dachau in Bavaria (see no. 13). Moving on to the ticket hall of the Südbahnhof on Landstrasser Gürtel, rebuilt in 1960, there can be found another sculptural fragment. Here, in the main ticket hall, is a battered sandstone lion, one of eight that once adorned the roof of the original glass-roofed building constructed in 1869. The lion is called the *Markuslöwe* after the Evangelist St. Mark, patron saint of Venice, who since the 9th century has been represented as a winged lion. Sculpted by Franz Melnitzky the lions hark back to the strong connections between Vienna and Venice in the days of the Habsburg monarchy (a winged lion also adorns the Italianate *Dogenhof* on Praterstrasse; see no. 57). They also remind the visitor of Venetian engineer Karl Ritter

A stone lion of St. Mark that once stood on the roof of the old Südbahnhof

von Ghega, builder in 1848–54 of the world's first Alpine railway that ran south from the Südbahnhof across the Semmering Pass (a plaque on the corner of Lugeck and Rotenturmstrasse marks the building where Ghega died of Tuberculosis in 1860). Directly next-door to the Südbahnhof once stood the delicately pavilioned Ostbahnhof (or Staatsbahnhof) but this was bombed the heaviest during the Second World War because of its importance in servicing Germany's military fronts. Trains from today's Südbahnhof (now effectively two stations in one but with separate platforms and timetables) still go to Italy, as well as servicing south and central Europe, including the South of France, Hungary, Poland, the Czech Republic and Slovakia. Somewhat surprisingly Vienna itself lacks a dedicated railway museum, though amongst the few related pieces to be found in the Museum of Technology (*Technisches Museum*) (see no. 73) is an intricate model of the Nordbahnhof, another of Vienna's lost railway stations. Opened in 1865 in the Moorish-Tuscan style and said to have had the most beautiful façade of any station in the world, the Nordbahnhof (known also as Kaiser-Ferdinands-Bahnhof) became the most important and busiest of Vienna's stations, connecting the capital with its eastern Crown lands, Prague and Warsaw. It lay at the end of Praterstrasse along which newcomers arriving at the station would travel to reach the *Innere Stadt*. It was also at the very heart of the entertainment area of Leopoldstadt where the Viennese, travelling in the opposite direction, would go to relax at the Prater (see no. 59). The Second World War changed all that and the station's sorry bombed-out shell was eventually dynamited in 1965. Unlike the two stations listed above, not a single architectural fragment remains of the once glorious Nordbahnhof. The anonymous-looking Wien Nord/Praterstern station that handles predominantly local traffic now occupies the site. Only the nearby Tegetthoff monument, commemorating Austria's naval victory against the Italians at the Battle of Lissa in 1866, stands witness to the former grandeur of this once vibrant crossroads. That just leaves Alsergrund's classical-pedimented Franz-Josefs-Bahnhof and Brigittenau's magnificently columned Nordwestbahnhof. The latter, once prickling with statuary, has now been entirely obliterated and relegated to use as a freight terminal. The Franz-Josefs-Bahnhof was lost also but has today been replaced by a hi-tech steel and glass structure that dominates Julius-Tandler-Platz. On the wall of the modern foyer can be seen the incongruous sight of a huge gilded clock, all that's left of the grand old station that once stood here. Today, trains travel from here as far as Prague.

Other places of interest nearby: 44, 47

77 Vienna's First Concrete Church

16th District (Ottakring), the Parish Church of the Holy Ghost
(*Pfarrkirche zum Heiligen Geist*) on Herbststrasse;
take Tram 9 to Gersthof from Schweglerstrasse U-Bahn (U-3)

Of Vienna's very many churches about thirty are superb masterpieces of Gothic, Baroque and even Art Nouveau (*Jugendstil*) architecture. A few, however, are unique for other reasons and warrant special attention by the explorer. These tend to be the city's parish churches (*Pfarrkirchen*), worthy of any city centre and yet hidden away in Vienna's suburbs. They are rarely given any mention in the standard guidebooks and are well off the usual tourist routes.

A fine example is the superbly painted interior of the Altlerchenfeld parish church (1860) on Lerchenfelder Strasse in the 7th district of Neubau, designed by Johann Müller and Eduard van der Nüll who famously hung himself after his State Opera House received a critical mauling. Also definitely worth a visit is Josefstadt's Dreifaltigkeitskirche at Alser Strasse 17, with its incredible cloister gallery containing 4,500 votive wall plaques to St. Anthony.

A classic example is the Parish Church of the Holy Ghost hidden away in the working class district of Ottakring. It was designed in 1913 by Jože Plečnik, a Slovenian architect and student of Otto Wagner, responsible previously for the striking Zacherl House (1905) at Brandstätte 6 in the *Innere Stadt*. The church was Vienna's very first to be constructed of concrete and one cannot miss its massive

The concrete
Parish Church
of the Holy Ghost
in Ottakring

grey classical frontage. Needless to say it caused some controversy when it was unveiled prompting the Emperor's heir Archduke Franz Ferdinand to describe it as being a mixture »...of a temple to Venus, a Russian bath and a stable«! Once inside however, the true original-ity of the church is revealed in all its glory. Unlike the overblown gild-ed interiors of the old Baroque churches in the *Innere Stadt*, here is a bright and modern space, building on the tradition of early Christian basilicas, and illuminated by means of lovely stained-glass windows at first-floor balcony level. The stunning Viennese Art Nouveau (*Jugend-stil*) altar depicts a dove and angels rendered in aluminium against a golden sunburst, as well as a purple mosaic illustrating the seven attributes of the Holy Ghost – from *Frömmigheit* (piety) to *Gottes-furcht* (fear of God). On either side of the altar are concealed stairs leading down into a concrete crypt. The shadowy and mysterious underworld to be found here reminded this author of the Megalithic rock-hewn chambers of prehistoric Malta. The main room has an altar flanked by pale Klimt-esque murals (*Rachel Weeping for her Dead Children* and *The Creation of Water*) and in the corner is a font whose golden lid is alive with sculpted fish from which rises a figure holding a cross. Finally, at the back of the crypt there is a trio of grottoes, one of which, behind a chande-lier of green and red lights, contains a sar-cophagus with a life-sized figure of Christ that is periodically revealed from below its shroud.

The font with its ornate golden lid

More than sixty years later another con-troversial church was built in concrete, this time on Georgenberg at Maurer Lange Gasse 137, out in the 23rd district of Liesing. Built to a design by the atheist sculptor Fritz Wotruba, the Church of the Most Holy Trinity (*Kirche zur Heiligsten Dreifaltigkeit*) is made up of 152 concrete blocks stacked seemingly haphazardly. Referred to sometimes as the Wotruba Church (*Wotruba-kirche*) it illustrates the designer's concept that from apparent chaos comes harmony.

Other places of interest nearby: 47

78 From the Outer Suburbs to Outer Space

16th District (Ottakring), the Kuffner Astronomical
Observatory (Kuffner-Sternwarte)
on Johann-Staud-Strasse 10;
take U-3 to Ottakring and then Bus 46B to Ottakringer Bad

It comes as no surprise to learn that a city of learning such as Vienna has long had an interest in the study of astronomy. Indeed the Urania

The Urania observatory on Stubenring with Wien River lantern in the foreground

building, moored like a great white ship on the banks of the Danube Canal at the end of Stubenring, contains Austria's very first public observatory (*Sternwarte*). It was designed in 1910 by architect Max Fabiani as an adult education centre for the enlightenment of the people, a role it continues to fulfil to this day. Should the city's light and air pollution be too great or the sky overcast, budding astronomers can head for the Planetarium at the Volksprater. Here, by means of a 2.5 ton Zeiss projector, the stars and planets of the night sky can be reproduced perfectly on the inside of a 13 metre-high domed ceiling.

Of course for those after the real thing Vienna has several full-size observatories to offer, two of which are built on suitable highpoints free of dust and smoke in the northwestern suburbs. The University Observatory (*Universitätssternwarte*), for example, lies behind the high walls of Sternwartepark on Sternwartestrasse, close to Türkenschanz-park in the 18th district of Währing (note: visitors to the grounds are warned not to stray off the path due to beehives and overhanging trees!). The grand brick building was constructed in 1880, its porti-coed entrance to shelter arriving carriages leading via a grand stair-case and long residential wing to the observatory proper. The main central dome contains a large refractor telescope (i.e. one whose main focussing element is a lens) seated on a 15 metre-high, structurally independent column in order to minimise vibrations. Made in Dublin it was the largest telescope in the world when first installed. Smaller refractors terminate the building's three shorter wings, one of which is a so-called Comet Catcher.

To the southwest, on the slopes of the Gallitzinberg, is the charming Kuffner Observatory erected in 1886 as a private observatory by Moriz von Kuffner, a Jewish brewer whose family were responsible for reversing the declining fortunes of the famous Ottakringer Brewery (the impressive grave of Wilhelm Kuffner, brewery proprietor, can be found in Group i1 of the Döbling Cemetery (*Döblinger Friedhof*) on Hartäckerstrasse). Now restored beautifully, one of the observatory's

The twin domes of the Kuffner Observatory in Ottakring

two domes has glazed plaques incorporated into it, bearing the names of history's great astronomers, such as Copernicus and Galileo.

It is a device repeated in the Chemical Institute on Schottentor (e.g. Bunsen and Liebig) as well as the Natural History Museum (e.g. Marco Polo and James Cook) and the Kunsthistorisches Museum (e.g. Rembrandt and Leonardo Da Vinci). Since 1946 the Kuffner Observatory has been used as an education centre where visitors may observe the night sky using Kuffner's own original telescope and other high quality instruments.

Also providing a good view of the night sky (though only visible today from the outside) is a fine brick-built *belvedere* tower on a hillock in Währing's Türkenschanzpark, built to celebrate the 200th anniversary of the expulsion of the Turks (see no. 2), as well as the forty-year reign of Emperor Franz Josef I (1848–1916).

Other lookouts include the Jubiläumswarte on the Satzberg (433 metres) next to Johann-Staud-Strasse 80 in Ottakring, and the Hubertuswarte on top of the Kaltbründlberg (508 metres) in Hietzing's Lainzer Tiergarten, a former Imperial hunting reserve where Emperor Franz Josef I built the romantic Hermesvilla for his wife Elisabeth (*Sisi*). Grandest of all is the fairytale Habsburgwarte, a Habsburg tower constructed in 1888 on the Hermannskogel at the edge of Döbling, which at 542 metres is the highest point within Vienna's city

limits. It is possible to climb its narrow spiral stairs to the top from where a wonderful view of the surrounding Vienna Woods (*Wienerwald*), with their ground cover of aromatic wild garlic (*Bärlauch*), can be gained.

Other places of interest nearby: none

The Habsburg lookout tower
on the summit of the Hermannskogel in Döbling

79 Europe's Largest Landscape Garden

17th District (Hernals), Schwarzenbergpark on Neuwaldegger Strasse; take U-6 to Alserstrasse then Tram 43 to terminus at Neuwaldegg and enter via Waldegghofgasse/Schwarzenbergallee

Count Franz Moritz Lacy was born in St. Petersburg in 1725, his father Peter Lacy being a noteworthy Russian general and Irish political émigré. Together with many others he had left Ireland in the face of English suppression and religious intolerance, and offered his military and political services to the Catholic monarchs of Europe. These emigrants were known collectively as the »Wild Geese« (»*Wildgänse*«, or in Celtic »*Na Géanna Fiáine*«). Together with several others, Franz Moritz Lacy found his way to Habsburg Vienna during the long reign of ›Empress‹ Maria Theresa (1740–80). In time he became a high-ranking field marshal, his courage and military prowess helping preserve the empire established by her ancestors. He was awarded with the Military Order of Maria Theresa for services during the Seven Years' War with Prussia (1756–63) and went on to become a close adviser to Emperor Josef II (1765–90).

In 1765 he purchased a swathe of land in Neuwaldegg occupying what is today the western end of the district of Hernals, in the foothills of the Vienna Woods (*Wienerwald*). Here, following the principles of the »back to nature« movement popular in the late-18th century, the by now wealthy field marshal and statesman created what at the time was Europe's largest landscape garden. Known as the Lacy Park (today's Schwarzenbergpark), the planned naturalism of its landscaping was somewhat similar in concept to the idealised vistas produced for the great country estates of England by garden designer Lancelot »Capability« Brown. Lacy's planned landscape of rolling hills included streams and ponds, trees and coppices, as well as deliberately placed open spaces. Notable too were the number of garden features and novelties he incorporated, including decorative stone vases, a Chinese pavilion, a miniature Garden of Eden and the *Hameau*, a model hamlet where the simple pleasures of country life could be played out, albeit under stage-managed conditions. After his death in Vienna on 24th November 1801 the estate was inherited by the

Schwarzenberg family, one of Austria's most powerful, whose Baroque palace lies at the far end of Schwarzenbergplatz, just outside the Ring. It was Prince Karl von Schwarzenberg who led the Austrian and allied armies to victory against Napoleon at the Battle of Leipzig in 1813 (hence his equestrian statue occupying the square since 1867 and the plaque marking his birthplace in 1771 at Neuer Markt 8). Somewhat ironically, the prince had been the first ambassador to visit the court of Napoleon in Paris, in 1809 in order to negotiate the French emperor's marriage to the daughter of Emperor Franz I (the carriage he used can be seen at Schloss Schönbrunn's Wagenburg carriage museum).

Unfortunately, it was only a matter of time before Lacy's park returned to the true natural state it was so cleverly trying to imitate, its design once again engulfed by the trees of the Vienna Woods. However, with a little imagination, the visitor can still experience something of the Count's original vision, especially when entering via the grand obelisk gateway along the chestnut-lined Schwarzenbergallee. Half way along, on the right-hand side, can be seen a white marble statue that once adorned the original garden. Beyond lay the park proper identified today only by its woodland pathways and the

Obelisks marking the entrance to the former Lacy Park in Hernals

The grave of Count Lacy hidden in the woods of Schwarzenbergpark

occasional overgrown pond. Lacy himself is actually buried here in a tiny classical temple surrounded by beech and birch trees, signposted along a track that runs up from Hohenstrasse.

Note: another notable member of the Austrian Wild Geese was Max O'Donnell of Castlebar, adjutant to Emperor Franz Josef I (1848–1916). Together with a Viennese butcher called Josef Ettenreich, he saved the emperor's life during an assassination attempt by János Libényi, a travelling tailor and Hungarian nationalist, on February 18th 1853. As a result, opposite the exact spot at Schottentor where the event occurred, construction began in 1854 on the twin-spired Votivkirche in the style of the great Gothic cathedrals of Cologne and Chartres.

Other places of interest nearby: none

80 Vienna's *Via Dolorosa*

17th District (Hernals), the Calvary Church
(*Kalvarienbergkirche*) on Kalvarienberggasse;
take U-6 to Alserstrasse then Tram 43 to Elterleinplatz

The visitor approaches the Kalvarienbergkirche in Hernals by way of
Jörgerstrasse, named after a Protestant family of noble ancestry who
lost their estate here to the Chapter of St. Stephan during the Counter
Reformation of the 17th century. As a result, the Chapter laid out a
Way of the Cross that ran from the Stephansdom in the *Innere Stadt*
all the way out via Schottentor to the parish church of Hernals – a

The Kalvarienbergkirche from the old market place in Hernals

distance exactly the same as Jerusalem's own Way of the Cross, the *Via Dolorosa*. Consecrated in 1639 it was Emperor Ferdinand III (1637–57) himself who laid the foundation stone of a »Holy Grave« at the church. This inevitably provided the ultimate goal for the many penitential processions that began using the route thereafter, despite the destruction of the church by the Ottomans during the second Turkish siege of Vienna in 1683 (see no. 2). The church was rebuilt in 1709–14 at which time it was given its now famous Calvary, surely one of the most unusual in all Austria. Its most curious feature is the series of original wooden reliefs, now nearly 300 years old, which represent the seven deadly sins (Envy – dogs attacking Jesus; Pride – a strutting peacock; Covetousness – a money-grabbing raven; Gluttony – a greedy hyena; Lust – a billy goat; Anger – a lion ravaging a lamb; and Sloth – a sleeping donkey). As the number of pilgrimages increased so the Calvary was extended in 1766–69 to accommodate them. However, in 1782 Emperor Josef II (1765–90) dissolved the Pauline Order that had administered the Calvary as well as its church and all further pilgrimages were banned. In fact the reform-mad Emperor dissolved nearly one in five of Austria's monasteries believing them to be engaged in activities that did not benefit the state. In the years that followed pilgrimages resumed once more and the church was remodelled again, with some final modifications made to the Calvary in 1894. By this time pilgrims were making a good day out of their visit to the Calvary at Hernals, enjoying the hospitality of the numerous surrounding inns as well as the shopping opportunities offered by the burgeoning market in the church square in front.

Wall plaque
to Franz Schubert

Either side of the building's façade are staircases that lead up the unusual rough-hewn masonry of the ground floor to the Calvary above, symbolising the climb that Jesus made to his crucifixion site on the hill of Golgotha (hence the name *Kalvarienberg*). A plaque nearby records that on 3rd November 1828 Schubert (1797–1828) heard his last music performed here, namely the Latin *Requiem*, written for his brother Ferdinand in the hope that he would one day be recognised as a serious composer.

Other places of interest nearby: none

81 A Japanese Garden Paradise

19th District (Döbling), the Setagaya Japanese Garden
(*Setagayapark*) at the junction of Hohe Warte and
Barawitzkagasse; take U-6 to Nussdorferstrasse then Tram 37
to Barawitzkagasse

It is not surprising that a city like Vienna, which experiences long hot summers and is built on rich alluvial deposits and well-draining sandstone, can boast a large number of attractive parks (occupying 868 hectares) for both inhabitants and visitors to enjoy. These include the French formality of Schönbrunn's Schlosspark, the English gentility of the Stadtpark, the Baroque terraces and Alpine Garden (*Alpengarten*) of the Belvedere Palace (note the huge Plane tree outside Rennweg 14 planted in 1780 by the director of the nearby Botanical Gardens), the glorious scented roses of the Volksgarten, the lakes and mature trees of Türkenschanzpark and the simple green space of the Fridtjof Nansen Park in Liesing, commemorating the Norwegian polar explorer, statesman and 1922 Nobel Peace Prize winner.

However, for something rather unusual, the explorer should head to the leafy 19th district of Döbling where, tucked into a compact space next to a retirement home, there lies the unexpected Setagaya Japanese Garden. Designed in 1992 by Japanese landscape gardener the late Dr. Ken Nakajima, it celebrates the long-standing cultural ties between Döbling and the Tokyo district of Setagaya. The park can be identified from the outside by its telltale bamboo railings and engraved Japanese *Furomon* stone signalling to the passerby that a paradise garden lies beyond.

Once through the gate, the visitor is transported immediately to a world of calm and serenity reflecting the deep Japanese love of nature, as well as the Shinto faith in which divinities are believed to inhabit rocks, trees and water. From the charming teahouse (*Chaniwa*) set amongst a grove of bamboo at the water's edge there is a lovely view across a lily-strewn lake towards a gracefully arching bridge. This in turn is set off perfectly on one side by a white gravel beach in the *Suhama* style, planted with iris and dotted with turtles basking in the sun. Paths wind harmoniously through the park past an elegant *Yukimi* stone lantern, dense plantings of seasonal blossoms, as well as Japanese Maple, Cherry, Azalea and Magnolia trees.

Past a gushing waterfall the path reaches a high point where there is a summerhouse in a miniature mountain setting. Close by is a simple cube of stone (»the source«) from where all the garden's water originates. One channel feeds into a carefully pivoted piece of bamboo (*Shishiodoschi*) that when full swings down hitting a stone below, the resultant knocking sounds interrupting deliberately and regularly the otherwise hypnotic peace of the garden.

On leaving this earthly paradise, whose stated aim is that »people should observe this work of art in tranquillity and try to find their own inner peace«, be sure to track down the incredible former insect powder factory around the corner at Nusswaldgasse 14, constructed in the style of a Persian mosque!

Vienna has three other Japanese gardens one of which, next to Schönbrunn's Palmenhaus (see no. 69), was so choked with ivy in 1996 that it took a Japanese woman living in Vienna (whose father by chance was a gardener) to re-discover it! Subsequent restoration revealed a so-called »dry« Japanese garden (*Kare-sansui*) built from rock and sand in 1913 by Austrian gardener Anton Hefka. It contains stone formations representing the lucky Crane and Tortoise and was re-opened in 1999.

A factory in the style of a mosque on Nusswaldgasse

Another example of a Japanese garden in Vienna is the Takasaki Park (Takasakipark) at Laaerbergstrasse 21 in the Kurpark Oberlaa in the 10th district of Favoriten. It is to a design by Professor Ikeda Tadashi and based on a temporary Japanese garden built in 1974 by Professor Kunsaku Nakame as part of the Viennese International Horticultural Show. The new garden was opened in 1992 by citizens from the Japanese city of Takasaki at whose suggestion it was built. Finally, at Donizettiweg 29 in the 22nd district of Donaustadt, there is the School of Horticulture's Asia Garden. Opened in 2001 it is an edu-

Lake, bridge and lantern in the Japanese Setagayapark in Döbling

cational garden designed to introduce both pupils and public to the basic elements of East Asian garden culture.

A second *Kare-Sansui* garden, created in 1999 in Courtyard 2 of Alsergrund's Old General Hospital (Altes Algemeines Krankenhaus), celebrates the 60th anniversary of the founding of the University's Japanese Faculty; its miniature landscape of mountain, river and sea is constructed from actual Japanese stones brought from Kyoto, Kobe, Shikoku Island and Mount Ikoma.

Other places of interest nearby: 81

82 Karl Marx and Red Vienna

19th District (Döbling), the Karl-Marx-Hof
on Boschstrasse; take U-4 to Heiligenstadt

With the end of the Great War in 1918 and the collapse of the Habsburg Empire, Austria's First Republic was declared under Karl Renner, albeit reluctantly as many Austrians had wanted union with Germany. The loss of so many of its former territories in one fell swoop brought severe economic hardships, widespread unemployment and famine – even the legendary Vienna Woods (*Wienerwald*) were felled for fuel. In 1919 the vote was extended to all Viennese adults, a fact which, when combined with the rise of a powerful labour movement led by the Austro-Marxists, led to a landslide electoral victory in Vienna's City Council for the Social Democrats. Thus Vienna became the world's first city to be administered by socialists and, in 1922, the city was made a separate Austrian federal province (*Bundesland*), distinct from conservative Lower Austria of which it was formerly a part.

Despite inevitable tensions with the Conservatives, who held sway in the Austrian countryside, the city council of so-called Red Vienna (*Rotes Wien*) embarked on Europe's most intensive programme of social reform, throughout the twenties and early thirties. Nowhere was this more apparent than in the task of re-housing a quarter of a million workers who were living in antiquated and overcrowded tenements. These were replaced with 398 new city-owned housing complexes (*Gemeindebauten*) that provided 58,667 apartments with basic comforts (including running water and WC) at a low rent, together with a previously unknown infrastructure of public amenities. Some of these huge structures were quite literally fortresses (or palaces) for the people, such as the Reumann-Hof in Favoriten, Friedrich-Engels-Hof in Brigittenau, Sandleiten-Hof in Ottakring and Raben-Hof in Landstrasse. However, the true architectural flagship of Red Vienna was the mighty Karl-Marx-Hof in Döbling, designed by Karl Ehn, a pupil of Otto Wagner, and named after the founder of Scientific Socialism. The complex is over a kilometre long (an indication of its great length being the fact that the road in front was earmarked as a possible airstrip in case the Berlin Airlift of 1948 spread to Vienna!) and contains nearly 1,400 apartments together with laundries, kindergartens, clinics, pools, and shops, as well as a youth centre, pharmacy and post office. Significantly the building itself occupies less than

(RIGHT) Detail of the archways leading into the inner courtyards

(BELOW) The Karl-Marx-Hof seen from the surrounding gardens

20% of the total area, the rest comprising courtyards and green spaces bringing therapeutic light and air into people's lives.

Also of interest are the rows of tiny hedged-in gardens (*Schrebergärten*) clustered along the nearby railway line. Named after Daniel Gottlieb Schreber, the 19th century German founder of the Small Garden Movement who designated them originally as children's playgrounds, in reality they were used as vegetable allotments during times of shortage. Now common in urban areas across Austria, the Schrebergarten has become the apartment-dweller's very own pleasure garden in miniature, replete with summerhouse, pond and tiny orchard (not to mention a scattering of gnomes and other ornaments).

Although the ornamentation of buildings such as the Karl-Marx-

Hof was minimal, it is interesting to see how it hints at the Socialist Realist murals depicting happy workers that would later appear on the walls of Vienna's council houses erected during the 1950s (e.g. Albertgasse 52 in the 8th district of Josefstadt).

During the Red Vienna period an impressive number of other public welfare institutions were also created, including swimming pools (see no. 65), dental clinics, libraries and playgrounds; even the former luxury villa the Wilhelminenberg became a children's home (see no. 75). The 63,736 apartments built between 1923 and 1934 were financed by taxes on unearned income (such as rents), luxuries like champagne, property and businesses. Unfortunately, by the early thirties Vienna's Socialist experiment was faltering in the face of rising National Socialism, global economic crises, mounting unemployment and worsening relations within federal Austria. Socialist Austria, namely Vienna, had become increasingly polarised from the conservative Catholics of greater Austria and tensions climaxed in a brief three-day civil war in February 1934. Two thousand members of the socialist workers' militia (*Schutzbund*) died during fighting with superior conservative forces (*Heimwehr*), the Karl-Marx-Hof itself being bombed into submission. As a result, the federal Chancellor Engelbert Dollfuss, who opposed both Marxism and Nazism, established an authoritarian Austro-fascist regime in an attempt to contain the situation. Shortly afterwards, on July 25th, outlawed Nazi rebels attempted an abortive coup (*Juliputsch*) and murdered Dollfuss in his office on Ballhausplatz, the couch on which he expired being preserved in Vienna's Museum of Military History (see no. 40). Although succeeded by the Austro-Fascist Kurt Schuschnigg, Austria had begun its inexorable slide into the hands of Hitler's Nazi Germany, and for the next eleven years the progressive socialist reform policies of Red Vienna lay dead and buried (see. no.13).

Fifty years later and Viennese architects are again designing housing complexes on a huge scale, this time on the outskirts of the city, as witnessed by the incredible Wohnpark Alt-Erlaa in the 23rd district of Liesing, where 3,181 apartments have each been given a leafy sun terrace resulting in what looks like a modern version of the Hanging Gardens of Babylon!

Other places of interest nearby: 81, 83

83 The Taming of the Blue Danube

19th District (Döbling), the Nussdorf Weir and Sluice
(*Nussdorfer Wehr- und Schleusenanlage*)
at Brigittenauer Sporn; take Tram D to Nussdorf

It was during the last Ice Age that layers of gravel were deposited by glacial melt water across the Vienna Basin. The River Danube, together with its numerous tributaries, gradually eroded these gravels into a series of terraces. It was on one of these terraces (the so-called City Terrace), c.20 metres above the present level of the Danube Canal, that Bronze Age man first settled and where the Romans later built their garrison fort of Vindobona (see no. 12). Later still the streets of the medieval *Innere Stadt* would also occupy this plateau, safe from the river's fickle flow and with the churches of Maria am Gestade (see no. 9) and St. Ruprecht occupying its steep outer edges. Much of the surrounding land, however, remained at the mercy of the Danube and its sprawling tributaries, creating swampy river meadows in summer and icy marshes in winter. Bearing in mind the fact that 82 great floods were recorded over 900 years it was obvious that for Vienna to grow the mighty Danube would have to be tamed.

From Babenberg times the river had gradually been shifting its course northeastwards, away from the *Innere Stadt*. However, the first serious attempt at river regulation in 1598 took place on a major tributary (the Wiener Arm) that still flowed right past the old city wall, where the Franz-Josefs-Kai now runs. This was in part a response to the need by city traders for a safe navigable waterway (see no. 9) made necessary by the silting up of the once navigable Salzgriesarm. Continued flooding of low-lying areas, especially in 1787, 1830 and 1862, led to a complete channelling between Nussdorf and Albern in 1870-75, using techniques perfected during the digging of the Suez Canal. This tributary became known as the Danube Canal. At the same time the Danube proper was also straightened allowing large vessels to dock safely. By 1875 this had left several dead tributaries in the Prater (e.g. Heustadelwasser) as well as a curved arm of the original river marooned and cut off to the east. The latter, straddling Floridsdorf and Donaustadt, is known today as the Old Danube. Long popular with bathers (see no. 65), it is curious for being the only part of the Danube that actually appears blue (certainly when viewed from

Kahlenberg) – the rest being greyish green due to the current churning up lime from the riverbed.

Continued flooding in 1897, 1899 and 1954 led finally to the cutting in 1972 of a brand new channel (the New Danube) parallel to the Danube proper. A by-product of this work was the creation of the Danube Island (*Donauinsel*), a 20 kilometre-long spit of land that never exceeds 400 metres in width. Needless to say, the Viennese love to use it for sunbathing, cycling and swimming, claiming it to be Europe's biggest urban park.

In conjunction with these major river-management projects there have also been constructed a number of harbours, sluices and weirs. Between 1878 and 1916, for example, harbours for over-wintering Danube vessels were built at Kuchelau and Freudenau, whilst after 1938 docks were built at Lobau (for petroleum) and Albern (for grain). By far the most striking of these river facilities is at Nussdorf where Otto Wagner's magnificent lion-topped weir and sluice (1894-98) controls the flow of water into the Danube Canal. As if to symbolise the might of the monarchy in taming such a river the granite structure bears the Emperor's motto *Viribus Unitis* (With United Strength). Further down the Canal, at Obere Donaustrasse 26, is Wagner's pretty Floodgate House (*Schützenhaus*) (1904-08), erected on the site of the old Kaiserbad bathing facility in an attempt to convert the Canal into a trade and winter port. Although never completed, the building's projecting cockpit remains intact, from where overhead

A sculptured lion on Otto Wagner's Nussdorf sluice

cranes would have been controlled to raise a sluice gate from the riverbed. Designed in the Modernist style it has a simple white-tiled exterior broken up by a pretty blue wave pattern.

Finally, where the Canal joins the Danube proper, there is the modern Freudenauer sluice and hydroelectric power station (*Kraftwerk Freudenau*) built in 1992-98.

Also worthy of mention here is the regulation of the 17 kilometre-long River Wien that drains part of the Vienna Woods and repeatedly flooded the Schönbrunn Palace on its way down to what is now the Danube Canal. Although the Romans made attempts at controlling the river, it was not until 1897 that much of the river was culverted in conjunction with the building of Otto Wagner's Metropolitan Railway that follows the same course (see no. 42). Upstream, between Auhof and Hütteldorf, are a series of purely functional retention basins with locks and spillways to contain potential floodwaters (they have a capacity of 1.6 million cubic metres). By contrast, after a covered section between the Naschmarkt and the Stadtpark U-Bahn station (used for scenes in the film *The Third Man*, see no. 1), the tamed river re-emerges in the Stadtpark itself by means of a stunning Viennese Art Nouveau (*Jugendstil*) portal designed by Friedrich Ohmann and Joseph Hackhofer, and completed in 1906.

Note: the walls of the U-Bahn station at Dresdner Strasse and Floridsdorf on the U-6 carry a fascinating series of old maps and illustrations showing the various phases of river straightening on the Danube.

Other places of interest nearby: 82

84 The Secret of Dreams

19th District (Döbling), Freud monument on Bellevuehöhe;
take U-4 to Heiligenstadt and then Bus 38A
to Parkplatz Am Cobenzl

The father of psychoanalysis Sigmund Freud was born in Moravia (now the Czech Republic) in 1856 and died in London in 1939 having been forcibly exiled by the Nazis. He spent most of the intervening years in Vienna where his second-floor house and practice still exists at Berggasse 19 in the 9th district of Alsergrund (note the beautifully etched maidens on the ground floor doors leading into the courtyard, see page 4). Now a museum (*Sigmund-Freud-Museum*), but sadly lacking the famous couch that followed him to his new practice in London (today also a museum), Freud's Berggasse rooms can boast the great man's hat, coat and walking stick.

He was an inveterate walker, and smoker, and it is said that he enjoyed a brisk stroll along the nearby Ringstrasse most days. On Sundays he would don traditional Alpine walking clothes and head with his daughter Anna to the picturesque Vienna Woods (*Wienerwald*). It is here that a little-known monument to Freud, erected in 1977 at Bellevuehöhe (388 metres above sea level), can be discovered. Alighting from the bus at Am Cobenzl car park the visitor must follow the main road back out of the car park and then turn right, walking down onto Himmelstrasse; then turn right again (this time signposted »Zur Bellevuestrasse«), finally walking left up unmarked steps and alongside an old avenue of trees. At the far end will be found a stone bearing the following words: »Letter to Wilhelm Fliess, Bellevue, 12th June 1900 – Do you suppose that someday a marble tablet will be placed on the house inscribed with these words: In this house on July 24th 1895 the Secret of Dreams was revealed to Dr. Sigmund Freud? At this moment I see little prospect of it« (Fliess was a Berlin doctor and admirer of Freud's work). The house referred to was the Schloss Bellevue, a »Kurhotel« that once stood here but which was destroyed during the Second World War. So Freud was right in thinking that the building would not get its plaque, but even after the Second World War there was little official recognition of his academic achievements. Freud himself commented dryly on the Viennese reticence to acknowledge his work, notably when he was made University Professor of Neurology in 1902 by Emperor Franz Josef I, saying it was as if »the role of sexuality had suddenly been officially recognised by His Majesty, the significance of dreams confirmed by the council of ministers and the necessity of psychoanalytical therapy for hysteria passed by a two-thirds majority in parliament«. Thankfully, his contribution to the study of psychology is today unquestioned, indeed it was Freud who pioneered the analysis of a patient's dreams as a means of unlocking coded meanings that might help to understand a patient's troubled mind. His book *The Interpretation of Dreams* (1900), whilst largely ignored on publication, is now considered a classic and his concepts of ego and the subconscious are taken for granted around the world. It was Freud too who pioneered the use of »free association« now so common in the counselling of patients suffering mental illness. A bust of Freud was eventually erected in the cloisters of the University (*Universität*) on Karl-Lueger-Ring, alongside Vienna's other academic worthies, and he even got a park in Vienna named after him (*Sigmund-Freud-Park*), directly in front of the Votivkirche – just around the corner from Berggasse and his old apartment that he was never to see again.

Looking out across Vienna from the aptly-named Bellevuehöhe where Sigmund Freud once strolled

Sitting on the grassy hillside at Bellevuehöhe, where Freud himself once walked a century ago, is the perfect place to finish this odyssey during which some of the more unusual and unsung corners of Vienna have been explored. Looking out from the woods and vineyards, across the sprawling suburbs to the *Innere Stadt* and the Danube beyond, gives the satisfied explorer the opportunity to reflect on the culture, characters and contradictions encountered in this legendary city lying at the crossroads of Europe.

Opening Times

Amalienbad, 10th District,
Reumannplatz 23, Tue 9am-6pm,
Wed & Fri 9am-9.30pm, Thu 7am-9.30pm,
Sat 7am-8pm & Sun 7am-6pm

**Asia Garden of the School of
Horticulture**, 20th District, Donizettiweg 29,
Apr-Oct first Thursday in the month
10am-6pm)

Austrian Museum of Applied Arts
(MAK), 1st District, Stubenring 5,
Wed-Sun 10am-6pm, Tue 10am-midnight

Austrian Museum of Folk Art, 8th District,
Laudongasse 15-19, Tue-Sun 10am-5pm

Austrian National Library, 1st District,
Josefsplatz, Prunksaal, daily 10am-6pm,
Thu 10am-9pm, closed Mon

Büchereien-Wien Library, 7th District,
Urban-Loritz-Platz,
Mon-Fri 11am-7pm & Sat 10am-2pm

Burggarten, 1st District,
Burgring/Opernring,
daily Apr-Sep 6am-10pm;
Oct-Mar 6am-8pm

Butterfly House, 1st District, Burggarten,
Apr-Oct Mon-Fri 10am-4.45pm,
Sat & Sun 10am-6.15pm;
Nov-Mar 10am-3.45pm

Calvary Church, 17th District,
Kalvarienberggasse, church open daily,
Calvary only open in March during the
Lenten period, between Ash Wednesday
(Aschermittwoch) and Easter Monday
(Ostermontag)

Catacombs, 1st District, Stephansplatz,
Stephansdom, guided tours only
Mon-Sat 10-11.30am & 1.30-4.30pm,
Sun 1.30-4.30pm

Cathedral Museum, 1st District,
Stephansplatz 6, Tue-Sat 10am-5pm

Central Cemetery, 11th District,
Simmeringer Hauptstrasse,
daily May-Aug 7am-7pm,
Mar, Apr, Sep & Oct until 6pm,
Nov-Feb 8am-5pm

**Chimney Sweeps' Museum in the
Wieden District Museum**, 4th District,
Klagbaumgasse 4, Sun 10am-noon

Clock Museum of the City of Vienna,
1st District, Schulhof 2, Tue-Sun 10am-6pm

**Collection of Ancient Musical
Instruments**,
1st District, Heldenplatz, Neue Burg, daily
10am-6pm, closed Tue

Collection of Religious Folk Art,
1st District, Johannesgasse 8,
Mar-Dec 9am-4pm, Sun 9am-1pm

Contemporary Art Tower (CAT),
3rd District, Arenbergpark Flak tower,
May-Nov Thu 3-7pm

Court Pavilion, 13th District,
Schönbrunner Schlossstrasse,
Sun 10.30-12.30am

Court Silver and Porcelain Collection,
1st District, Hofburg, Michaelertrakt,
daily 9am-5pm, Jul-Aug to 5.30pm

Criminal History Museum, 2nd District,
Grosse Sperlgasse 24, Thu-Sun 10am-5pm

Desert House, 13th District, Schlosspark
Schönbrunn, daily Jan-Apr 9am-5pm,
May-Sep 9am-6pm, Oct-Dec 9am-5pm

**Doderer Memorial Room in the
Alsergrund District Museum**, 9th District,
Währinger Strasse 43,
Wed 9-11am & Sun 10am-noon;
closed Weds in Jul & Aug

Fiaker Museum, 17th District,
Veronikagasse 12 (2nd floor), first
Wednesday of each month, 10am-noon

Figaro House, 1st District, Domgasse 5,
daily 10am-8pm

Fire Brigade Museum, 1st District,
Am Hof 7/10, Sun & holidays 9-12am,
weekdays by appointment tel. 01 531 99

Fools' Tower, 9th District,
Old General Hospital, Courtyard 13,
Wed 3-6pm, Thu 8-11am & first Sat of the
month 10am-1pm

Globe Museum, 1st District,
Palais Mollard, Herrengasse 9, Mon-Wed,
Fri and Sat 10am-2pm; Thu 3-7pm

House of the Sea, 6th District, Esterházypark Flak tower, daily 9am-6pm

Imperial Carriage Museum, 13th District, Schlosspark Schönbrunn, daily Apr-Oct 9am-6pm; Nov-Mar Tue-Sun 10am-4pm

Imperial Court Furniture Depot, 6th District, Mariahilfer Strasse 88/Andreasgasse 7, Tue-Sun 10am-6pm

Imperial Treasury, 1st District, Hofburg, Schweizerhof, daily 10am-6pm; closed Tue

International Esperanto Museum, 1st District, Palais Mollard, Herrengasse 9, Mon-Wed, Fri & Sat 10am-2pm, Thu 3-7pm

Johann Strauss Museum, 2nd District, Praterstrasse 54, Tue-Thu 2-6pm, Fri-Sun 10am-1pm

Jewish Museum of the City of Vienna, 1st District, Dorotheergasse 11, daily 10am-6pm, Thu until 8pm; closed Sat

Judenplatz Museum, 1st District, Judenplatz 8, Mon-Thu & Sun 10am-6pm, Fri 10am-2pm; closed Sat

Kaisergruft, 1st District, below the Kapuziner Church, Neuer Markt/ Tegetthoffstrasse, daily 9.30am-4pm

Karlskirche, 1st District, Karlsplatz, Mon-Fri 7.30am-7pm, Sat & Sun 9am-7pm

Klimt Villa, 13th District, Feldmühlgasse 15a, from 2007 the villa will be operated by the Belvedere and will re-open in 2008 as a memorial and research centre

Kuffner Astronomical Observatory, 16th District, Johann-Staud-Strasse 10, Sat 5pm; also Apr-Sep Tue, Fri & Sat 9pm; Oct-Mar 8pm; see the published seasonal timetable at the gate

Kunsthistorisches Museum, 1st District, Burgring5/Maria-Theresien-Platz, Tue-Sun 10am-6pm, Thu to 9pm

Marzipan Museum, 1st District, Kohlmarkt 14, Demel's Confectionery Shop, Thu-Fri 11am-4pm

Museum in the Documentation Centre of Austrian Resistance, 1st District, Old Town Hall, Wipplingerstrasse 8, Mon, Wed & Thu 9am-5pm

Museum of the Institute for the History of Medicine, 9th District, Währinger Strasse 25, Mon-Fri 9am-3pm

Museum of Medieval Legal History, 6th District, Esterházypark, daily 10am-6pm

Museum of Military History, 3rd District, Arsenal, Objekt 18, daily 9am-5pm except Friday

Museum of Ethnology, 1st District, Heldenplatz, Neue Burg, daily 10am-6pm; closed Tue

Natural History Museum, 1st District, Burgring 7/Maria-Theresien-Platz, daily 9am-6.30pm, Wed until 9pm; closed Tue

Neidhart Frecoes, 1st District, Tuchlauben 19, Tue 9am-1pm, 2-6pm, Fri-Sun 2-6pm

Otto Wagner Pavilions, 4th District, Karlsplatz, Apr-Oct Tue-Sun 9am-6pm

Palm House, 13th District, Schlosspark Schönbrunn, May-Sep 9.30am-5.30pm, Oct-Apr 9.30am-4.30pm

Papyrus Collection, 1st District, Heldenplatz, Neue Burg, Oct-Jun Mon, Wed-Fri 10am-5pm, Jul-Sep Mon, Wed-Fri 10am-4pm

Pasqualatihaus, 1st District, Mölkerbastei 8, Tue-Sun 10am-1pm, 2-6pm

Prater Museum, 2nd District, Oswald-Thomas-Platz 1, Tue-Sun 10am-1pm, Fri & Sat 2-6pm

Roman Remains Below Am Hof, 1st District, Am Hof 7/10, currently closed for restoration

Roman Museum, 1st District, Hoher Markt 3, Tue-Sun 9am-1pm & 2-5pm

Russian Orthodox Church, 3rd District, Jaurèsgasse 2, Vigil held each Sat at 5pm and the Holy Liturgy each Sun at 10am

Schlosspark Schönbrunn, 13th District, daily 6am-sunset

Schnapps Museum, 12th District, Wilhelmstrasse 19-21, by appointment only tel. 01-815-73-00

Schubert's Death House, 4th District, Kettenbrückengasse 6, Fri-Sun 2-6pm

Setagaya Japanese Garden, 19th District, corner of Hohe Warte and Barawitzkagasse, daily 7am-dusk; closed Dec-Feb

Sigmund Freud Museum, 9th District, Berggasse 19, daily July-Sep 9am-6pm; Oct-June 9am-5pm

Snowstorm Museum, 17th District, Schumanngasse 87, by appointment only tel. 01-486-43-41

St. Mark's Cemetery, 3rd District, Leberstrasse 6-8, daily Apr & Oct 7am-5pm; May & Sep 7am-6pm; June-Aug 7am-7pm; Nov-Mar 7am-dusk

St. Michael's Church, 1st District, Michaelerplatz, guided tours only of the crypt usually Mon-Fri 11am, 1pm, 2pm, & 3pm, though this changes seasonally; see the notice board at the entrance

St. Stephen's Cathedral, 1st District, Stephansplatz, daily 6am-10pm

St. Virgil's Chapel, 1st District, U-Bahn station Stephansplatz, visible from an overhead gallery in the U-Bahn station

Steinhof Church, 14th District, Baumgartner Höhe 1, Otto-Wagner-Spital, the exterior can be visited at any reasonable hour; guided tours only of the interior are on Saturdays at 3pm tel. 01 910 60 20031

Takasaki Park, 10th District, Laaerbergstrasse 21, Sat & Wed only 7am-dusk; closed Dec-Feb

Technical Museum, 14th District, Mariahilfer Strasse 212, Mon- Fri 9am-6pm, Sat-Sun 10am-6pm

Third Man Private Collection, 4th District, Pressgasse 25, Sat 2-6pm, tel. 01 586 48 72 for appointments at other times

Tramway Museum, 3rd District, Ludwig-Kössler-Platz, May-Oct Sat & Sun 9am-4pm

Treasury of the Order of the Teutonic Knights, 1st District, Singerstrasse 7 (Staircase 1, 1st floor), Tue, Thu & Sat 10-12am, Wed & Fri 3-5pm

Undertakers' Museum, 4th District, Goldeggasse 19, Mon-Fri noon-3pm for guided tours by prior appointment only tel. 01 501 95 4227

Vienna Museum (formerly the Historical Museum of the City of Vienna), 1st District, Karlsplatz, Tue-Sun 9am-6pm

Vienna Shoe Museum, 8th District, Florianigasse 66, Tue 2-4pm

Viennese Brick Museum in the Penzing District Museum, 14th District, Penzinger Strasse 59, Wed 5-7pm, Sun 10am-noon; closed Jul-Aug

Viniculture Museum in the Döbling District Museum, 19th District, Döblinger Hauptstrasse 96, Sat 3.30-6pm & Sun 10am-noon; closed Jul-Aug

Wagner Apartment, 7th District, Döblergasse 4, by appointment only tel. 01 523 2233

Wagner Villa I (Ernst Fuchs Private Museum), 14th District, at the junction of Bujattigasse and Hüttelbergstrasse, by appointment only Mon-Fri 10am-4pm tel. 01 914 85 75;
Wagner Villa II is not open to the public

Water Tower, 10th District, Windtenstrasse 3, the exterior can be seen from the road; the interior may be visited during occasional open days and on guided tours by appointment only tel. 01 599 599 4131

Wotruba Church, 23rd District, Georgenberg, Maurer Lange Gasse 137, Sat 2-8pm; Mar-Oct Mon-Fri 2-5pm, Sun 9am-6pm; Nov-Feb Tue-Fri 2-4pm, Sun 9am-5pm

Bibliography

GUIDEBOOKS

The Rough Guide to Vienna 3rd ed.
(Rob Humphreys), Penguin Books, 2001

Eyewitness Travel Guide Vienna
(Gretel Beer, Caroline Bugler, Deirdre
Coffey & Fred Mawer), Dorling Kindersley,
1999

Vienna City Guide
(Käthe Springer and Manfred Horvath),
Christian Brandstätter Verlag, 2002

Kompass Guide Vienna
(Dr. Ingrid Fleischmann-Niederbacker),
Fleischmann & Mair Gmbh, 1994

The Green Guide Vienna (Various),
Michelin Travel Publications, 2002

Lonely Planet Vienna 3rd ed.
(Mark Honan and Neal Bedford),
Lonely Planet Publications, 2001

Time Out Vienna 2nd ed (Various),
Time Out Guides Ltd, 2003

Visible Cities - Vienna (Annabel Barber),
Somerset Ltd., 2002

*In Search of Vienna: Walking Tours of the
City* (Henriette Mandl), Christian
Brandstätter Verlag, 1995

Wanderung rund um Wien
(Fritz Peterka), Bergverlag Rudolf Rother
Gmbh, 1995

ILLUSTRATED BOOKS

*Mystisches Wien – Verborgene Schätze,
Versunkene Welten, Orte der Nacht*
(Robert Bouchal & Johannes Sachslehner),
Pichler Verlag, 2004

Vienna – Strolling Through an Unknown City
(Ernst Hausner), Edition Wien/Pichler
Verlag, 1996

Wien (Ernst Hausner), Jugend und Volk
Verlagsgesellschaft m.b.H., 1988

Wien (Vienna) - mit den Augen des Adlers
(Alfred Havlicek & Horst Friedrich Mayer),
Pichler Verlag, 2002

*This Pearl Vienna – A Book of Pictures
Taken From Vienna's Most Dreadful Time*
(Hans Riemer), Jugend und Volk G.M.B.H.,
1946

ARCHITECTURE AND MONUMENTS

*Architecture in Vienna 1850-1930
Historicism Jugendstil New Realism*
(Bertha Blaschke & Luise Lipschitz),
Springer-Verlag, 2003

Jugendstil in Wien
(János Kalmár & Andreas Lehne),
Pichler Verlag, 1998

Vienna: A guide to Recent Architecture
(Ingrid Helsing Almaas),
Ellipsis/Könemann, 2001

*Denkmal – Wiener Stadtgeschichten vom
Walzerkönig bis zur Spinnerin am Kreuz*
(Matthias Settele), Deuticke, 1996

Album of Socialist Vienna
(Hans Riemer), Wiener Volksbuchhandlung
Julius Deutsch & Co., 1947

Flaktürme – Berlin, Hamburg, Wien
(Hans Sakkers), Fortress Books, 1998

CHURCH, CEMETERY
AND MUSEUM GUIDEBOOKS

St. Stephan's Cathedral in Vienna 2nd rev. ed.
(Reinhard H. Gruber), Church Office of
St. Stephan's Cathedral, 2001

Stephansplatz and the Virgilkapelle
(Dr. Ortolf Harl), City of Vienna Museums
Publications, undated

*Graves of Honour at the
Central Cemetery in Vienna*
(Robert Budig, Gertrude Enderle-Burcel
and Peter Enderle), Compress Verlag, 1998

Imperial Furniture Collection Pocketguide
(Eva B. Ottilinger), Schloss Schönbrunn
Kultur- und Betriebsges.m.b.H, 2000

*The Kunsthistorisches Museum Vienna
Guide* (ed. by Martina Haja),
Kunsthistorisches Museum/Christian
Brandstätter Verlag, 1988

*The Kunsthistorisches Museum Vienna -
The Imperial and Ecclesiastical Treasury*
(Manfred Leithe-Jasper & Rudolf
Distelberger), Scala Publishers/Verlag
C. H. Beck, 1998

*Kunsthistorisches Museum Vienna
Wagenburg (Carriage Collection) at
Schönbrunn Palace* (Georg Kugler),
Kunsthistorisches Museum, 1999

TMW – Technisches Museum Wien
(ed. by Gabriele Zuna-Kratky),
Prestel Verlag, 2002

*Vienna by MAK – Applied
Arts/Contemporary Art*
(ed. by Peter Noever),
Prestel Verlag, 2002

The Treasury of the Teutonic Order
(Wolfgang Krones), Office of the
Hochmeister of the Teutonic Order –
Museum and Treasury, 2000

Gustav Klimt – Last Studio
(Gustav Klimt Memorial Society),
Zeitschrift der Österreichischen Gesellschaft
für Denkmal- und Ortsbildpflege in
Verbindung mit dem Verein Gedenkstätte
Gustav Klimt, September 2000

*The Neidhart Frescoes ca.1400 The Oldest
Secular Mural Paintings in Vienna*
(Eva-Maria Höhle, Renata Kassal-Mikula,
Oskar Pausch & Richard Perger), Museums
of the City of Vienna, undated

*The Treasures of Montezuma –
Fantasy & Reality*
(Ferdinand Anders), Wilfried Seipel/
Museum für Völkerkunde, 2001

The Park at Schönbrunn Palace
(Elfried Iby), Schloss Schönbrunn
Kultur- und Betriebsges.m.b.H, 2001

MISCELLANEOUS

The Habsburg Monarchy, 1809–1918
(A. J. P. Taylor), Penguin Books, 1964

Danube Encounters
(Hellmut Andics), Jugend und Volk
Verlagsgesellschaft m. b. H., 1976

Discovering Vienna Through Legends
(Hannelore Tik), Hannelore Tik, 2000

The Cooking of Vienna's Empire
(Joseph Wechsberg and Fred Lyon),
Time Life Books, 1979

Die Heurigen von Wien
(Wolfram Siebeck),
Wilhelm Heyne Verlag, 1997

Xenophobe's guide to the Austrians
(Louis James), Oval Books, 2000

Looking for Wolfgang Amadeus Mozart
(Walter M. Weiss),
Christian Brandstätter Verlag, 1997

WEBSITES

www.vienna.info
(the official Vienna Tourist Board site)
www.wien.gv.at
(the official City of Vienna site)

www.wienguide.at
(details of walking tours through Vienna)

www.austriatoday.at
(site for Austria's weekly English-language
newspaper)

www.wienerzeitung.at
(weekly news and culture digest for Vienna
in English)

www.wienerlinien.at
(details of Vienna's public transport system)

www.virtualvienna.net
(site for Vienna's English speaking
expatriate community including a useful
series of articles on Viennese legends and
curiosities by Billie Ann Lopez)

**Old lantern in the Central Cemetery,
Simmering (see no. 63)**

Acknowledgements

First and foremost I would like to thank the staff of my Viennese publisher Christian Brandstätter Verlag, not only for their initial belief in my work but also their professionalism, enthusiasm and good humour in bringing it to the shelves of the city's bookshops. In this respect I am especially grateful to Elisabeth Hölzl and Elmar Trampisch, Eva Gruber and Beatrix Kutschera not forgetting Brigitte Hilzensauer for her excellent translation of the text for the German edition.

For kind permission to take photographs, as well as arranging for access and the provision of information, the following people are very gratefully acknowledged:

the staff of the Aioli Restaurant (Haas-Haus); Michael Hugh-Bloch (Alte Leopoldsapotheke, Plankengasse); Raoul Brunner (Amalienbad); the staff at Antiquarische Fundgrube (Fuchsthallergasse); Elisabeth Edhofer (Austrian National Library); Frau Ledl (Bestattungsmuseum); the staff of the Büchereien Wien library (Burggasse-Stadthalle); Mag. Helga Farukuoye (Internationales Esperanto Museum); Gabriele and Michael Kornherr (Confiserie zum süßen Eck, Währinger Strasse); the staff of Steinmetz-Gastro (Währinger Strasse); Ingrid Scholz-Strasser (Freud Museum); Dr. Georg Becker (Gustav Klimt Memorial Society and Klimt Villa); Günter Rott (Graz); Jan Mokre (Globenmuseum); Christian Schreitl and Angela-Jacqueline Rakuscha (Hofpavillon Hietzing); Mag. Josefa Haselböck and Wolfgang Smejkal (Kaiserliches Hofmobiliendepot); Mag. Benedikt Haupt (Kunsthistorisches Museum); Dr. Günther Woratsch and Julius Reiter (Landesgericht für Strafsachen, Wien); Alexander Marwan and Marion Schuller (Michaelerkirche); Claudia Österreicher (Wien Museum, Karlsplatz – Neidhart Fresken, Pratermuseum, Römische Ruinen unter dem Hohen Markt and Virgilkapelle); Dorothea Nahler and Prof. Bernd Lötsch (Naturhistorisches Museum); Dr. Franz Grieshofer and Dr. Margot Schiller (Österreichisches Museum für Volkskunde); Walter Schmidt (Palais Coburg Residenz); Cornelia Römer (Papyrus Collection); Hofrat Franz Kraljic (Schatzkammer des Deutschen Ordens); Helmut Lackner (Technisches Museum); Gerhard Strassgschwandtner (Third Man Private Collection); Stefan Müller (Virgilkapelle); the staff of the Wiener Würstelstand (Kupfschmiedgasse); and the staff of the Central Library (Arts and Social Sciences Dept.) in Sheffield, England.

For the supply of film, high-quality processing and technical advice thanks to Foto Wachtl (Graben) and Foto Eduard Risavy (formerly Schottengasse).

The following friends, family, colleagues and acquaintances are much appreciated for their support, advice, assistance and inspiration:

In Vienna, new acquaintances Natascha Backes and Eric Jedrzejek, Birte von Benckendorff, Hans Berger and Andrea Mayr, Harold Beyerley, Ewald Bineder, Emanuel Boesch, the Brunner Family (Leogang), Lee Eypper; Eva Fischer, Thomas Fischer, Melanie Gufler and Jan Rupp (the latter for his selfless services over and above the call of duty in creating my first website), Dr. Simon Heathcote-Parker, Karin Höfler, Sven Hollmann and Viki Kiss, Susan von Kloos, Robert Kraska and Christa Bock, James Linkogle and Kristin Teuchtmann, Silvia McDonald (Virtual Vienna), Christian Mikosch, Gabriele Peterlin and Eva Prenner (Ruefa Reisen), Meri Stanković, Barbara and Brigitte Timmermann (Vienna Walks and Talks), Franz Trischler, Christoph Urtz, Marco and Lisa Villard, Wolfgang Zankl and Angelika Bruckner, Martina Horvath and especially my good friend Stefan ›Sy‹ Gebharter, for his tireless searching of the internet on my behalf as well as his technical assistance with computer-related problems – to him I will always be grateful.

Also Roswitha Reisinger for her invaluable assistance in translating German articles, coming up with the title and generally putting up with me and my mania for all things unusual; and not forgetting the Reisinger family in Freistadt, Upper Austria for their affection and unending hospitality.

In England, my loving parents Mary and Trevor, brother Adrian, auntie Catherine and great cousins James, Sally and Janet; also old friends who have sustained me from afar including Philip Adsetts, Peter and Dorothy Askew, Paul Billington and Kerry Newman, Rose and Mike Blackadder, Lisa Blanchflower, Mandy Boughton, Philippa Chapman, Margaret and John Connors, Diane Cooke, Catie Evans and Mark Pitcairn, Andrew Farrer, Zoe Gibson, Jenny Glazebrook, Jean and David Gledhill, Tim and Jane Hale, Judith Hall, Caroline and David Hepworth, Phil Higgins, Lisa-Jane Izatt, Joanne Jagiellowicz, Karen Jagiellowicz and Neil Burkinshaw, Marie-Christine Keith and Bob Barber, Simon, Nadine, Fran and Madeleine Laffoley, Rosalie and Georgia Nelson, Amy Pluckrose and Paul Taylor, Victor Povid, Marek Pryjomko, Roman Pryjomko, Tracey Richmond, Teresa Robinson, Diane Rocket and Adrian Ripley, Jill Sleaford, Nick Smith and Ellie Tordoff, Alan and Pauline Varney, and Tricia and David Ware – my thanks go to you all.

Finally, very special thanks to my father Trevor, not only for proof-reading and correcting my text, but for inspiring me to track down unusual locations in the first place – thanks Dad for making it all such fun!

Statue of W. A. Mozart in the Burggarten, moved here from Augustinerplatz in 1953

Page 2: Lookout tower in Türkenschanzpark, Währing
(see no. 78)

2nd Edition
Graphic Design:
Beatrix Kutschera, Atelier 21, Vienna
Technical Supervision and Reprographics:
Atelier 21, Vienna
Editor: Brigitte Hilzensauer
Maps: APA, Vienna
Printed and bound by: Gorenjski Tisk, Kranj

ISBN 3-85498-413-8

Christian Brandstätter Verlag
GmbH & CoKG
A-1080 Wien, Wickenburggasse 26
Telephon (+43-1) 512 15 43-0
Telefax (+43-1) 512 15 43-231
E-Mail: info@cbv.at
www.cbv.at